Intelligence, Destiny and I

GW00538247

How sound is the notion of general intelligence on which intelligence testing has been based? And if the idea cannot be justified, can it at least be explained? How did it originate? What are its historical roots?

In *Intelligence, Destiny and Education*, John White argues that these roots draw sustenance from the puritan tradition and its heirs on both sides of the Atlantic. Beginning with the works, family histories and socio-religious assumptions of Galton, Pearson, Burt, Goddard, Terman, and others, he traces the story back to traditional puritan beliefs in predestination, salvation, the elect, and the power of logical thinking. On the way, he shows how the traditional subject-based school curriculum, whose history has been so closely intertwined with that of intelligence testing, has sprung from the same roots.

Intelligence, Destiny and Education casts surprising new light not only on the history of psychology, but also on schooling in Britain and the USA in our own times, its selection devices and curriculum.

John White is Emeritus Professor of the Philosophy of Education at the Institute of Education, University of London, UK.

Intelligence, Destiny and Education

The ideological roots of intelligence testing

John White

Routledge
Taylor & Francis Group

LONDON AND NEW YORK

First published 2006
by Routledge
2 Park Square, Milton Park, Abingdon, Oxon OX14 4RN

Simultaneously published in the USA and Canada
by Routledge
270 Madison Ave, New York, NY 10016

Routledge is an imprint of the Taylor & Francis Group

© 2006 John White

Typeset in Goudy by
HWA Text and Data Management, Tunbridge Wells
Printed and bound in Great Britain by
MPG Books Ltd, Bodmin

British Library Cataloguing in Publication Data
A catalogue record for this book is available from the British Library

Library of Congress Cataloging-in-Publication Data
A catalog record for this book has been requested

ISBN10: 0–415–36892–8 (hbk)
ISBN10: 0–415–39493–7 (pbk)

ISBN13: 9–78–0–415–36892–6 (hbk)
ISBN13: 9–78–0–415–39493–2 (pbk)

Contents

Acknowledgements

There are a number of people who have helped me on specific aspects of this work and to whom I am most indebted. They are: Lord Kenneth Baker, for correspondence on the origins of the 1988 National Curriculum; Christopher Brand, formerly of Edinburgh University, and Richard Lynn, Professor Emeritus of the University of Ulster, for advice about family backgrounds of contemporary psychologists working in a broadly Galtonian tradition; Ann and Alan Clarke, for discussions about Cyril Burt; Raymond Fancher, of York University, Canada, for correspondence on Galton's possible link with Combe; Norman Franke, of Toronto, Canada, for his help on Cyril Burt's Congregationalist ancestry; Jim Garrison, from Virginia Tech, USA, for advice on Dewey's views on intelligence testing and the curriculum; Jane Green, doctoral student at the Institute of Education in London, for first putting into my head the idea that Piaget's psychology may have puritan roots; Roy Lowe, who is Visiting Professor at the same institute, for his comments on a draft of my chapter on the history of the English school curriculum; Douglas McKnight, from the University of Alabama, USA, for correspondence arising out of his work on Ramus and the puritan origins of American school curricula; Henry Minton, of the University of Windsor, Ontario, Canada, for advice on Lewis Terman's family genealogy; Lewis Terman, President, IBM Academy of Technology, USA, for his comments on his grandfather's likely puritan ancestry; and Thierry Veyron, of the Bibliothèque Municipale de St Etienne, France, for his kindness in sending me material on Jean Piaget's English ancestry. I am also most grateful to colleagues and students from the Institute of Education, University of London for their helpful comments following talks I gave at seminars in curriculum studies, philosophy, psychology and sociology.

Introduction

This book has two foci: the psychology of intelligence; and the school curriculum. The two go together, intellectually and practically. The latter is evident at the level of policy. For much of the last century it was widely believed, not least in Britain and the United States, that people differ in innate intelligence as measured by the IQ. For much of that period, too, it was widely held that secondary schools for the more intelligent require a more academic curriculum than schools for other children. Abstract thinking was the link between the two ideas. Intelligence tests were constructed around linguistic, logical and mathematical abilities especially prized by selective schools.

Today, intelligence is still bound up with the school curriculum, but often differently. In England, for instance, the academic curriculum – once only for a few – is now, in the shape of the National Curriculum, the daily experience of all. IQ tests have receded, and with them the idea that intelligence is a unitary ability for abstract thinking. In their place many teachers now believe that children come hard-wired with combinations of *multiple* intelligences. These closely fit the areas of the traditional curriculum – not only at its more abstract end, but also in artistic and other subjects like physical education. Non-abstract thinkers can now be bright, too: a curriculum for all coheres with a theory of intelligence for all.

In these ways intelligence and curriculum are, and have been, linked at the level of policy. But the intellectual connexion between them goes far deeper. It is this book's purpose to explore this.

The argument takes off from philosophical doubts about the justifiability of both these core beliefs. Psychologists from Francis Galton to Cyril Burt, Lewis Terman and beyond have claimed that we are all born with individually differing levels of innate general intelligence. Educational administrators and ministers, from Robert Morant at the beginning of the twentieth century to Kenneth Baker at its end, introduced a school curriculum based on a broad range of academic subjects, originally for selected secondary pupils and recently for every state school child from five to sixteen. However influential the two core notions have been, if you look for sound supporting arguments behind them, you will be disappointed. There are no solid grounds for innate differences in IQ; and there are none for the traditional subject-based curriculum.

Yet if the two ideas are so wanting, how is it that they became such powerful drivers of educational policy over the last hundred years? To answer this means leaving philosophical critique behind and turning to history: where justification is lacking, we must turn to explanation.

The *leitmotif* of this book is its suggestion that the two ideas have common origins. Roots of both go back to the protestant Reformation of the sixteenth century. More specifically, they are late fruits of the more radical forms of protestantism which formed the puritan and dissenting communities of the seventeenth century and afterwards on both sides of the Atlantic.

I build up the case for this across the six chapters of this book, looking first at the psychology of intelligence and then at the school curriculum.

In Chapter 1, I begin by showing how very *odd* an account of intelligence the traditional view is that we find in Galton, Burt and Terman. Aspect after aspect of it collapses when examined closely. Hence the shift from philosophy to history. How is it that such a powerful, and powerfully wrong-headed, idea could ever have arisen in the first place?

The post-Galton story of intelligence testing and its connexion with eugenic ideas has often been told. Although I go over parts of that story, my interest is more in a more deep-rooted explanation. Why did intelligence testing and eugenics grow up in the first place? What are their origins?

The first part of the trail is easy to follow. Everything leads back to Galton's views on the heritability of intellectual eminence in his *Hereditary Genius* of 1869 (Galton 1978). We can press back another four years: the origins of his eugenic thinking in that book can be traced to a magazine article he wrote in 1865. But there the trail seems to stop. Did his ideas just come to him out of the blue? We know that he read his cousin Charles Darwin's *Origin of Species* after it was published in 1859, but the use to which he put evolutionary notions was idiosyncratically his own. Did he invent it? Or does his eugenic vision have deeper roots?

In the hands of Galton's followers in the UK and in the USA, intelligence tests rapidly became a social institution. They were used to identify the mentally subnormal and the intellectually gifted; to fit pupils to appropriate tracks within elementary schools; to assign them to élite or non-élite secondary schooling; to exclude undesirable immigrants; to help in vocational selection. Some years ago it struck me – as it had struck the American journalist Walter Lippman decades before – that predestination was as much a key feature of intelligence testing as it had been of Calvinism and its puritan offshoots. In both systems, where one will end up in life – or after life – is wholly or largely fixed at birth, whether by God or by nature. There is no way a person destined for damnation can come to be saved, just as there is no way a child of very low IQ can hope to become a doctor or a lawyer. This set me to wondering how far other elements of the puritan thought-world also had eugenic counterparts. Is there any connexion between the modern notion of an educated élite and the notion of an elect of those destined for salvation? Is the puritan dichotomy between the saved and the damned in any way reflected in the tendency of most of the intelligence pioneers to focus on the gifted at one end of the spectrum and the so-called feeble-minded at the other? Does reference to 'the gifted' and 'talented' in Terman, Galton and others carry any echo of the puritan insistence that individuals are called by God to discover and put to good use the innate gifts which He has given them? Is the interest that Burt and others have shown in vocational selection residually associated with this older sense of vocation?

I discuss these and other questions in Chapter 2. The intelligence pioneers I look at in the book came from the UK and the USA. Is it significant that these were the two countries in which eugenic intelligence testing became most firmly established? Is it a coincidence that both countries have deep puritan roots?

If Chapter 2 is long on questions but short on answers, Chapter 3 is more informative. It consists of a study of the family backgrounds of the leading intelligence pioneers, to see if this shed any light on the parallels, outlined above, between psychological and religious thinking. It documents the remarkable fact that nearly every early well-known psychologist of intelligence in the Galtonian tradition in Britain and in America had a puritan or puritan-related ancestry. Among religious denominations, Congregationalism and Quakerism are especially prominent. This also applies to a psychologist of intelligence not in the Galtonian tradition but equally interested in abstract thinking, Jean Piaget, whose mother, Rebecca Jackson, was a descendant of an immigrant English Quaker. The only major exception to a puritan or post-puritan link among mainstream scholars appears to be Charles Spearman, although evidence about him is uncertain. As far as the others in this mainstream are concerned, could it be that a nineteenth-century upbringing in a family shaped by puritan thinking helped create a cast of mind especially susceptible to eugenic ideas? Is there any direct evidence that religion played a part in the pioneers' work? I explore these questions, too, in Chapter 3, also looking further into counter-evidence and relating the overall argument to Nicholas Pastore's fifty-year-old thesis that the hereditarian beliefs of the early intelligence psychologists (among other scientists) broadly correlate with the conservative political views which most of them shared.

Chapter 4 takes the investigation deeper. As I hinted earlier, the Galton-Burt concept of intelligence has some odd features. Although in the real world we act intelligently in all sorts of areas, from fitting bathrooms to mending relationships, the eugenicists' concept is specifically about *intellectual* ability, especially of an abstract sort. The prominence of logical, classificatory and mathematical puzzles in test items is an illustration of this. I had no idea, until I looked into Perry Miller's writings on the puritan thought-world of seventeenth-century New England, how central abstract thought in general and logic in particular were to this religious outlook and how strong their hold still was in the nineteenth century.

Why logic? What have Aristotelian syllogisms to do with ascetic protestantism? The answer is: not very much. The kind of logic that meant so much to it is not Aristotelian at all, but traceable to a French sixteenth-century scholar called Pierre de la Ramée, or Ramus. He mapped out in a highly systematic manner the knowledge of God's created universe that the protestant individual, freed from the authority of the old priesthood, came to require as a condition of personal salvation. He did this by a largely *a priori* process of repeated dichotomisings from the most abstract categories towards increasing particularity. Ramus was extraordinarily influential among puritan groups in both theological and, as we shall see in Chapter 5, educational circles. Although his own ideas fell into the background with the rise of empirical science, logic as a subject remained central to English (Old) dissenting, Scottish presbyterian, and American puritan religious and academic thinking throughout the eighteenth and well into the nineteenth century. Closely connected to it was a study called 'pneumatology', which revealed the nature both of the human and of the divine mind. I show how this element of the puritan tradition was transmuted into the earliest form of academic psychology in US universities – on which, via their teacher G. Stanley Hall, Henry Goddard and Lewis Terman, as well as a third pioneer, James McKeen Cattell, were reared. The same line of enquiry also suggests a possible answer to the question left hanging over from Chapter 1 – why the search for the origins of intelligence testing seems to stop with Galton's magazine article of 1865.

While looking into the matters explored in Chapter 4, I came to see their relevance not only to the history of intelligence testing but also to the history of the school curriculum. Since 1988 England has had a statutory curriculum based around ten or more school subjects. In their original form these were almost identical to the subjects which Robert Morant at the Board of Education prescribed for the new state secondary schools in 1904. How did this subject-based curriculum originate? Chapter 5 tries to find out. One line of thought has located its beginnings in the Dissenting Academies of the eighteenth century, but this account needs to be heavily qualified. Even so, there does seem good evidence that the (old) dissenting communities more generally, if we include within them those of presbyterian Scotland, play a lead role in the story. Again, the story itself goes back to Ramus's maps of knowledge, their neat, non-overlapping classifications, and the methodical ways – primarily from general to particular – in which items of knowledge were to be taught. It also features the tight timetabling – with shifts from subject to subject at the end of every learning period – which this way of carving up educational content required; and the place which examination, including self-examination, had in Old Dissent. By the mid-eighteenth century the outlines of a modern curriculum, comprehensively based on the major areas of knowledge, natural philosophy and mathematics not least, and markedly different from the classical curriculum favoured by the Anglican establishment, were clear. I trace its later history through the nineteenth century to the Taunton Commission recommendations of the 1860s and the Morant regulations of 1904. It was linked throughout this period with the notion of middle-class education and to a large extent with Dissent. It may be significant in this connexion that, as shown in Chapter 3, Morant himself came from impressive puritan stock.

Chapter 6 brings us forward to the present day. How do things stand now? The traditional notion of intelligence and the traditional school curriculum are both still with us, although not unchallenged. Are there any vestiges of puritan/ dissenting influence on our thinking in these areas? While contemporary notions of intelligence, including the educationally very popular theory of 'multiple intelligences', referred to above, yield little if any positive evidence for this, the British government's current 'Gifted and Talented' initiative has features in common with the eugenic programmes of Galton, Terman and Burt and may share, to some extent, in their ancestry.

The subject-based school curriculum which has been mandatory in England since 1988 has faced repeated attacks on its justifiability. This is not surprising, because it was introduced without any accompanying aims to speak of: ministers seemed to take it as read that it was a good thing, without onus of further backing. In its eighteenth-century beginnings, its rationale was very clear. Ignorance was a vice which one had to overcome as a condition of one's salvation. Understanding the overall structure of God's creation and seeing how each detail fits into the whole picture was theologically and educationally ideal. Over the centuries this rationale has fallen away and nothing compelling has taken its place. This became very evident when overall school aims *were* finally published in 1999: mismatches between these and the internal goals of many of the traditional subjects were now glaring. There have been recent moves in various quarters to begin curriculum planning from broad aims, rather than subjects, the latter thus becoming just one way among many possible other ways of realising these aims.

This alternative way of thinking about the curriculum puts the spotlight on aims themselves. What would a desirable set of school aims look like? This is a big question, but there will be little disagreement that equipping pupils to lead a successful life and help others to do so should be among them. The last part of Chapter 6 explores two notions of success. In one manifestation, it is a concept deriving from our puritan heritage, in which getting on in the world and the duty of unremitting hard work are central features. I urge that we detach ourselves from this older perspective and turn to a more acceptable version of a successful life. This revolves around a very different notion of personal fulfilment which has been hammered out in recent philosophical ethics. The chapter, and thus the book as a whole, suggest that our educational thinking, like our ethical thinking more generally, should begin with this pivotal concept.

Before we leave this introduction, a comment about terminology used in the rest of the book. As will have already been apparent in this introduction, it is often difficult to describe religious groupings in a non-controversial way. This is largely because of the multiplication of sects and subdivisions within the world of ascetic protestantism from its earliest days. Should the term 'puritan' cover, for instance, the Quakers, or should it be restricted to groups believing in predestination? By the late eighteenth century, the term 'dissenter' was used in England to embrace not only older puritan groupings, including for this purpose the Quakers, but also many Methodists. In places later in the book I shall use 'Old Dissenters' to stand for the former – i.e. the group consisting mainly of English Congregationalists, Presbyterians, Baptists and Quakers. But 'Old Dissenter' is inappropriate to describe eighteenth-century Scottish presbyterians, since 'dissent' in this context is dissent only from the laws of England. This is why I shall speak sometimes of communities 'of puritan descent'. Again, are Dutch Calvinists to be labelled 'puritans', or is the latter a term to be used only of English-speaking communities? Is there a single term to include Anglo-American puritanism, nineteenth-century Danish Lutheranism and evangelicalism in Switzerland? The phrase used earlier in this paragraph – 'ascetic protestantism' – is a helpful catch-all (taken from Weber 1930) and I shall rely on it here and there. But there is no perfect solution to these problems. I shall do my best to cope with them, hoping that the context will make it reasonably clear which groupings I have in mind.

1   An unexplained theory of intelligence

Two shapers of an educational system

Among fifty recently celebrated major thinkers on education between Confucius and John Dewey are four Englishmen born in the second half of the nineteenth century (Palmer 2001). They are Cyril Burt, Robert Morant, Bertrand Russell and Alfred North Whitehead.

Russell's and Whitehead's educational ideas, influential as they were, were not central to their work, their main achievements having been in mathematics and philosophy. But Morant and Burt are in a different class. They were both leading professionals, Morant in educational administration and Burt in educational psychology. Although, unlike Whitehead and Russell, they never collaborated, their achievements dovetailed. No two people did more to give state education in England in the twentieth century its characteristic shape.

That shape is élitist. At the turn of the twentieth century, state education was in theory still provided only at the elementary level. But the post-1870 system was rapidly moving beyond the basics: pupils who progressed through the 'standards' in the three Rs were often able to study more advanced subjects, including subjects of a practical/vocational sort, frequently in what were called 'higher grade schools'.

This pressure from below could have been reflected in policy. All young people could have been encouraged to go on learning as far as they wished, whether in practical/vocational directions or for more intrinsic reasons. Once one level of learning had been attained, the way could have been open to move on to another.

Theoretically, the English educational system could have moved in that direction after 1900. From time to time during the twentieth century short-lived attempts were made to push it that way. But such a policy required governments committed to furthering the education of every child and prepared to fund this. These were rare. At the beginning of the twentieth century the Conservative administration then in power was far from meeting these criteria.

Robert Morant

A key figure at the Board of Education at the turn of the twentieth century was Robert Morant (1863–1920). He was made Permanent Secretary to the Board in

1903, having played a leading part in setting up the 1902 Education Act, which put secondary as well as elementary education under public control for the first time, in the shape of newly created 'local education authorities'. In 1904 Morant introduced both a new code for the elementary school as well as regulations for the new state secondary schools. The effect of these two measures was to make a deep division between the two systems. This was most evident in their curricula. Each secondary school was normally to teach 'English language and literature, at least one language other than English, geography, history, mathematics, science, drawing, manual instruction (boys), domestic subjects (girls), physical exercise and organised games' (Aldrich 1988: 22). The subjects normally taught in elementary schools were: English language; arithmetic; drawing; practical instruction in handicraft, gardening, domestic and other subjects; observation lessons and nature study; geography; history; singing; hygiene; PT and moral instruction. This meant that for the 75 per cent of children who went to elementary school (McKibbin 1998: 208) there would be no provision for learning a foreign language, for mathematics beyond arithmetic, for science beyond nature study, or for a systematic introduction to English literature. Theirs was a curriculum designed to prepare them for work with their hands, not their brains.

It is hard not to agree with Eric Eaglesham's verdict on Morant's reforms, that they created a sharp division between 'education for leadership' and 'education for followership' (Eaglesham 1967: 51–61). Rather than building on the bottom-up growth under the old elementary system (where, for instance, the amount of science teaching in London had increased astonishingly between 1890 and 1900 (White 1975: 36, note 7)), 'Morant aimed at and achieved a standstill in elementary education' (Eaglesham 1967: 51). Henceforth, for the next sixty years and in part through to our own day, England's education system would be highly selective. A small minority of children would, at least in intention, receive a broad professional- and university-orientated education at secondary schools (later secondary grammar schools), while the vast mass would experience the academically undemanding curriculum of the elementary (later secondary modern) school.

The chasm between the two systems was not unbridgeable. The 1904 Elementary Code (Board of Education 1929: 9) stated that:

> It will be an important though subsidiary object of the School to discover individual children who show promise of exceptional capacity, and to develop their special gifts (so far as this can be done without sacrificing the interests of the majority of the children), so that they may be qualified to pass at the proper age into Secondary Schools, and be able to derive the maximum of benefit from the education there offered them.

Thus began the twentieth-century tradition of a 'ladder' of opportunity for exceptionally able children to pass into selective schools, the tradition that produced the '11+' exam in the middle of the century as well as the 'assisted places scheme' for entry into independent schools towards its end – and is more than vestigially alive in several forms in 2005.

Cyril Burt

Mention of the '11+' exam brings us to Cyril Burt (1883–1971), who contributed so much to its introduction. Although they never worked together, Burt shared with Morant an interest in clear-cut classification and grouping of the school population in line with pupils' likely future occupations and ways of life. Part of a memorandum on 'backward children' he wrote while working as a psychologist for the London County Council in 1925 was attached as an appendix to the *Handbook of Suggestions for Teachers* (i.e. elementary school teachers), which went through many reprints until as late as 1944. In it he stated:

> The ideal plan would perhaps comprise a 'treble-track' system – a series of backward classes for slow children, a series of advanced classes for quick children, both parallel to the ordinary series of standards for children of ordinary average ability.
>
> (Board of Education 1929: 422)

Although some movement between tracks was possible, just as some movement out of the elementary school into more advanced kinds of schooling was possible, Burt made it quite clear that both kinds were exceptional (ibid.: 422, 423). His advocacy of streaming in the elementary school did not remain purely theoretical. 'There is abundant evidence that this pattern was subsequently adopted in junior schools, particularly in the cities where they were sufficiently large. It is from the early 1930s … that streaming becomes *de rigueur*' (Simon 1974: 244).

Burt's attachment to streaming sprang directly from his views on intelligence. The report of the Spens Committee on secondary education in 1938 reflects his submission to it:

> Intellectual development during childhood appears to progress as if it were governed by a single central factor, usually known as 'general intelligence', which may be broadly described as innate all round intellectual ability. It appears to enter into everything which the child attempts to think, to say, or to do, and seems on the whole to be the most important factor in determining his work in the classroom. Our psychological witnesses assured us that it can be measured approximately by means of intelligence tests. We were informed that, with a few exceptions, it is possible at a very early age to predict with some degree of accuracy the ultimate level of a child's intellectual powers.
>
> (quoted in Simon 1974: 249–50)

Burt supported treble-tracking in elementary schools because he believed that children's intellectual level is relatively unchangeable, being fixed by heredity. As Simon (p. 250) points out, the Spens Report translated the general idea of treble-tracking (if not the details) to the school system as a whole. This appeared in their view that 'if justice be done' to the 'varying capacities' of children, there should be three different types of secondary school. After 1945 this took shape as the 'tripartite' system of secondary education, based largely on selection by IQ. Burt's theory of intelligence provided the major rationale for the 11+ examination which allocated children to different types of school (Gould 1981:293–6). Burt wrote of this:

> It is essential in the interests alike of the children themselves and of the nation as a whole, that those who possess the highest ability – the cleverest of the clever – should be identified as accurately as possible. Of the methods hitherto tried out the so-called 11+ exam has proved to be by far the most trustworthy.
>
> (Burt 1959: 117, as recorded in Gould 1981: 293)

Morant's introduction in 1904 of different school systems for children with different intended destinations in life was not backed by intelligence testing and the psychological theory surrounding this. It was only in this year that Alfred Binet, the French psychologist, who invented the first intelligence test as we now know it – and who influenced not only Burt and other British psychologists, but also Terman, Goddard and other pioneers in the USA – was approached by the French government to devise a test to pick out children intellectually unable to profit from ordinary schooling. His intelligence test was published in 1905.

Between the wars, however, as Simon tells us:

> ... the Morant outlook also received strong support from mental testing as operated within the existing system. Formerly apologists had stressed the overriding need of society for manual workers, even that manual work down the generations depressed intelligence beyond hope of improvement by education, as unavoidable social fact. This form of argument was never politically desirable and when it became politically impossible the doctrine of unequal distribution of 'intelligence' came very appropriately to hand. Here was an act of God, to which the sensible and knowledgeable necessarily bowed, as against the crank or visionary who sought to change the order of nature by social action. Essentially it was the same kind of argument, from assertion of a *status quo* (or natural order) that cannot be altered, as the old functional one which pointed to the given outlines of the social order to which education must conform.
>
> (Simon 1974: 292)

Burt, Galton and intelligence

The short period of 40 years between Morant's division of school curricula in 1904 and the tripartitism introduced after 1945 crystallised a system of state education based largely on social class, in which virtually the only prospect of avoiding a life of manual labour for able children from the working classes was to win a scholarship to secondary (later grammar) school, with further hope of entry to university and a professional career beyond.

It is difficult for us in 2006, still caught up in the residues of this system, to realise that there was nothing inevitable about its entrenchment. Its all-but-unscalable walls need never have existed; instead, there could have been open gateways at every turning.

The role of intelligence testing in providing an ideological rationale for the Morant system is central. So is the career of its main British architect, Cyril Burt.

Since his death in 1971 Burt's work on intelligence has been largely discredited, owing to claims that he fabricated data on the IQs of identical twins reared apart – the key plank in his claim that intelligence is innate – as well as inventing non-existent co-workers. Here I am less interested in the fraudulence than in the provenance of his ideas.

Burt's great intellectual hero had always been Francis Galton (1822–1911). It was Galton who first claimed, in an article in *Macmillan's Magazine* in 1865, that intellectual ability is inherited. His fuller and more celebrated exposition of his theory appeared in his 1869 book *Hereditary Genius* (Galton 1978).

Even as a schoolboy in the 1890s Burt knew much about Galton and his achievements. Burt's father was a doctor in Warwickshire and used regularly to visit a relative of Francis Galton.

> When my father had visited one of his more eminent patients, he would try to fire my ambition by describing their achievements or those of their relatives … Darwin Galton, an ailing old man of 80, lived three miles away at Claverdon, where Sir Francis Galton now lies buried. And since, as family physician, my father called there at least once a week, I heard more about Francis Galton than anyone else. Next to Milton and Darwin, he was, I think, my father's supreme example of the Ideal Man; and as a model he had the further merit of being really alive. So it was that, on returning to school, I got from the library Galton's Inquiries into Human Faculty, and I still recollect a superstitious thrill when I noticed on the title-page that it first saw daylight in the same year that I was born.
>
> (Burt 1952: 58–9)

Some years later Galton was more directly influential in shaping Burt's career. Burt's first ventures into psychological research, as an Oxford undergraduate and later, were on Galtonian topics, especially innate abilities (ibid.: 60–2). He corresponded with Galton and owed his appointment as educational psychologist to the London County Council (LCC) partly to Galton's support for the scheme in general (ibid.: 63). In addition, he had several intellectual and personal contacts from his Oxford days onwards with Karl Pearson, Galton's close associate and later biographer.

Burt's conception of intelligence was essentially Galtonian. For Burt intelligence was definable as 'innate, general, cognitive ability' (Burt 1955: 265).

> The degree of intelligence with which any particular child is endowed is one
> of the most important factors determining his general efficiency all throughout
> life. In particular it sets an upper limit to what he can perform, especially in
> the educational, vocational and intellectual fields.
>
> (ibid.: 281)

There are several elements to this notion, all of which are present in Galton.
The latter did not use the word 'intelligence', writing instead about 'genius' (a
term he later regretted (Galton 1978: viii)), or 'natural ability', but the underlying
concept is the same as Burt's. Galton's 1865 article was triggered by his cousin
Charles Darwin's *Origin of Species*, published six years before. Its basic idea is that
intellectual ability is inherited. Galton supports this by a demonstration of how
intellectual eminence is manifested among close family members in a range of
fields and occupations. *Hereditary Genius* fills out the idea with further evidence
of family connexions among the highly able.

The notion of *limitations* on ability is prominent in this work. In the preface to
the 1892 edition, Galton wrote:

> At the time when the book was written, the human mind was popularly
> thought to act independently of natural laws, and to be capable of almost
> any achievement, if compelled to exert itself by a will that had a power of
> initiation. Even those who had more philosophical habits of thought were
> far from looking upon the mental faculties of each individual as being limited
> with as much strictness as those of his body, still less was the idea of the
> hereditary transmission of ability clearly apprehended.
>
> (Galton 1978: vii)

In the book itself he wrote:

> I acknowledge freely the great power of education and social influences in
> developing the active powers of the mind, just as I acknowledge the effect of
> use in developing the muscles of a blacksmith's arm and no further.
>
> (ibid.: 14)

He went on to a vivid account of how a boy who believes himself capable of
any intellectual challenge, gradually acquires through life a more realistic
perception of his limitations, until:

> he limits his undertakings to matters below the level of his reach, and finds
> true moral repose in an honest conviction that he is engaged in as much
> good work as his nature has rendered him capable of performing.
>
> (ibid.: 16)

The Galtonian conception of mental ability, which Burt took over, thus
contains the notion of innately determined limits, differing from one individual

to another, and parallel to those with which we are all familiar in our bodily development, as shown in Galton's own example of muscle power.

Burt also followed Galton in two other respects. For Burt (1955: 265) intelligence 'is (in the broad sense of the word) an *intellectual* quality – that is, it characterizes the cognitive rather than the affective or conative aspects of conscious behaviour'. Galton mentions 'the intellect' and includes phrases like 'the enormous difference between the intellectual capacity of men' on page after page of *Hereditary Genius*. Much of the book is taken up with examples of 'eminence' in the families of scientists, judges, divines, poets and other professions, beginning its analysis with data on senior wranglers in mathematics at Cambridge (Galton 1978: 16–23).

For both writers, finally, intelligence (or natural ability) is *general*. People have specific abilities in mathematics or other fields, but underlying these is something more all-encompassing. In a passage from *Hereditary Genius* which Burt is fond of quoting (e.g. Burt 1955: 264), Galton tells us that his data show:

> in how small degree eminence … can be considered as due to purely special powers … People lay too much stress on apparent specialities, thinking over-rashly that, because a man is devoted to some particular pursuit, he could not possibly have succeeded in anything else. They might just as well say that, because a youth had fallen desperately in love with a brunette, he could not possibly have fallen in love with a blonde … It is as probable as not that the affair was mainly or wholly due to a general amorousness of disposition.
>
> (Galton 1978: 23–4)

He also writes, in another favourite gobbet of Burt's:

> Without a special gift for mathematics, a man cannot be a mathematician; but without a high degree of general ability he will never make a *great* mathematician.
>
> (quoted in Burt 1955: 264–5)

The oddness of the Galtonian conception of intelligence

To sum up, both Burt and Galton understood intelligence in basically the same way – as innate, intellectual, general and limited ability. It may seem remarkable that Burt should have taken over *all* these features of the concept from his mentor, since *each one of them* is radically problematic.

I have provided my reasons for this verdict more fully elsewhere (e.g. White 2002a: ch. 5) but will give the gist of them here.

Intelligence as intellectual

Was Albert Einstein more intelligent than David Beckham is? Neither Galton nor Burt would have had any doubts about his superiority, but that was because they were writing intellectual ability into their concept from the start. Intelligence, as we usually understand this – at least, if we are not already caught up in the Galtonian thought-world that has come down to us via intelligence testing – can be displayed in areas far removed from the pursuit of truth, assuming this is what 'intellectual' activities have as their aim. Plumbers can work on leaks intelligently or unintelligently; so can spouses striving to keep a fragile relationship intact. As we normally understand it, intelligent activity has to do with the flexible adaptation of means to ends, whether those ends are winning goals in football or working out problems in theoretical physics.

Burt and Galton approached things differently. The field that first suggested itself to Galton in explaining his theory was advanced mathematics as examined in the Cambridge honours degree, closely followed by classics, literature and the law; while for Burt, as we have seen, a schoolchild's level of intelligence is tied to whether he or she is secondary school material or, if not, it is tied to the upper, middle or lower track he or she should ideally be following in the elementary school. For both writers the prime locus is the academic institution – school or university.

This is not meant as a *criticism* of their theories (or rather 'theory', given what I have said about the similarity of their basic claims). People use terms in different ways, and there is no reason why either writer should have felt constrained to include in his range the good judgement of a tennis player or the flexible behaviour of a domestic cat when a habitual path to a goal has been blocked, both of which other authors might label 'intelligent'. The interesting question – and one to which we shall return – is *why* they both concentrated on the academic.

Intelligence as general

The same sort of conclusion is in order under this new heading. If, as suggested, intelligence is commonly understood in terms of flexible adaptation of means to ends, the most obvious way of taking it is as having to be contextualised in relation to the kind of end in question. It does not make sense, on this view, to talk of someone as 'intelligent full stop'. If she plays tennis intelligently, she makes good judgements on the way to trying to win a match. Someone else may be displaying their intelligence in relation to a different end and in a different field – say in making good judgements about how to keep their garden in good order. We have no reason to think that those who are good at tennis playing are likely to be good at gardening. They may or may not be: we would have to test this out case by case.

Galton's claim that natural ability is general appears to be more of an assumption than a conclusion based on evidence. His point, quoted favourably by Burt, and cited above, that people wrongly think that 'because a man is devoted to some particular pursuit, he could not possibly have succeeded in anything else' is true enough, but has no bearing on whether there can be such a thing as general ability. Just because a person is good at tennis, it would, I agree, be wrong to conclude that she could not possibly have succeeded as a gardener; but one could still hold that if she showed intelligent behaviour in both areas, this was specific to each.

Once again, the interesting question – at least in the context of this book – is not whether Galton and his disciple were right or wrong in their claim about general ability, but *why* they were so inclined to believe it.

Intelligence as innate

To act intelligently in playing football, in politics or in doing crosswords depends on understanding all sorts of things about these fields and having the skills and dispositions which they severally require. This requires some induction into the area. In this sense intelligence depends on training, learning, culture and 'environment'. But it also depends on something innate, for if we were born without brains and without more specialised brain features we would be unable to learn these things. We must at least have the innate ability, or capacity, to acquire them. All this is obvious and uncontroversial. When Galton and Burt wrote about intelligence as innate they obviously meant more than this. To see what this was, we have to move on to the next category.

Intelligence as limited

Galton began *Hereditary Genius* with these words:

> I propose to show in this book that a man's natural abilities are derived by inheritance, under exactly the same limitations as are the form and physical features of the whole organic world.
>
> (Galton 1978: 3)

The implication here is that natural abilities, being innate, also set limits on what we can achieve. Just as a person's height or the muscles in a blacksmith's arms are not only inherited but also reach a ceiling beyond which no more growth or strength is possible, the same is true of natural ability. We have already encountered Burt's belief that the degree of intelligence with which a person is innately endowed 'sets an upper limit to what he can perform, especially in the educational, vocational and intellectual fields'. The patterning of intelligence on height or muscle strength brings with it the thought, central to Burt's and Galton's theories, that there are individual differences in innate intelligence, from giftedness through to backwardness and beyond.

How can one show that intelligence shares these characteristics with height, strength and other physical features? In particular, how can one show that we all have individually different ceilings of ability? Despite Galton's agenda-setting opening sentence, the evidence he adduces in his book is scarcely convincing. The fact that some families, taken over time, contain several eminent people is capable of another and more plausible explanation than hereditary transmission of exceptional ability: that cultures develop inside the family which favour and celebrate outstanding achievements, especially in certain areas. Galton's own remarkable family is a case in point (as we shall soon see in more detail).

Burt's own preferred type of evidence for the innateness of intelligence is the close correlation among the IQs of identical twins 'brought up in different environments almost from birth' (Burt 1955: 273). In the work just mentioned Burt, as in other writings from the last years of his life, claimed to have collected 53 such cases, which together showed a high 'final assessment' correlation of 0.87 for the twins in each pair. It is now clear from minute analysis of Burt's data that they are radically untrustworthy (Kamin 1977: 55–71).

In an exchange of correspondence with Burt in late 1969 and early 1970 – not knowing of the as-yet-undetected problems with the data on the 53 cases – I put to him, among other matters, the following suggestion. Suppose it had been possible to give one of the twins from each pair intensive coaching which resulted in an average IQ increase for all who participated of, say, 15 points. This would have significantly reduced the correlation for the twins in each pair. So it must be an *assumption* made by the theorist – i.e. Burt – in claiming a correlation of 0.87, that coaching could not significantly affect the IQ scores. Burt replied 'I doubt whether, had we returned a second time, the coaching would have affected our correlations'.

It would appear that neither Galton nor Burt provided good evidence for their key claim. The proposition that, for all of us, there are individually differing ceilings of ability seems to be an *assumption* behind their position, rather than a conclusion based on telling grounds.

I have discussed elsewhere (White 1974, 2002a: ch. 5) what could count as evidence for this proposition, and concluded that it is neither verifiable nor falsifiable. It is not verifiable. The mere fact that a child appears not to be able to get beyond, say, elementary algebra and into advanced algebra is not evidence of a ceiling. The failure of this or that variation in teaching approach fares no better, since it is always possible for a teacher to try some different approach to help the learner get over the hurdle. (With some children, so neurologically damaged that they seem incapable of language, it may seem that the point where options run out for the teacher is easier to establish than it is for other children. But the proposition in question is supposed to apply to all of us: we are all said to have our own mental ceiling; and for non-brain-damaged people the existence of a ceiling seems impossible to demonstrate.) It is not falsifiable, since for even the cleverest person in the world, for whom no ceiling has been discovered, it is always possible that it exists somewhere. As an untestable – unverifiable and unfalsifiable – proposition, the claim that we each have a mental ceiling has, if we follow Karl Popper (1963: ch. 1), no role in science. It is like the proposition that God exists or that all historical events are predetermined, both of which are equally untestable. As such, it may play a foundational role, as these two propositions have played, in some ideological system of belief, but has no place in empirical science.

As with the other features of Galtonian intelligence, its intellectual nature and its generality, we need to ask about the claim that it is innate/limiting: *why* did both Galton and Burt believe this? An easy – too easy – answer is that they believed it because they took it that intelligence is patterned on physical differences between individuals like height or muscle power. But this only pushes the quest for explanation one stage back. *Why* did they think that mental differences work in the same kind of way as physical differences?

How did Galton's conception come about? His eugenic project

We have examined one by one the various features of Galtonian intelligence and seen that each is problematic. Intelligence is said to be an intellectual affair; but no good reason is given why intellectual activities are picked out within the far wider class of means–end activities. It is also supposed to be general; but no good reason is put forward for this either, in the face of the enormous heterogeneity of forms of intelligent behaviour from bowling to biological theory to bricklaying. The contention that it is innate in a limiting way is no more secure in its credentials.

In each case the question arises: *why* are Galton and then Burt attached to these features? What deeper-level explanation can be given for this?

Before exploring this, it will be helpful to connect the points made about the notion of intelligence with Morant's and Burt's work in reshaping English state education. Simon wrote, as we saw, that 'the Morant outlook also received strong support from mental testing as operated within the existing system'. We can now see in more detail how this was possible. Rationalising the post-1904 divided educational system needed three kinds of theoretical input. There had to be a way of selecting pupils for the new, *intellectually* orientated secondary schools. There had to be a way of selecting them not for their aptitude in geography or science or any other subject of the secondary curriculum, but for secondary education *in general*. There had to be a way of showing that children not selected for secondary education could not have profited by it because they would never be capable of engaging with it. A notion of intelligence as innate (i.e. limiting), general, intellectual ability was ideal for the purpose. All that was needed was a way of ensuring that the degree of intelligence which any child possessed could be accurately determined. This is what intelligence testing, as developed by Burt and his colleagues, professed to deliver.

Mental testing also helped to defuse the criticism of the Morant system that selective schools were largely for middle-class children, leaving aside the very few from the working class who were able to change class via scholarships. In his contribution to *Black Paper Two* (Burt 1969: 20) Burt agreed that the average IQ of children whose fathers follow one of the higher professions is well over 120 while for those born to unskilled labourers it is less than 90. But,

> One reason for these class differences in average intelligence is obvious. To become a doctor, lawyer, or teacher, it is necessary to pass certain qualifying examinations; and these demand a high level of innate ability. The ability of parents who have entered one of these professions tends to be transmitted to their children.

I turn back now to the deeper-level exploration of why Galton and Burt thought as they did. To begin this, we need a fuller picture of Galton's project. Here again is the first sentence of *Hereditary Genius*:

> I propose to show in this book that a man's natural abilities are derived by inheritance, under exactly the same limitations as are the form and physical features of the whole organic world.
>
> (Galton 1978: 3)

And here is the next sentence:

> Consequently, as it is easy, notwithstanding those limitations, to obtain by careful selection a permanent breed of dogs or horses gifted with peculiar powers of running, or of doing anything else, so it would be quite practicable to produce a highly-gifted race of men by judicious marriages during several consecutive generations.

Galton's project is in what he later came to term 'eugenics'. He believed, as he went on in the same paragraph to say, that for each generation 'it is a duty we owe to humanity' to investigate the power we have 'over the natural gifts of those that follow', and 'to exercise it in a way that, without being unwise to ourselves, shall be most advantageous to future inhabitants of the earth'.

The origins of Galton's eugenic project lie in his article on 'Hereditary talent and character' in *Macmillan's Magazine* for 1865, the whole text of which is available on the web at http://psychclassics.yorku.ca/Galton/talent.htm. It is worth reading in full, having been characterised by Karl Pearson, Galton's biographer, as 'an epitome of the great bulk of Galton's work for the rest of his life' (Fancher 2001: 15). It is also franker and more unbuttoned than his later, more considered, formulations.

As the title of the article indicates, in 1865 Galton was interested in the eugenic possibilities of breeding not only for intellectual ability but also for moral character (which he also called 'mental aptitude'). Both in his view have a hereditary basis. In *Hereditary Genius* his attention is almost wholly on intellectual ability, but he also states, and elaborates on the theme, that 'the table of the distribution of natural gifts is necessarily as true of morals as of intellect or muscle' (Galton 1978: 282).

The article is built around the idea of improving the human race through selective breeding. One purple-tending passage is worth quoting at length:

> Let us, then, give reins to our fancy, and imagine a Utopia – or a Laputa, if you will – in which a system of competitive examination for girls, as well as for youths, had been so developed as to embrace every important quality of mind and body, and where a considerable sum was yearly allotted to the endowment of such marriages as promised to yield children who would grow into eminent servants of the State. We may picture to ourselves an annual

ceremony in that Utopia or Laputa, in which the Senior Trustee of the Endowment Fund would address ten deeply-blushing young men, all of 25 years old, in the following terms :—

'Gentlemen, I have to announce the results of a public examination, conducted on established principles; which show that you occupy the foremost places in your year, in respect to those qualities of talent, character, and bodily vigour which are proved, on the whole, to do most honour and best service to our race. An examination has also been conducted on established principles among all the young ladies of this country who are now of the age of twenty-one, and I need hardly remind you, that this examination takes note of grace, beauty, health, good temper, accomplished housewifery, and disengaged affections, in addition to noble qualities of heart and brain. By a careful investigation of the marks you have severally obtained, and a comparison of them, always on established principles, with those obtained by the most distinguished among the young ladies, we have been enabled to select ten of their names with especial reference to your individual qualities. It appears that marriages between you and these ten ladies, according to the list I hold in my hand, would offer the probability of unusual happiness to yourselves, and, what is of paramount interest to the State, would probably result in an extraordinarily talented issue. Under these circumstances, if any or all of these marriages should be agreed upon, the sovereign herself will give away the brides, at a high and solemn festival, six months hence, in Westminster Abbey. We, on our part, are prepared, in each case, to assign £5,000 as a wedding-present, and to defray the cost of maintaining and educating your children, out of the ample funds entrusted to our disposal by the State.

If a twentieth part of the cost and pains were spent in measures for the improvement of the human race that is spent on the improvement of the breed of horses and cattle, what a galaxy of genius might we not create! We might introduce prophets and high priests of our civilization into a world as surely as we can propagate idiots by mating *crétins*. Men and women of the present day are, to those we might hope to bring into existence, what the pariah dogs of the streets of an Eastern town are to our own highly bred varieties.

The feeble nations of the world are necessarily giving way before the nobler varieties of mankind; and even the best of these, so far as we know them, seem unequal to their work. The average culture of mankind is become so much higher than it was, and the branches of knowledge and history so various and extended, that few are capable even of comprehending the exigencies of our modern civilization; much less fulfilling them. We are living in a sort of intellectual anarchy, for want of master minds. The general intellectual capacity of our leaders requires to be raised, and also to be differentiated. We want abler commanders, statesmen, thinkers, inventors, and artists. The natural qualifications of our race are no greater than they used to be in semi-barbarous times, though the conditions amid which we are born are vastly more complex than of old. The foremost minds of the present day seem to stagger and halt under an intellectual load too heavy for their powers.

(Galton 1865: 165–6)

There are two sides to Galton's selective breeding. One is, as we have seen, to improve the stock of those most naturally gifted. The other is to diminish the numbers of the less endowed to the point of their elimination. This comes out in a further passage in the 1865 article (ibid.: 319):

It may be said that, even granting the validity of my arguments, it would be impossible to carry their indications into practical effect. For instance, if we divided the rising generation into two castes, A and B, of which A was selected for natural gifts, and B was the refuse, then, supposing marriage was confined within the pale of the caste to which each individual belonged, it might be objected that we should simply differentiate our race – that we should create a good and a bad caste, but we should not improve the race as a whole. I reply that this is by no means the necessary result. There remains another very important law to be brought into play. Any agency, however indirect, that would somewhat hasten the marriages in caste A, and retard those in caste B, would result in a larger proportion of children being born to A than to B, and would end by wholly eliminating B, and replacing it by A.

There is also a racial element in Galton's thinking as his reference above to 'the feeble nations of the world' indicates. Take, for instance, his comparison of native American Indians and West African blacks (ibid.: 321):

Their characters are almost opposite, one to the other. The Red man has great patience, great reticence, great dignity, and no passion; the Negro has strong impulsive passions, and neither patience, reticence, nor dignity, He is warm-hearted, loving towards his master's children, and idolised by the children in return. He is eminently gregarious for he is always jabbering, quarrelling, tom-tom-ing, or dancing. He is remarkably domestic, and he is endowed with such constitutional vigour, and is so prolific, that his race is irrepressible.

From this and from his fuller review of the world's races in the chapter on 'The comparative worth of different races' in *Hereditary Genius*, it should come as no surprise to learn that Europeans – not least protestant Europeans from the north of the continent – come top. Not that they have always been so worthy: as he puts it in the closing words of his 1865 article, talking about the human race as a whole (ibid.: 327): 'our forefathers were utter savages from the beginning; and ... after myriads of years of barbarism, our race has but very recently grown to be civilized and religious'.

It is important to realise the *grandiosity* of Galton's eugenic vision. The ending of *Hereditary Genius* is sympathetic to the view that:

> the constitution of the living Universe is a pure theism, and ... its form of activity is what may be described as cooperative ... all life is single in its essence, but various, ever varying, and interactive in its manifestations, and ... men and all other living animals are active workers and sharers in a vastly more extended system of cosmic action than any of ourselves, much less of them, can possibly comprehend ... they may contribute, more or less unconsciously, to the manifestation of a far higher life than our own, somewhat as – I do not propose to push the metaphor too far – the individual cells of one of the more complex animals contribute to the manifestation of its higher order of personality.
>
> (ibid.: 376)

Galton clearly believed that steps could and should be taken through selective breeding to further this cosmic process and to remove the obstacles to it posed by what he saw as the danger of degeneration resulting from the prolificness of inferior stock, both nationally and globally. Britishers – of the right stock – have a peculiar responsibility in this grand design as they belong to a race at the pinnacle of human development.

Burt takes up Galton's baton

Galton's vision may seem a world away from Burt's treble-track conception of the English elementary school half a century later. But the two ideas mesh well together. Recall Burt's statement in his autobiographical sketch that 'next to Milton and Darwin, he was, I think, my father's supreme example of the Ideal Man'. For many people towards the end of the nineteenth century Galton was an inspirational figure. We know that these included Burt himself. It is underestimating the latter to see him simply as an educational psychologist as we understand this term today – as a local government official with statistical expertise who played a leading role in the organisation and reorganisation of English schools. No doubt he was this. But he was more. In 1937 and 1957 he was also on the Consultative Council of the Eugenics Society which Galton had founded in 1908. Classifying children so that they followed the eugenically appropriate course for them was his lifetime's work. Educational selection was one facet of that 'careful selection' mentioned by Galton in his account of planned breeding at the opening of *Hereditary Genius* (see above). Burt's Galtonian theory of intellectual ceilings helped to ensure that pupils were not placed in tracks, and later schools, which were beyond their capacities, thus degrading the quality of work at that level.

Burt's eugenic preoccupations emerge in the very different attitudes he shows towards the education of the élite and that of the masses – the 'refuse' in Galton's terminology quoted above. In his contribution to *Black Paper Two* (Burt 1969: 22), he rails against the slack approach to 'discipline and work' that he associates with opponents of a selective school system and their predilection for child-centred methods. He quotes Galton to the effect that high intelligence is not enough for success. It needs to be reinforced by 'sustained and laborious toil'. And he quotes from a story by Ian Hay, in which the headmaster says 'Make them work like niggers. That's education in a nutshell'. Compare that with his Appendix on 'The Backward Child' in the post-1925 reprints of the *Handbook of Suggestions for Teachers*.

> For the majority of these children, the ultimate objects in view should not be too ambitious ... Dispense with all that does not either (a) appeal to the natural interests of the child himself, or (b) bear closely upon his work or leisure in later life ... Discipline in such schools and classes should be as free as possible.
>
> (Board of Education 1929: 422–7)

Galton would have applauded Burt's remarks in *Black Paper Two* (Burt 1969: 22) that:

> the types of pupils who seem to be nearly always overlooked are what have been termed the 'exceptionally gifted' ... The moral would seem to be that, instead of pursuing a policy which demands a greater uniformity in the nation's schools, we should aim at a greater diversity.

He would also have welcomed Burt's defence of the 11+ selection of the 'cleverest of the clever' for grammar school education as a wise step for 'warding off the ultimate decline and fall that has overtaken each of the great civilisations of the past' (Burt 1959: 117, as recorded in Gould 1981: 293).

For both writers, the élite came first. For both, examinations and scholarships to selective schools were a key eugenic mechanism. Burt would have applauded – or perhaps did in fact applaud, Galton's remark in *Hereditary Genius* that:

> The best form of civilisation in respect to the improvement of the race, would be one ...where every lad had a chance of showing his abilities, and, if highly gifted, was enabled to achieve a first-class education and entrance into professional life, by the liberal help of the exhibitions and scholarships which he had gained in his early youth.
>
> (Galton 1978: 362)

The Galtonian project in the USA

Selective secondary education in England and the wide use of Galtonian intelligence testing in that country are historical contingencies. They might never have happened. The same is true of intelligence testing more globally.

It was in the United States that Galtonian ideas had most impact. The pioneers

here are widely acknowledged to have been H.H. Goddard (1866–1957) and
Lewis Terman (1877–1956).

H.H. Goddard

Goddard was a student of G.S. Hall at Clark University and from 1906 until
1918 was psychological director of the Vineland Training School, an institution
for the feeble-minded in New Jersey. In 1908 he was the first American to recognise
and develop the potential of intelligence testing as invented by Binet in 1905 – a
few years before Burt began his own work on the use of the Binet tests in England
(Burt 1952: 67). Over the next years he became a vigorous advocate of the Binet
approach, using his own version of the tests in public schools in 1911, and in
1913 with immigrants arriving at Ellis Island. By 1918 he had helped to introduce
intelligence testing into the US Army.

As with Burt, Goddard's testing activities were in the service of larger purposes.
Like Burt, he was a eugenicist, and in his own case a member of the American
Eugenics Society. He held similar views to those of Galton and Burt about the
hereditary nature of intelligence and about social reform via the strengthening of
a stratified society led by the most intelligent:

> It is no useless speculation that tries to see what would happen if society
> were organized so as to recognise and make use of the doctrine of mental
> levels … it is quite possible to restate practically all of our social problems in
> terms of mental level …The great advantage of having every man doing
> work on his own mental level would prove fundamental.
>
> (Goddard 1920: vi)

Goddard is well-known for his study of the 'Kallikak Family' (Goddard 1912),
which sought to prove the hereditarian thesis in the contrast between two families
of some 400 individuals each which were descended from the same man. One
family, descended from a liaison with a feeble-minded woman, included over 100
feeble-minded people; while the other, descended from the man's normally
intelligent wife, contained no feeble-minded members at all.

Among the conclusions that Goddard drew from his study were that ways had
to be found of preventing feeble-minded people, who he claimed were multiplying
at a faster rate than normal people, from putting brakes on social progress. He
recommended that colonies should be set up where they could lead segregated
lives. The fact that in his Ellis Island work he detected very low average IQs in
various cultural groups of immigrants from southern and eastern Europe helped
to lead to the Immigration Restriction Act of 1924.

Lewis Terman

Lewis Terman, like Goddard, was a pupil of G.S. Hall at Clark University and a
follower of Galton. He wrote in his autobiography: 'Of the founders of modern
psychology, my greatest admiration is for Galton' (Terman 1932: 331). He is famous

in the history of intelligence testing for several reasons. First, for his publication in 1916 of *The Measurement of Intelligence*. This introduced the Stanford-Binet test, a revised version of the Binet test appropriate for American children. Second, for bringing the notion of the IQ into intelligence testing with the Stanford-Binet (Terman borrowed the idea from Stern). And third, for his work, conducted over several decades, on the intellectually gifted.

As with Goddard, Burt and Galton, Terman's work was in the service of wider social ends – essentially the *same* ends as theirs. He, too, was a eugenicist, having been a member of the Advisory Council of the American Eugenics Society from 1922 until 1935. Kamin (1977: 20) quotes from the first chapter of *The Measurement of Intelligence*:

> ... in the near future intelligence tests will bring tens of thousands of these high-grade defectives under the surveillance and protection of society. This will ultimately result in curtailing the reproduction of feeble-mindedness and in the elimination of an enormous amount of crime, pauperism, and industrial inefficiency. It is hardly necessary to emphasise that the high-grade cases, of the type now so frequently overlooked, are precisely the ones whose guardianship it is most important for the State to assume.
>
> (Terman 1916: 6–7)

A few years later (Terman 1923, quoted in Minton 1988: 98), Terman expressed his agreement with the view that:

> ... the differentiation of curricula and the classification of school children according to ability, far from being undemocratic measures, are absolutely essential if the public school is to be made a real instrument of democracy ... true democracy does not rest upon equality of endowment, but upon equality of opportunity ...

In another paper (Terman 1922: 657–9, quoted in Minton 1988: 99), he stated that:

> ... all the available facts that science has to offer support the Galtonian theory that mental abilities are chiefly a matter of original endowment ... It is to the highest 25 percent of our population, and more especially to the top 5 percent, that we must look for the production of leaders who will advance science, art, government, education, and social welfare generally...The least intelligent 15 or 20 percent of our population ... are democracy's ballast, not always useless but always a potential liability ...

The intelligibility gap: why Galtonianism?

This book is not a comprehensive history of intelligence testing. For one thing, it discusses Robert Morant, whose work was exclusively in educational administration. The fuller story of intelligence testing has been told many times already. The American part of that story, in particular, includes many well-known names which have not come into the account so far – Yerkes, Thorndike, Thurstone, and more recently Jensen, Herrnstein and Murray. These will figure in later chapters. I have also said nothing about the decline in enthusiasm for eugenics in Britain and the USA after it was taken up by the Nazis in the 1930s with results we all know; or about the rekindling of interest in alleged racial differences in intelligence with the work of Arthur Jensen in the late 1960s, and Herrnstein and Murray's (1994) *The Bell Curve* in the mid-1990s. What is interesting about these last two developments is that they show the *resilience* of the Galtonian perspective, its ability to survive for over a century despite what seem gross flaws. How far is this connected with the point made above, that the existence of Galtonian intelligence, with its notion of individually varying limits of ability, is *unfalsifiable*?

This brings me to the purpose of the discussion so far – much of which will have been familiar to those with an interest in the early history of modern psychology. My aim has been to suggest a gap in intelligibility. *Why* did these pioneers on both sides of the Atlantic develop the theories and tests and educational arrangements they did? What impelled them to make the comments quoted from them in this text?

I have tried to bring out the *peculiarity* of their positions – the patent oddity, unacceptability, and even inhumanity of some of their statements, the deeper unfoundedness of others. It may be hard for us to see all this at first, since we live in a culture so significantly shaped by theories of intelligence and practices connected with them like educational selection. I will finish this section by a reprise and further elaboration of the points at which fuller explanation is necessary.

Most of these take us back to Galton – not surprisingly, since many of the oddities in others' positions can be explained by their Galtonian origin. Galton was the first of the line. If we can understand more clearly what motivated *him*, we will be in a good position to understand the others.

Although he used other terms for it, Galton was the creator of the notion of intelligence which has been transmitted from him through all our famous names down to Herrnstein and Murray of *The Bell Curve* and beyond. Why did he invent it? No one before him had come up with the thought that we all possess different degrees of an ability which is intellectual, general and limited. The idea of such an ability is odd. Why these elements? Why *them*, especially when their credentials, when examined closely, are so wanting?

As we have seen, the interest in this ability is part of Galton's broader interest in eugenics. But this satisfies the desire for intelligibility only to a point. We still need to know why Galton – and his disciples – were attracted by eugenics in the first place. Not only this: we also need to know why the eugenic ideas took the form they did.

Why the emphasis on abstract thinking?

Why was there such emphasis on the intellect? Why did intelligence come to be associated particularly with the logical, mathematical and linguistic areas examined by intelligence tests? If the main task of eugenics was to produce leaders of society in different fields, why not work with a broader and less abstract notion of the kinds of ability required, including, not least, the kinds of practical ability needed in running large organisations?

Part of the answer lies, no doubt, in the belief that mental ability is general – and that the training of the intellect in some unqualified sense will generate the more specific abilities needed in statesmanship or generalship. But, again, the eugenic outlook is detachable from the notion of general ability. Building on Galton's Utopia, one could imagine a eugenic prize-giving ceremony for youths and maidens of quality in their early twenties based on how well they have achieved in any of the 'multiple intelligences' of Howard Gardner (1983). So the explanation in terms of eugenics fails fully to satisfy the desire for intelligibility. We still need to know why abstract intellect and general ability were the focus.

Incidentally, talking of Galton's prize ceremony, how fanciful are its details? The offer of a cash reward (of £5,000) for couples willing to marry and of free state education for their children did not remain Utopian. James McKeen Cattell (1860–1944) – an American who studied with Galton when a lecturer at Cambridge, England in 1886, became a Galtonian, and introduced an interest in measuring individual differences to America – 'promised his seven children $1000 each if they would marry sons and daughters of college professors' (Schultz and Schultz 2000: 209).

Why the preoccupation with examinations and tests of ability?

A related feature of Galton's Utopia is its reliance on public examinations. The young men have come top in the exam for 'talent, character, and bodily vigour', while the women's exam 'takes note of grace, beauty, health, good temper, accomplished housewifery, and disengaged affections, in addition to noble qualities of heart and brain'. Again, this is not merely fanciful. Examinations played a large part in Galton's life and in his picture of a good society (Fancher 1984). As we have seen, the first case study in *Hereditary Genius* is a detailed analysis of the final honours mathematics exam at Cambridge, especially of the top-scoring Wranglers and Senior Wrangler. Galton himself attempted honours in mathematics at that university and had hopes of a Wranglership himself; but he suffered an emotional breakdown and ended up with a 'poll' (non-honours) degree. Fancher's paper suggests that this experience helps to explain his fascination with competitive honours-level examinations – as well as with anthropometric testing – throughout his career. But his interest in the idea of examining went further than the scholastic, as is evident in this passage near the start of *Hereditary Genius* (Galton 1978: 6):

I look upon social and professional life as a continuous examination. All are candidates for the good opinions of others, and for success in their several professions, and they achieve success in proportion as the general estimate is large of their aggregate merits. In ordinary scholastic examinations marks are allotted in stated proportions to various specified subjects – so many for Latin, so many for Greek, so many for English history, and the rest. The world, in the same way, but almost unconsciously, allots marks to men.

Although Galton's own eugenic visions pivoted around examinations, and although school examinations as well as mental tests were prominent in the work and thought of Cyril Burt and other eugenicist psychologists, there is no necessary link between eugenics and exams, least of all with scholastic exams. Eugenicists can and do dream of identifying those in whom they want to encourage or discourage breeding via their genes, not by seeing how they perform on three-hour papers or the Stanford-Binet. Once again there is an explanatory gap in the story. Why did *these* eugenicists put such weight on examinations and intelligence tests? Does it all go back to Galton's student breakdown? Or is there more to it??

Darwin's work is obviously a major factor in explaining the origins of intelligence testing. *The Origin of Species* appeared in 1859 and Galton's magazine article, with its Darwinian themes, in 1865. (See Fancher 2001 for the Darwinian circles in which Galton moved in the intervening six years.) But Darwinian influences cannot be the whole explanation. Not all Darwinians, by any means, who were exercised by the implications of the theory for human society, were eugenicists. So we need an answer to the question why Galton and his followers moved in *that* direction. We also need, as we have seen, explanations of why they built into their version of eugenics such contingent features of it as intellectual and general ability, as well as examining and testing.

Why the polarised interest in extremely high and extremely low ability?

There are other puzzling aspects of Galtonianism. Its attitude, for instance, towards the *non*-eminent, the *non*-gifted. Sometimes it seems that its only interest is in the highly able – just as horse breeders are only interested in the kind of horse who will win races and simply ignore the rest. Except that this is not quite the whole story. Horse breeders do indeed ignore the rest: they do not have any *attitude* towards them. But Galton and his followers *do* have an attitude towards the non-gifted. In a passage quoted above, Galton wrote about dividing 'the rising generation into two castes, A and B, of which A was selected for natural gifts, and B was the refuse'. As we have seen, too, for Terman 'the least intelligent 15 or 20 percent of our population … are democracy's ballast, not always useless but always a potential liability'. This dismissive attitude, as here, applies especially towards the least intelligent. It comes out in talk of their segregation in colonies, being debarred from immigration, and perhaps in Burt's suggestion that not too much should be expected of 'backward' children.

A related point is the Galtonians' tendency to focus on extremes. Their chief concern is with the highly able. Their next is with the least able – the 'feeble-minded' or the 'backward'. The rest – those close to average intelligence – come a poor third. The highs and the lows are often described in *evaluative* language, as good as opposed to bad. For example, Goddard's work 'Kallikak' is his own invention, formed from the Greek words *kallos* (beautiful) and *kakos* (bad). These match the two contrasting branches of the Kallikak family. Galton's own work is full of ethical epithets. In his 1865 work the more able and the less able are distinguished not only by intellect but also by character. In *Hereditary Genius*, character differences are less prominent, but the book abounds in ethical discriminations. It comes out in his phrase 'the extreme classes, the best and the worst' (Galton 1978: xxii). He describes his favoured class as 'eminent', 'those who have honourably succeeded in life' (ibid.), 'presumably … the most valuable portion of our human stock' (ibid.). Those at the other end are evolutionary laggards, way behind the gifted but ahead of lower races, the lowest of whom are 'recent converts from barbarism' (ibid.: 350). Traces of uncivilisedness appear in the 'Bohemian spirit of our race' (ibid.: 347), which disinclines people from 'the monotony of daily labour' and turns them towards the public house and towards crime; but fortunately 'the social requirements of English life are steadily destroying it' (ibid.). These traces can also be seen 'in the excitement of a pillaged town' where 'the English soldier is just as brutal as the savage. Gentle manners seem, under those circumstances, to have been a mere gloss thrown by education over a barbarous nature' (Galton 1865: 326).

Why the grandiosity?

Among items calling for explanation, therefore, is the polarisation in Galton's and others' thinking between high ability and virtue on the one hand and low ability and vice on the other. Another item is about what I have called 'grandiosity'. Why did Galton write that 'the constitution of the living Universe is a pure theism', that 'men and all other living animals are active workers and sharers in a vastly more extended system of cosmic action than any of ourselves, much less of them, can possibly comprehend'? Why in the Preface to the 1892 edition of *Hereditary Genius* (Galton 1978: xxvii) did he applaud the prospect of 'gradually raising the present miserably low standard of the human race to one in which the Utopias in the dreamland of philanthropists may become practical possibilities'? Were these comments merely rhetorical exaggerations – or is there some other explanation?

Why does the trail stop in 1865?

There is a final puzzle. Like an intellectual version of one of Galton's eminent families, the teachers and disciples of the new science had by 1930 generated amongst themselves a complex lineage of interconnecting relationships. All this had happened within the previous thirty-odd years. In both Britain and the USA the movement had become a powerful force not only in academic psychology but also in educational and social policy. If we look for its origins, we find them, as all the psychological textbooks do, in Galton. When we reach Galton's texts, we trace his ideas back from *Hereditary Genius* to the magazine article on 'Hereditary Talent and Character'. Yet there, in 1865, the trail stops. The ideas of intelligence as innate, general intellectual ability, of the polarity of giftedness and feeble-mindedness, of eugenics as the saviour of the human race all appear to have been conceived in that year. Agreed, Darwin was a major influence, but as already stated, one cannot derive the peculiar features of Galtonianism only from Darwin. Where else may they have originated?

Conclusion

In the practical realm, Cyril Burt's work contributed to the development of a selective secondary school system in England, building on the earlier achievements of Robert Morant. Theoretically, Burt built on the work of his mentor, Francis Galton, in asserting that intelligence is innate, intellectual ability which sets individually differing limits to mental achievement. Philosophical analysis reveals serious difficulties in this conception. For want of an adequate justification of it, it makes sense to ask instead for an explanation of how the notion arose in the first place. Interest in eugenics provides part of the answer. Most of the early intelligence pioneers, in Britain and in the USA, were eugenicists; and the seeds of eugenics go back to Galton's first publication in the area in 1865. But this satisfies the demand for explanation only to a point. Why was intelligence identified with *intellectual* ability, especially of an abstract sort? Why were the eugenicists especially interested in the extremes of the ability range? Why did they place so much weight on examinations and tests? And can the historical narrative be extended backwards in time beyond 1865?

2 Parallels

Intelligence and predestination

In 1969 I wrote a short article in the *Times Educational Supplement* which either I or the paper's sub-editor entitled 'Intelligence – the new Puritanism' (*TES* 24 October 1969: 4). The justification for the title was slim. Most of the piece was a critique of contributions by Burt and Eysenck to *Black Paper Two*, which had just appeared (Cox and Dyson 1969). But towards the end of my essay I added a flourish to what I had been saying about the doctrine that for each of us there are limits to our intelligence. The substantive point is the one I made in Chapter 1.

> Is there any reason to think that we each have our own intelligence ceilings, as the official doctrine asserts? None whatsoever ...
>
> That we all have ceilings is not an unintelligible proposition; but it is as unverifiable and unfalsifiable as the proposition that God exists. God, indeed, is not unfittingly compared with intelligence. The proposition that all men have genetically determined intelligence is not unlike the Calvinist belief that for all of us our future state is predestined by God. In both, one finds the notion of a mysterious something, either 'out there' or 'in the genes', which sets limits to what men will do.
>
> The official doctrine of intelligence is a modern re-edition of an older Puritanism. Nature has replaced God; an élite, the elect; Mensa the community of the saved; and intelligence testers, the Puritan high priests. It is time we shook such primitive notions out of our minds.

Eysenck replied with 'Environment – the new dogmatism' (*TES* 12 December 1969: 4) and said nothing about my remarks on puritanism, perhaps taking them as the unsupported journalistic extravagance they were.

I found out recently that the comparison I suggested with predestination had been made a long time before – also in journalism. In 1922–3 Walter Lippman, the American columnist, wrote a celebrated series of six articles for *The New Republic*, followed by a reply to a response by Terman. Lippman's target was intelligence testing as practised by Terman and others. This had recently risen to national notice owing to the involvement of psychologists, including Yerkes and

Goddard, in the classification of the mental level of recruits to the US Army after the USA entered World War I in 1917:

> Psychological testing won its own victory in the war, the success of public acceptance. Millions of employees, schoolchildren, and college applicants soon faced batteries of tests, the results of which could determine the course of their lives. In the early 1920s, up to 4 million intelligence tests were being purchased every year, mostly for use in public schools. Terman's *Stanford-Binet* sold over a half million copies by 1923. In the United States, the public education system was reorganised around the concept of the intelligence quotient, and IQ scores became the most important criterion for student placement and advancement.
>
> (Schultz and Schultz 2000: 215–16)

This was the background to Lippman's scorching critique. Its details do not concern us here, only the fact that he mentions predestination in three different parts of his argument:

> … most of the prominent testers claim not only that they are really measuring intelligence, but that intelligence is innate, hereditary, and predetermined. They believe that they are measuring the capacity of a human being for all time and that this capacity is fatally fixed by the child's heredity. Intelligence testing in the hands of men who hold this dogma could not but lead to an intellectual caste system in which the task of education had given way to the doctrine of predestination and infant damnation.
>
> (Lippman 1922: 298)

and

> What their footrule does not measure soon ceases to exist for them, and so they discuss heredity in school children before they have studied the education of infants. But of course no student of human motives will believe that this revival of predestination is due to a purely statistical illusion.
>
> (ibid.)

And in his reply to Terman

> Finally, a word about Mr Terman's notion that I have an 'emotional complex' about this business. Well, I have. I admit it. I hate the impudence of the claim that in fifty minutes you can judge and classify a human being's predestined fitness in life.
>
> (ibid.)

Lippman must have had Calvinist puritanism in mind, judging by his reference to 'infant damnation' and his mention of the 'revival' of predestination. But it is hard to know whether he really saw some historical connexion between the religious doctrine and the psychological, or whether he was simply adding further colour to his journalist's account.

Journalism aside, is there any evidence for or against a historical connexion? In the rest of this chapter, I will sketch out some resemblances between ideas to do with intelligence and ideas of puritan provenance. Predestination is one such focus, but there are others. Chapters 3 and 4 will discuss further evidence and counter-evidence. Meanwhile, to set the scene, here is a thumbnail account of the puritan background.

Puritanism in Britain and America

It was especially in Britain and in the United States that intelligence testing of a Galtonian kind found a home. It is true that Binet, who was from France, comes into the story in a big way. But he is important because of the use that Goddard and especially Terman made of his 1905 test, incorporating new versions of it into a Galtonian, eugenic scheme. Binet himself had no such grand plan. He devised his test in response to the French government's request for a method of identifying those children who could not benefit from attending public schools. The test was built around academic elements akin to features of the school curriculum. Its purpose was thus narrowly delimited, having nothing to do with wider matters to do with the innate basis of intelligence, ceilings of ability, or eugenic encouragement of the gifted. As Stephen Jay Gould (1981: 155) points out, 'the scores are a practical device; they do not buttress any theory of intellect'. In addition, Binet believed in the improvement of intelligence through special training, not in low scores as indications of low intellectual ceilings. Binet has a different cast of mind from the theorists studied in this book, virtually all of whom were from Britain or the USA.

Both these are countries with deep puritan roots. From the break with Rome under Henry VIII until the voyage of the *Mayflower* in 1620 the roots are common. They are found in the more radical forms of protestantism that grew up during that period. These grew increasingly apart from the ideas and practices of the official Church of England, although no clear-cut distinctions can be made here. Central to the protestant rejection of Roman Catholicism is its stricter attitude to salvation. Salvation is not something that can be promoted by the sale of indulgences; and neither is it to be mediated via an ecclesiastical hierarchy. Each person is to be his own priest. Compared with Roman Catholicism, both Lutheranism and especially Calvinism stressed predestination – to salvation or damnation – rather than free will, the Church of England under Elizabeth being probably nearer to Calvinism (George and George 1961: 54). The growing detachment of more thorough-going Calvinist communities from the Anglican church in the late sixteenth and early seventeenth centuries led to the formation of the first puritan groupings, notably the Presbyterians, Baptists and Independents (Congregationalists). The Baptists, who rejected infant baptism, became split on the issue of whether Christ died on the cross for everyone or only for the elect. In church organisation, while Congregationalists and Baptists believed in the autonomy of each local congregation, Presbyterianism had a more centralised structure. In Scotland the Presbyterians were already the dominant group, following John Knox's reforms after his return from Calvinist Geneva in 1559. After the founding of the New England colonies in the early seventeenth century, the history of the two countries, Britain and America, began to diverge, although immigration from Old to New England continued throughout that century.

Puritanism brought with it a revolution in the picture of the ideal Christian life. For the Roman Catholics this had been the contemplative life of the monk or nun, withdrawn from the world in a monastic community. For the puritan what became central was, in Charles Taylor's words, 'the affirmation of ordinary life' (Taylor 1989: Part III). The best way to live as a christian was not remote from the everyday world but in the thick of it, fully absorbed in family life and earning a living (see Weber 1930: 81, 108, 158–9). Hard work in one's God-assigned calling, care for one's children and their upbringing, scrupulousness in one's day-to-day moral responsibilities were the new hallmarks. They were associated not only with personal salvation, but also with a collective goal, the creation of the 'New Jerusalem'. Social as well as individual improvement was a powerful puritan motive. More details on all these matters will be filled in later in this chapter and later in the book.

Britain

In Britain from the sixteenth to the eighteenth century, while Presbyterianism became the dominant form of religion in Scotland and helped to shape the separate legal and educational systems of that country, puritan beliefs among the English became confined to a minority. Under Cromwell in the mid-seventeenth century, puritans seized state power, but in the reaction after the restoration of the monarchy in 1660, a series of punitive measures known as the Clarendon Code debarred those refusing to swear allegiance to the Church of England from municipal government offices and from teaching in schools and universities.

These dissenters, as they came to be known, now included the Quakers, a sect founded by George Fox around 1652. Unlike Calvinist groups like the Congregationalists, Presbyterians and some Baptists, Quakers did not believe in predestination and in an absolute gulf between God and man. They held that in every human soul is implanted an element of God's own spirit, called the 'inner light' or the 'seed of Christ'. Salvation is in our own hands, depending on how responsive we are to this inner light, that is, on how far we nourish the seed of God so that it becomes the controlling force in our lives.

Although the overt persecution of dissenters, not least the Quakers, was largely checked by the Act of Toleration after the accession of William III in 1688, they continued to live to some extent apart from mainstream English society until legislation and other developments in the nineteenth century brought them back into it. One reason for this re-integration was the success of so many dissenting families in commerce and industry following their exclusion from other professions. This exclusion had also caused them to organise their own systems of secondary/

higher education, not least in the Dissenting Academies, which, from the late seventeenth century onwards, often provided a general education for laymen as well as a theological training for ministers. Close links were also made by the eighteenth century with higher education institutions in Presbyterian Scotland. The 'modern' curriculum taught in the leading English and Scottish colleges included scientific and mathematical subjects which were put to good use by the new industrial entrepreneurs.

In England, the dissenting communities formed the backbone of the 'middling classes', some of whom rose to great wealth during the industrial revolution, sandwiched between the Anglican establishment and the poorer classes below. Swelled from the mid-eighteenth century onwards by the followers of Methodism – founded within the Church of England but influential also among dissenters – the middle classes increased in power and influence throughout the nineteenth century, coming to share them with the old landed class of aristocrats and gentry, with whom the upper middle class gradually merged. In an increasingly fuzzy-boundaried and increasingly secular form, the middle classes dominated English political life throughout most of the twentieth century.

America

While in England the puritans were a minority community and for many years excluded from the mainstream, in America, from the *Mayflower* onwards, they *constituted* the new society. This has meant that puritan attitudes have been able to shape the general culture of America throughout much of its history. Ten years after the *Mayflower*, in 1630, John Winthrop arrived aboard the *Arbella* with other puritans, largely Congregationalists, intent on constructing 'a Citty upon a Hill' which would witness a new spiritual age. Winthrop became the first leader of the Massachusetts Bay Colony. This was a tight-knit theocratic community, based on the Congregationalist belief in an elect predestined for salvation. By the beginning of the eighteenth century other immigrant groups from the British Isles were forming communities outside the heartland of New England, Quakers, for instance, in Pennsylvania and Scots-Irish Presbyterians from Ulster, who set up farms in the Appalachians, from which they spread out to the south and much of the mid-west.

Puritanism, now weakening in fervour, now undergoing revival, was still the dominant force by the nineteenth century, although increasingly challenged by secular ideas, especially in the period following Darwin. Catholic immigration from Ireland, followed by Jewish and other immigration from Europe from the late nineteenth century, and in the late twentieth century Asian and Latin American immigration have helped to erode the continuing influence of puritanism in the culture, especially on the north-eastern and western seaboards. Yet the hold of the older culture, especially in the south and mid-west, is still noteworthy in the early twenty-first century, as evidenced by the contribution of the protestant electorate in these parts of the USA to the re-election of President Bush in 2004.

Puritan beliefs have been rather less associated in America than in England with the aspirations of a particular social class, and rather more with the fortunes of the community as a whole. In England the puritans and their descendants saw themselves as a group apart from both the upper classes and from the rabble below them, thus defining themselves as the virtuous 'middling classes' free from the idleness and luxury of the one and the undisciplinedness and criminal inclinations of the other. In America, at the time of the earliest settlements there were no such contrasting groups in that society, and the folk memory of aristocratic vices back in England soon faded. Contrast with puritan virtue was supplied at first by the pagan practices of native Indians beyond the frontier, and later by the perceived vices of African slaves. On the other hand, the growth of commercial and later industrial society, for which puritan attitudes were themselves partly responsible, led to something of the same stance towards the poor among the successful classes as occurred in England – and in addition, of course, racial differences were also seen in class terms.

Conversely, the late nineteenth century growth of the British Empire, which coincided with the increasing political power of the middle classes, spawned views, including those of Galton, about the racial superiority of Anglo-Saxons over black Africans and others. Yet earlier historical influences were and are still powerful – in the greater incidence of overt social class snobbery in contemporary England than in the USA, as well as in the greater prominence of racial discrimination in twentieth-century America.

It has been argued that the early puritan notion of 'an errand into the wilderness' to erect a 'city upon a hill' created an image of a communal destiny which, in changing forms, has accompanied the history of America, and helped to form American national identity down to our own times. The preservation of a godly community in the face of paganism, an oppressive imperial power, and the inhumanity of slavery are all chapters in this story, as is twentieth century participation in two world wars and many smaller ones to preserve democracy and rid the world of the evils of German militarism, Nazism, and later communism and global terrorism. Intertwined with this political narrative has been the astonishing economic growth of the USA, especially from the end of the nineteenth century, its emergence as a world leader and recently as *the* world leader in this field. As in Britain, the influence of puritan virtues like industriousness, discipline, frugality and punctuality on the growth of capitalism has been important. All these aspects of American self-identity have been reflected in the public education system, not least from the end of the nineteenth century onwards, as new immigrant groups have had to be rapidly socialised into American ways (McKnight 2003). The notion of America as a mighty force for good in an evil world is under increasing challenge from the liberal left; but its continuing political resonance shows how powerful the puritan legacy still is.

Parallels

The sketch of the rise of Puritanism and its divergences has been a necessary background for exploring its connexions, if any, with intelligence testing. No evidence has been provided as yet for any such links. All we have been given so far are the loosest of comparisons – between the terms 'elect' and 'élite', between predestination and the fixedness of the IQ. Can anything more be done, here and in other cases, to strengthen the case for a historical connexion? We can now examine parallels between the religious and the psychological notions in more detail.

Predestination

I start with the notion of predestination. Although some element of a belief in this, arising from the omniscience and omnipotence of God, is embedded in Christian thought in general (George and George 1961: 53), it is especially strong in Lutheranism and particularly Calvinism (ibid.: 54). Conversely, the room for human beings' free will to shape their destinies – the counterbalancing element in all Christian thought – is correspondingly weaker in these two forms of protestantism, and especially again Calvinism.

The predestinarian doctrine was prominent in English protestantism in the late sixteenth century, especially in its more radically Calvinist circles. It has a double aspect: some are predestined to salvation, the others to damnation. There is no middle ground. The saved, moreover, are few in number and the many are damned. The saved are the 'elect', those whom God has selected for eternal life. The damned are those of whom the protestant came to say, formerly with more literalness than most of us using the phrase today, 'There but for the grace of God go I' (ibid.: 55).

There is an obvious problem with this way of thinking. For people to make the remark just quoted, they must have some assurance that they are indeed among those selected. But how can they have this? How can they discover what is only in God's power to know? How can they be sure that, as sinful creatures like all mankind, their sins will not be such as to condemn them to perdition? This problem exercised the minds of Calvinists from Elizabethan times across the centuries. We will return to it.

There are pale echoes of these points – which may be mere resemblances – in ideas associated with the IQ and with school selection. Look again at this quotation from Burt:

> The degree of intelligence with which any particular child is endowed is one of the most important factors determining his general efficiency all throughout life. In particular it sets an upper limit to what he can perform, especially in the educational, vocational and intellectual fields.
>
> (Burt 1955: 281)

Or this one:

> This general intellectual factor, central and all-pervading, shows a further characteristic, also disclosed by testing and statistics. It appears to be inherited,

or at least inborn. Neither knowledge nor practice, neither interest nor industry, will avail to increase it.

(Burt 1937: 10–11, as recorded in Gould 1981: 273)

There is certainly a *negative* predestination here. For all of us, there are limits which we cannot transcend, which will affect our performance in life. Our lives have been predestined in this way by our heredity, by Nature as revealed by post-Darwinian science, rather than God. People of low IQ are predestined never to become doctors or teachers or judges or engineers. Whatever teaching they receive cannot get them beyond the Pons Asinorum implanted in them by their genes.

The theory does not allow us such a definite verdict with regard to those of high IQ. Whether they are successful in life will depend on what they do with their inborn talent. Some may be too slothful, too easily open to temptation, to make best use of it. For some, personal circumstances may be stacked against them.

Is there any surer way, in principle, of knowing that a person will succeed? Galton thought so. In one place in *Hereditary Genius* he holds that not only intellectual ability, but also 'zeal' and 'capacity for hard labour', are inherited (Galton 1978: 38). His view was that with really exceptional innate talent *and* these other innate qualities one was bound to come through, whatever misfortunes one endured: 'It is incredible that any combination of circumstances could have repressed Lord Brougham to the level of undistinguished mediocrity' (ibid.). 'If a man is gifted with vast intellectual ability, eagerness to work and power of working, I cannot comprehend how such a man should be repressed' (ibid.: 39).

Elsewhere, while still proclaiming the necessity of 'sustained and laborious toil', Galton seems to see this as (at least partly) in the sphere of nurture rather than nature:

> Without a determination to achieve and the habits of self-discipline and industry, natural ability alone seldom leads to eminence; and, unless these habits have been ingrained during childhood, no man can develop to the full whatever potentialities he may have inherited or contribute his best to the community in which he lives.
>
> (quoted in Burt 1969: 22. I have not been able to track down the quotation in Galton himself; and Burt gives no reference.)

Cyril Burt, as indicated in Chapter 1, follows the second of these claims, the one memorably enshrined in Michael Young's satire on intelligence testing *The Rise of the Meritocracy* (Young 1958: 74) as 'Intelligence and effort together make up merit (I + E = M)'.

The first of these views of Galton's sees success in life as wholly dependent on heredity (at least in the case of the exceptionally able), the second as dependent on heredity plus human effort. The first believes achievement in life is completely predetermined by the genes; the second is less uncompromising. Abstractly speaking, there is something of a parallel here with the fissure among the puritans, given that many, if not all, veered towards predestination, between those more inclined and those less inclined to emphasise the role for free human action – e.g. in virtuous living, self-monitoring, baptism within a church, hard work – in gaining some assurance of salvation. I say more below about the place of hard work within both theological and the psychological theorising.

Heredity and innateness

As the argument in the last section has been making clear, although a belief in predestination brings with it a belief in innate mental faculties the converse of this is not necessarily true. This is evident from Quakerism, in which, as indicated earlier, the idea that the 'inner light' or 'seed of God' is implanted in all men is not accompanied by predestinarianism. This raises the possibility of another kind of parallel between the theological and psychological theories, in that both hold that mental faculties are innate. While for puritans, including non-predestinarians, it is God who has given us our distinctive intellectual talents, for the intelligence pioneers, it is nature.

In Galton's time it was not the similarity of these ideas which impressed his commentators, but, as Ruth Cowan (1977: 137) points out, the contrast between them:

> Viewed theologically, the notion that a man's mental faculties were bequeathed to him by his ancestors contradicted the notion that a man's mental faculties were bequeathed to him by God. In short, and this did not go unnoticed by Galton's critics, the idea of mental heredity denied the existence of a God-given soul.

What for Galton's contemporaries, and perhaps for Ruth Cowan herself, appeared a contradiction, may also be construed as the continuation of the same idea. Galton himself made a direct link between biological and theological notions of innate qualities. When discussing the idea that human beings differ as much as other animals in inherited characteristics, he wrote

> So it is with the various natural qualities which go towards the making of the civil worth in man. Whether it be in character, disposition, energy, intellect, or physical power, we each receive at our birth a definite endowment, allegorized by the parable related in St.Matthew, some receiving many talents, others few.
>
> (Pearson 1914–30, Vol. IIIA: 227, quoted in Pastore 1949: 10)

In Galton's thinking religion and science are not easily separable.

Salvation and damnation

Meanwhile there is another point of comparison. This revolves around the division in puritan thinking between the saved and the damned, given that no one falls outside these categories. This distinction, too, is not necessarily tied to predestination, since the Quakers, to invoke them once again, believed in salvation but not predestination.

Can we usefully compare the saved/damned dichotomy with the perceived contribution of intelligence or the lack of it to success and failure in life, as conventionally understood? One thing telling against this is that intelligence testers claim to identify via IQ scores a *continuous gamut* of ability from lowest to highest. On the other hand, most of the pioneers in the field were, as we saw in Chapter 1, especially interested in the *far ends* of this range – in Galton's phrase 'the extreme classes, the best and the worst'. On the one hand there were the 'gifted', 'the eminent', 'those who have honourably succeeded in life', 'presumably … the most valuable portion of our human stock'. On the other, the 'feeble-minded', the 'cretins', the 'refuse', those seeking to avoid 'the monotony of daily labour', 'democracy's ballast, not always useless but always a potential liability'.

It is interesting in this connexion that Galton brings his good/bad polarisation into his acknowledgement of a continuous gamut of ability. Having said that the 'most prolific class' lies between 'the extreme classes, the good and the bad', he asks

> … Are the natural gifts of the most prolific class, bodily, intellectual, and moral, above or below the line of national mediocrity? If above that line, then the existing conditions are favourable to the improvement of the race. If they are below that line, they must work towards its degradation.
>
> (Galton 1978: xxii)

Overall, then, we find another parallel: between salvation and success, and between damnation and failure.

Many young people in our own societies are orientated towards 'success'. They work hard at school in order to get into good universities in order to get 'good jobs' in order to lead a successful life. Some are driven onwards by the thought of the shame and diminished life-chances in store for them should at any point they fail. The combination of hope and fear, as well as the constant sense of drivenness, have something in common with the psychology of puritan anxiety – of people hoping and working for election, yet knowing their sins could cast them down.

The idea that working-class English children can be 'rescued' from prospective drudgery by the scholarship system has been a staple of fiction and biography over the last decades. In a recent review of Melvyn Bragg's novel *Crossing the Lines*, Roy Hattersley quotes him as saying that the hero, Joe, was part of a generation who were 'the first of their kind to be off the land after centuries in thrall to it, first out of the mines and out of the factories'. His teachers saw themselves as leading their pupils into '… a new and better life through the salvation of scholarships' (*Guardian Review* 5 July 2003: 28). The language here does not jar when we read it. It seems quite natural.

Many parents these days encourage their children through all their hard work at school and college because they want them to do well. New England Puritans used the same language. The cover of Cotton Mather's tract *Cares about the Nurseries* shows that it consists of 'two brief discourses', the second of which offers 'some INSTRUCTIONS for CHILDREN, how they may DO WELL, when they come to Years of Doing for themselves' (Morgan 1944: 49).

In the puritan context 'doing well' in this life was related to salvation for the next. How do *we* understand 'doing well', as the term is commonly used? It is not any particular achievement, although particular achievements – in examinations, in professional life – facilitate it. It is success in one's life as a whole. But what is this? And is this global quality an essential element in an individual's well-being?

These are difficult questions, which take us into philosophical discussions of the nature of personal well-being. I will come back to them briefly in Chapter 6. Meanwhile, Galton himself has views, worth examining, on success in life in the shape of social recognition.

In *Hereditary Genius* (Galton 1978: 37) Galton explains what he means by 'natural ability': 'By natural ability, I mean those qualities of intellect and disposition, which urge and qualify a man to perform acts that lead to reputation'.

As to what kind of reputation he has in mind:

> By reputation, I mean the opinion of contemporaries, revised by posterity – the favourable result of a critical analysis of each man's character, by many biographers. I do not mean high social or official position, nor such as is implied by being the mere lion of a London season; but I speak of the reputation of a leader of opinion, of an originator, of a man to whom the world deliberately acknowledges itself largely indebted.

Galton's criterion of achievement is narrow. Few will fit it; and we do not know how far he held that what he elsewhere (ibid.: xxii) called 'those who have honourably succeeded in life' constitute a broader class. But at least we know that *reputation* is central to his thinking, in the qualified sense he describes.

Reputation in this sense shares features with a common puritan notion of salvation. In each case only few will achieve it. In each case one's character is favourably assessed, either by God or by men. In each case the assessors – God, or posterity – transcend one's own lifetime. In each case, the individual who is favourably assessed also lives on in a sense beyond his or her death – as an eternal soul, or as an eminent figure of history (like the generals, poets and statesmen whom Galton studied in his book).

We saw in Chapter 1 how important the notion of the examination is in Galton's thinking. Here we see another, and centrally important, example of this. The worth of one's life is determined by a 'critical analysis' of one's character by one's contemporaries and by posterity.

Galton's 'reputation' has a dimension which transcends individuality. Achieving it is important not only for the individual, but also – and more importantly – because it benefits humanity as a whole. 'I wish again to emphasize the fact that the improvement of the natural gifts of future generations of the human race is largely, though indirectly, under our control' (Galton 1978: xxvii). He goes on to talk about 'raising the present miserably low standard of the human race to one in which the Utopias in the dreamland of philanthropists may become practical possibilities' (ibid.).

This appears to make his vision *unlike* the puritan notion of salvation in so far as the latter is about the destiny of the individual. But although relative to Roman Catholicism the puritan believed in a personal, unmediated relationship to God, the communal element in puritanism was significant, too. 'The institutional structure of Puritan society was not set up to oppress one's free will, but actually made one's individuality and identity possible' (McKnight 2003: 46). Winthrop's 'City upon a Hill', the idea of which reverberates through American history, is reminiscent of Galton's utopian project.

…Yet this is not the end of the story. *Why* does Galton want a vastly more perfected human race? Remember his cosmological vision at the close of *Hereditary Genius*:

> the constitution of the living Universe is a pure theism, and … its form of activity is what may be described as cooperative … all life is single in its essence, but various, ever varying, and interactive in its manifestations, and … men and all other living animals are active workers and sharers in a vastly more extended system of cosmic action than any of ourselves, much less of them, can possibly comprehend … they may contribute, more or less unconsciously, to the manifestation of a far higher life than our own.
>
> (Galton 1978: 376)

'Reputation' is important, ultimately, for its contribution to this 'pure theism' which is 'the living Universe'. This brings it closer again to puritan salvation. If you were to ask an early – or indeed a later – puritan whether the salvation of the individual soul was important only in itself, the answer would surely be 'no'. The eternal life that the individual enjoys is one in which one's own spirit is ultimately part of the divine spirit in general.

A note, finally, on Terman. His evolutionary hopes refer more explicitly to salvation. In a late unpublished manuscript called 'My Faith', he writes about the devastating effects of 'the increased tempo of cultural change', especially in technological innovation. 'If we are to be saved from chaos it can only be by increasing the tempo of man's social and moral evolution' (Seacoe 1975: 237).

The work ethic

I mentioned above the often-expressed view among the pioneers of intelligence testing that inherited high intelligence is not a sufficient condition of doing well.

You also need what Galton called 'zeal' – or 'eagerness to work' and 'capacity for hard labour'. Burt echoes Galton in calling for these 'sterner virtues' (Burt 1969: 22); while Terman says of high-ability school children

> Unless they are given the grade of work which calls forth their best efforts, they run the risk of falling into lifelong habits of submaximum efficiency. The danger in the case of such children is not over-pressure, but under-pressure.
>
> (Terman 1919: 16)

This has a parallel – I am not claiming a causal connexion – with the role of the work ethic in puritan thinking. Perry Miller writes, in his account of the New England mind in the seventeenth century,

> that every man should have a calling and work hard in it was a first premise of Puritanism … even the man who has an income must work. Everyone has a talent for something, given of God, which he must improve.
>
> (Miller 1953: 40–1)

As Tawney (1926: 230, 240–6, 265) and other writers (e.g. Taylor 1989: ch. 13; see also Weber 1930: ch. 5) have argued, puritanism in England and America brought with it, as we have seen, a rejection of the medieval belief that the highest form of Christian life was governed by the monastic ideal of contemplation. Instead, it argued for full involvement in the occupations of everyday life – farming, craft, commerce, and for women, home-making. Life was to be lived in the pursuit of one's particular calling, which was at the same time both temporal and spiritual. Work came to be the central element in a holy life.

Being predestined for salvation is not, therefore, on this view, a sufficient condition of doing well. Human beings are sinful creatures and, to be saved, must show that they have struggled against their nature and lived a virtuous life. Continuous hard work is a crucial sign of this.

There is a parallel, therefore, between the psychological and the theological doctrines. In each case, what is given innately must be accompanied by habits of industry if success is to be possible.

The converse is also true. Children born with low IQs have been held to have no hope of a professional, well-paid job. If they are capable of joining the workforce at all, they must find their niche as unskilled workers. It would be wrong to press them too hard academically, as Burt urged in a passage quoted in Chapter 1. Terman (1919: 4) writes about 'wasting energy in the vain attempt to hold mentally slow and defective children up to a level of progress which is normal to the average child' and says:

> they are never able to cope successfully with the more abstract and difficult parts of the common-school course of study. They may master a certain amount of rote learning, such as that involved in reading and in the manipulation of

number combinations, but they cannot be taught to meet new conditions effectively or to think, reason and judge as normal persons do.

(Terman 1919: 6)

In other words, these children are still expected to work, but not with the same intensity and at such abstract matters as other children. The rote learning enjoined on them will no doubt fit the low-level, mentally undemanding jobs many of them will be doing as adults. Many of the feeble-minded, however, will not acquire such disciplined habits of work. According to Terman, they have a tendency towards delinquency: 'not all criminals are feeble-minded, but all feeble-minded are at least potential criminals. That every feeble-minded woman is a potential prostitute would hardly be disputed by any one' (ibid.: 11).

This is reminiscent of Galton's comment, quoted in Chapter 1, about the 'Bohemian spirit of our race' which disinclines some people from 'the monotony of daily labour' and tempts them 'to the public house, to intemperance, and, it may be, to poaching, and to much more serious crime' (Galton 1978: 347).

In puritan thinking, too, there is a general expectation that everyone should work: 'Man is made for Labour, and not for Idleness' (quoted in Miller 1953: 41). Everyone must have some warrantable calling 'though it be but of a day-laborer' (quoted ibid.). But not all live up to this expectation. Many drift into poverty and idleness. 'Poverty is a great affliction, and Sin the cause of it' (quoted ibid.: 396).

> If the Poor will but Work, they would make a better hand of it in this Country [i.e. New England], than in almost any under the Cope of Heaven. What Pity 'tis, that such a Hive should have any Drones in it.
>
> (quoted ibid.: 397)

Vocation

The intelligence pioneers all had a great interest in vocational matters. Galton's *Hereditary Genius* is structured around eminent individuals in a range of top-flight professions. (Oddly, he also includes wrestlers and oarsmen alongside his judges, generals, scientists and poets, having received data from a correspondent in Tyneside who had details of family connexions in those areas.) Like most of his followers, Galton did not believe that specialised talents are inherited. As we have seen, he held that people wrongly think that 'because a man is devoted to some particular pursuit, he could not possibly have succeeded in anything else' (Galton 1978: 24). What is inherited is general intelligence. This fits one for a range of possible occupations, not for a specific vocation.

The same idea is found in Terman (1919: 17–18), who thought the time close when intelligence tests would be used for determining vocational fitness. He did not believe this could be done in any fine-tuned way, such that tests could say 'unerringly exactly what one of a thousand or more occupations a given individual is best fitted to pursue'. But he did hold that further researches will ultimately determine the minimum IQ needed for success in each main occupation. 'All classes of intellects, the weakest as well as the strongest, will profit by the application of their talents to tasks which are consonant with their ability' (ibid.: 21).

Goddard (1920: 128) and Burt thought similarly. Goddard's ideal of democracy required its highly intelligent leaders 'to so organise the work of the world that every man is doing such work and bearing such responsibility as his mental level warrants'. As for Burt, we have already encountered his belief (Burt 1955: 281) that one's level of innate intelligence sets a ceiling to what one can achieve vocationally. In 1919 Burt was one of the first people in Britain to hold a post in vocational psychology (Burt 1952: 67).

All this points to a society where occupational levels are correlated with IQ bands. And if intelligence is inherited, then the broad vocational destination most fitting for one is already implicit in one's genes.

The idea that vocations should be roughly related to one's innate talents or gifts is a *leitmotif* of the intelligence testers. The three terms just used, 'vocation', 'talent' and 'gift' are all of religious origin. The idea just mentioned has a close parallel in a key puritan belief.

A vocation is a 'calling' from God. It is a central concept in Calvinist thought, marking the revolution which this way of thinking made in overturning Roman Catholic beliefs (George and George 1961: 126–43). It takes two forms, the 'general' calling and the 'particular' calling. The former applies only to the elect: God has called them to keep faith with the gospel. The latter applies to everyone, saved and unsaved. Its chief form consists in an occupation – e.g. husbandman, merchant, physician, carpenter. A calling in this sense has two important features. It must be useful to society; and it must correspond to the individual's 'gifts' – the talents which he or she has been given by God. A calling is not simply a kind of job, as we would understand this today. What is important is how one sees the job. Performing it is a central religious duty. It is in this that the revolution from Roman Catholicism consists. As we saw above, the puritan celebrated everyday life in all its ordinariness as the chief site of religious duty. In the early puritan period, say before 1650, manual and mental toil are 'equated in the dignity of the calling' (ibid.: 131). As the puritan divine Perkins put it: 'Now if we compare worke to worke, there is a difference betwixt washing of dishes, and preaching the word of God: but as touching to please God none at all' (quoted ibid.: 138–9).

There is something of a similarity, therefore, between the vocational ideas of our two groups, the psychologists and the theologians. The similarity does not go all the way, for in the modern scheme of thought individuals do not have specific innate gifts matching exactly the most appropriate vocation for them, and parallel to the God-given gifts of the earlier doctrine. More roughly and generally, however, the idea of some kind of inborn match between gift and calling is present in both.

Family, equality and equality of opportunity

Family is an important concept for the intelligence theorists because of their belief in the heritability of intelligence (and also, sometimes, of capacity for and inclination to hard work). Galton's investigations in *Hereditary Genius* were into family relationships among eminent individuals. Goddard looked at the half-virtuous, half-vicious 'Kallikak' family; Davenport and others examined other families of 'degenerates' (Terman 1919: 9–11).

The conclusion that high, low or middling intelligence tends to run in families had implications for the testers' involvement in and attitudes towards public education. Burt defended the selective system in England – in justifying which his theories had played such a part, as we saw in Chapter 1 – against the charge that it was biased towards children from the 'non-manual' or 'middle' classes. He did not find it surprising that children from middle-class homes were present in such numbers in selective schools or in universities:

> To become a doctor, lawyer, or teacher, it is necessary to pass certain qualifying examinations; and these demand a high level of innate ability. The ability of parents who have entered one of these professions tends to be transmitted to their children.
>
> (Burt 1969: 20)

But there are also highly able children from working-class families; and it is, according to Burt, a major virtue of the use of intelligence testing in school selection that it has enabled them to be identified.

> As Professor Valentine has pointed out, 'there are hundreds of children from poverty-stricken and illiterate homes who have cause to thank the system of intelligence-testing for rescuing them from the stigma of mental deficiency which got attached to so many who were merely educationally backward, and still more who, owing to social handicaps, would otherwise never have found their way to university'.
>
> (ibid.)

The social ideal implicit in Burt's ideas, mirrored in other Galtonians' writings, is of a stratified, or class, society. As Burt says, 'class differences thus become inevitable in any civilised society' (ibid.). The 'doctrine of equality' must be rejected. At the same time, this is not a caste system, with no mobility between stratified groups. (The belief in classes but not castes was also held by nineteenth-century Congregationalism (Jones 1962: 192). For the possible significance of this fact, see the section on Burt in Chapter 3.) The scholarship system 'rescues' bright working-class children, providing a 'ladder' for them up which to climb to achieve successes otherwise unattainable. It is a social ideal based on 'equality of opportunity', not on equality in income, life-style or social regard. On its Galtonian assumptions, the system does not seem to be unfair.

Goddard is another believer in social stratification. He upbraids socialists for deploring inequalities of wealth, whereby someone can live in a luxurious and finely-furnished house while a labourer lives in a hovel. These critics, he says, fail to realise that the labourer would not be able to enjoy all the artistic decorations and fine furnishings and pictures unless he had the innate intelligence to do so (Goddard 1920: 100–1). Once again, destiny resides in one's innate gifts. As with his 'Kallikaks', the biological features one inherits from one's family are of crucial importance.

From the start, the puritans also placed the family at the centre of their thinking. Although the main part of one's 'particular vocation' (at least for men) has to do with one's occupation, another concerns one's duties as a family member, whether husband or wife, child or parent, master or servant (George and George 1961: 127). It is to the puritans that we owe the modern idea of marriage as something freely entered into by both parties and based on love and companionship (Taylor 1989: 226). Seventeenth-century puritanism 'heralds the shift, which takes place in the next two hundred years, from the patriarchal to the conjugal family, that is to the family centred on the married couple' (Walzer 1966: 188).

The puritan family provided the spiritual and economic structure within which individuals could perform the religious duties attached to all their particular callings – and thus, on any but the most extreme form of predestinarianism, make more secure their hope of salvation. *Children's* salvation was a central preoccupation. Puritan parents gave meticulous attention to education, both intellectual and moral. I discuss this in more detail below, as well as in Chapter 5. The main point here is that parents had a duty to equip their children with intellectual and moral virtues because they would need these as a condition of salvation.

Here we come to a crucial issue. More exactly, we come back to a question raised in a more general form in the section above on predestination. How can puritan parents *be certain* that their children will be saved? The proper answer, on the strictest Calvinism, is that this is something they *cannot* know. Only God can have this knowledge. In practice, for some puritans the intense desire for *assurance* about their children's salvation as well as about their own was assuaged by theological innovation in the late sixteenth and early seventeenth centuries.

In New England, as well as in Europe, this took the form of the 'Covenant of Grace' (Miller 1939: 365–97). The idea here is that of a *deal*, or contract, between God and individual human beings, and instigated by the former (ibid.: 379). Of his own volition, God agrees to limit his own power. He agrees to assure the other party that he or she will be saved, conditionally on the person having faith; and, as a token of that faith, fully performing the duties of his or her calling. Salvation is thus still predestined by God and is at the same time conditional on moral virtuousness. The latter is not enough on its own: one cannot be saved by good works, as the Arminians believed – any more than one can be saved by intensity of faith, as did the Antinomians. The puritan saint lived by both, but only because of their role in the deal with God.

In line with an early pronouncement in the Canons of Dordrecht 1618–19 (article 17), an important aspect of the Covenant of Grace for our discussion is that God made it:

> with a believer and his seed: He promised godly parents that He would save their children as well as themselves. As extended to the children, however,

the promise was not unconditional, for even a believer's children were born ignorant. The covenant did not give them an absolute claim to salvation, but it did give them a better chance than other children. If they were properly brought up, it was almost certain that the promise would be fulfilled … children who by their parents' covenant were half saved, might by education become wholly saved.

(Morgan 1944: 47)

Parents, to keep their part in the bargain, had to bring up their children well.

It was especially the Congregationalists who developed and lived by this covenant, extending the idea in New England via the Half-Way Covenant of 1662 to include the baptism of grandchildren as well as children within the scheme (Miller 1953: 89). The Congregationalist church was restricted to those presumed to be members of the elect, whether adults or children. The Presbyterians, who accepted the more traditional Calvinist view of predestination and therefore did not claim to know who was saved or not, objected to this restriction of baptism to members of saints' families, favouring the admission to their church of everyone, whether saved or reprobate.

For Congregationalists the effect of this bargain was that salvation could be, if not fully assured, at least partially assured, from one generation to the next. In the cliché used by New England preachers, 'God casts the line of election in the loins of godly parents' (Morgan 1944: 102). The agreement took care of the innate, predestined factor in salvation, as it were, leaving moral uprightness to do the rest. It is here that we see a parallel with Galtonianism. The presumption of salvation, just as later the presumption of eminence, was found in certain families, extended through time. The agent responsible for this transmission was, in the earlier case, God himself; and in the later, Nature.

Something of the spirit of Congregationalism was found among the Quakers, who formed their own group among the puritans in the mid-seventeenth century. In one way the Quakers were very different from the Independents. They did not believe in predestination as the source of salvation. Instead, as already mentioned, they held that everyone possessed the light of Christ within, but only those who consented to be guided by it could be among the saved (Watts 1978: 188). Like the Congregationalists/Independents, however, they tended towards exclusiveness. In their case this did not derive from the idea of a covenant, but rather from the efficient organisation and tight control that they soon managed to establish over their communities, in England on a nation-wide basis (Walvin 1997: 24–6). This included the detailed elaboration of rules and conventions, and a strict regime of disciplinary action against those who transgressed. One of these rules, in operation until 1858, forbade marriage with non-Quakers. As a result of this many Quakers were disowned by their Society (ibid.: 133). Richard Vann has calculated that by the mid-eighteenth century between 80 and 90 per cent of Quakers were themselves the children of Friends. He writes that 'the bias of Quaker institutions was against the conversion of the world and in favour of the organisation of family life for the conversion of Quaker children' (quoted in Watts 1978: 390).

The family thus became a central institution as much for the Quakers as for the Congregationalists. Although God's grace was not transmitted across the generations via a covenant, the transmission across them of Quaker beliefs and practices – which still included the division between the saved and the unsaved – meant that something like a presumption of salvation could be passed down the same Quaker families over the years. Although predestination was absent, there was still an innate element in this transmission in the shape of the light of Christ within, with which all men were thought to be endowed. Much more weight than in some other branches of Dissent was placed on free human action, especially in the shape of industry, frugality and mutual self-help, as a sign of guidance by this inner light.

The argument in this section has so far drawn parallels between the Galtonians' attachment to the family as a transmitter of high ability and puritan – especially Congregationalist and Quaker – reliance on the family to provide something like a lineage of the saved. The Galtonian scheme, as elaborated by Burt and others, also has room for the notion of 'rescuing' children from other, lower-class, families who give evidence of high intelligence. Is there anything similar to this notion in puritan thought and practice? Puritan philanthropy, from the sixteenth and seventeenth centuries onwards, was 'directed less toward the relief of beggars than toward the transformation of a selected number of religious paupers into self-sufficient and presumably self-disciplined men' (Walzer 1966: 217). 'Wealthy Puritans ... sought to provide not only direct relief, but also educational opportunity and apprenticeship training and sometimes capital or material for men who were willing, in effect, to become saints' (ibid.). Here is, clothed in religious terms, the same abstract notion as is embodied in the modern idea of a ladder out of the slums: the notion of helping selected members of the non-élite who have characteristics appropriate to the élite to find a place within it. 'Bright working-class children' correspond to 'the godly poor'.

Education

I recently attended the launch of a new book on contemporary attitudes towards education among the English middle class. An academic who was speaking about the book said she wondered why the middle class were so bothered about getting their children into 'good schools' if they really thought that ability was innate.

This somewhat misrepresents the doctrine of the intelligence-testers, as we have seen. None of them held that high innate ability is enough on its own. For Galton, one also needs 'the habits of self-discipline and industry'; as we have seen, Burt and Terman agreed with him.

In the English context, the locus for building up these 'sterner virtues' in high ability, mainly middle-class, children was the new secondary school created by the Morant reforms in 1904. Here they followed the broad curriculum he laid down, based mainly on discretely parcelled areas of theoretical knowledge, the content of which was heavily influenced by the requirements of universities. The secondary school provided the first training ground for future doctors, teachers, lawyers and other professionals. Burt, as we saw in Chapter 1, worked within and developed this selective system. Like Galton, he was attached to a highly intellectual form of education for the élite.

This pattern of education for an innately gifted élite destined for a successful life finds echoes in puritanism. Morgan's study of the seventeenth-century puritan family in New England shows the importance then paid to education. Indeed, he writes, in a passage reminiscent of the academic I mentioned above: 'For a people who believed in predestination and the absolute sovereignty of God the Puritans ascribed an extraordinary power to education' (Morgan 1944: 51).

Parents had a duty under the Covenant of Grace, and under local law, to educate their children so that they, too, could become worthy of salvation. In particular, parents had to help their sons to choose their particular calling. (For girls there was no choice since their calling was to be a housewife.) Boys usually chose between the ages of 10 and 14, being then apprenticed for seven years (ibid.: 29–30). It was important to make a good choice, since it was difficult to change one's mind later, especially given another long apprenticeship. Some boys, who were intelligent enough and whose parents were rich enough, might put off the choice of a calling until later by going to Harvard College. 'Anyone with a "liberal" education would adopt a "liberal" calling, that is, a calling which required no manual labor and no long period of apprenticeship' (ibid.: 30). Parents wanted their children to 'do well' (ibid.: 49), and had only fulfilled their obligations after they saw 'their Children well dispos'd of, well settled in the World' (quoted ibid.: 39), that is, well married and settled in their own home.

Very young children were allowed to spend their time in 'pastime and play', but probably well before seven began to be involved in useful work (ibid.: 29). Children learned to read and to acquire knowledge for religious reasons. As Protestants, they had to be able to read the Bible themselves (ibid.: 45–6). Lack of knowledge was seen as man's chief enemy – again a reaction to the perceived intention of the old Roman Catholic regime to keep people ignorant. For the puritan, the acquisition of knowledge, especially of the scriptures, was a necessary route to salvation (ibid.: 46). They thought it should begin early and intensively. New England ministers believed that 'Satan never hesitated to begin his assaults upon children in their infancy, " and therefore if you would prevent him, do not you delay, but be dropping in instruction as they are able, and as soon as they are able to understand any thing"' (ibid.: 53). 'Children were taught as fast as they could learn' (ibid.).

As well as being born ignorant, children were born evil. This meant an equally strict regime of discipline to match that of instruction. 'There was no question of developing the child's personality, of drawing out or nourishing any desirable inherent qualities which he might possess, for no child could by nature possess any desirable qualities' (ibid.: 53).

One reason for the preoccupation with early learning must have been the far greater probability than in our age of dying young. Given the comparative recentness of the assumption that most people in our society will live into old age, this thought must have exercised devout parents even into the twentieth century. Comenius, the Moravian educationalist and member of the radical protestant sect called the Moravian Brethren, who, like Morgan's New England families, lived in the seventeenth century, put forward as the first of his six reasons for beginning education early

> ... the uncertainty of our present life. For that we must leave it is certain, but when and how is uncertain. And that any should be snatched away unprepared is a danger greatly to be dreaded, since a man is thus doomed eternally. For, just as a man must go through life without a limb if he leave his mother's womb bereft of it, so, if, when we leave this world, our minds have not been moulded to the knowledge of and participation in God, there will be no further opportunity given us. And therefore, as the matter is of such importance, the greatest haste is necessary, lest any man be lost.
>
> (Comenius 1907: 57)

Despite its ancientness, several features of this upbringing will be easily recognisable in parental views of a certain kind today – the emphasis on hard work and firm discipline from an early age, being able to learn things as quickly as one can, reading as a basic skill, the plentiful acquisition of knowledge – especially factual/theoretical rather than practical knowledge, deciding early on one's vocational direction unless one is likely to go on to university – in which case decisions can be put off till later, wanting one's child to do well and to be well settled in the world. What is usually absent from today's version of this – apart from the disappearance of the well-founded belief that a human life is likely to be a short one – is the religious rationale for all these specifics. By and large, children are no longer educated in this way so that they can be saved – not in the traditional sense, anyway. There will be further discussion of educational ideas, particularly about intellectual orientation, in Chapter 4 and especially Chapter 5.

Race

It has been said that intelligence testing has tended to focus on social class differences in England and racial differences in the USA. Writing of Cyril Burt, Stephen Jay Gould states

> He did not feel that races varied much in inherited intelligence, and he argued that the different behaviors of boys and girls can be traced largely to parental treatment. But differences in social class, the wit of the successful and dullness of the poor, are reflections of inherited ability. If race is America's primary social problem, then class has been Britain's corresponding concern.
>
> (Gould 1981: 284)

There is something of a match between this divergence and the differing histories of the two puritan communities, as described above. Racial superiority was always more present to the minds of American puritans, given their relations with native Americans on the one hand, and black slaves on the other. In 1657, for instance, the New England divine Richard Mather, impressing on children their baptismal covenant, said that if they did not keep it, they would be 'no better than Turks, or Indians, or other "pagans"' (Miller 1953: 11–12).

In England, puritan communities defined themselves more *vis-à-vis* other classes – the Anglican establishment above and the masses below – than *vis-à-vis* other ethnic groups. This is not to deny what we would now call racist thinking among them, only to say that it was relatively less salient than in America. The celebrated eighteenth-century Congregationalist Isaac Watts (1792: 1), for instance, wrote:

> I could even venture to say, that the *improvement of reason* hath raised the learned and the prudent, in the European world, almost as much above the *Hottentots*, and other savages of *Africa*, as those savages are by nature superior to the birds, the beasts and the fishes. (italics in original)

The fact that on different sides of the Atlantic there were different degrees of concern about racial superiority is reflected in the history of psychology. Kamin (1977: ch. 2) documents how racist ideas were applied to immigration into the USA in the 1910–30 period, from Goddard's 1912 intelligence testing of immigrants on Ellis Island, which 'showed', for instance, that 83 per cent of the Jews were 'feeble-minded' (ibid.: 31); to Yerkes's work with army recruits in 1917, which claimed superior intelligence for those with a northern rather than southern or eastern European background (ibid.: 34); to the work of eugenicists like Carl Brigham on Nordic superiority (ibid.: 36ff). He also mentions Arthur Jensen's (1969) finding that 'on average, Negroes test about one standard deviation (15 IQ points) below the average of the white population' (ibid.: 50). Terman (1916: 91–2) also believed that a low level of intelligence is common among black Americans, as well as among Spanish-Indian and Mexican families of the southwest (Rose *et al.* 1984: 86).

Among British psychologists there is less, but still some, evidence of racialist thinking. Although Burt can be absolved, Galton cannot – as the passage quoted on this in Chapter 1 testifies. Neither can McDougall, whose book from the 1920s called *Is America Safe for Democracy?* was attacked for its racist eugenics (see below, p. 70). One of the most forthright of British psychologists on race was Burt's pupil, Raymond Cattell, who proclaimed, among many other comments 'I think the following provisional order of racial intelligence will not be far wrong: 1. Nordic and Jews; 2. Alpine; 3. Mongolian; 4. Mediterranean; 5. Negroes; 6. Lowest Races, Australian blacks, etc.' (Cattell 1933: 53).

On race there do, therefore, seem to be parallels between the beliefs of the puritans and those of the pioneers, although what weight one should put on these is a further question. The history of South Africa under apartheid may throw further light on this, given the role in this of the Dutch Reformed Church on the one hand and, on the other, the many psychological attempts to show that whites are superior in intelligence. For an account of the latter, see Mensh and Mensh (1991: 107–18).

As a final disclaimer, I hope it should go without saying that I am *not* saying that all puritan and puritan-derived communities have been and are racist. Especially in the last two centuries the groups, among and within themselves, have not been homogeneous in their political attitudes in a range of matters. For instance, although many dissenters in nineteenth-century Britain were socially conservative – being a main target of Matthew Arnold's (1869) excoriations in *Culture and Anarchy*, there were also many dissenting dissenters, as it were, including those who towards the end of the nineteenth century and into the next were prominent in the growth of the Labour Party. The desire to make society a better place, deeply etched into puritan thinking, can take many forms. On matters of race, at the end of the eighteenth century it was Quakers like Thomas Clarkson and William Wilberforce who led the way to the eventual abolition of the slave trade.

Gender

What, finally, shall we say of gender? Are there parallels here, too, between religious and psychological beliefs about the abilities of women as compared with men's? Puritan views revolve, as we have seen, around the idea of vocation. With few exceptions (e.g. those reported in Hufton 1995: 408–18), in New England as in other similar communities, while those boys who did not automatically follow their father's calling needed time to choose their own, girls were called only to become housewives, so their apprenticeship in sewing and other crafts could begin much earlier (Morgan 1944: 29). Outside a theological context, this does not necessarily show a belief in women's intellectual inferiority, for one could in principle be a good seamstress and a good reasoner. But within such a context, how could a woman be naturally endowed with, say, the powers of reasoning of a man from Harvard College, if gift correlates with vocation?

If there are gender parallels with psychology, one would expect the intelligence pioneers to deny the intellectual equality of the sexes. While G.S. Hall made no bones about doing so (Dyhouse 1981: 121–32), and while it may never have crossed Galton's mind to include any women in his long list of eminent individuals in *Hereditary Genius*, others among the pioneers were explicitly egalitarian, although not always in a clear-cut way. In a 1912 study of sex differences in intelligence, Burt and his schoolteacher co-author R.C. Moore wrote 'with few exceptions innate sex differences in mental constitution are astonishingly small – far smaller than common belief and common practice would lead us to expect' (Hearnshaw 1979: 28. See also the comment in Gould (1981) above). Similar results are reported by Terman (1919: 68–72). There is a hint in the passage just quoted – but this is not certain – that empirical data from test scores may have challenged Burt's own beliefs and that these may have been closer to traditional views. Similarly, there seems to be some evidence that Terman manipulated his results to lower girls' scores, having initially had data which showed that girls did better than boys (Mensh and Mensh 1991: 68). Despite these occasional suggestions of conventional attitudes, the evidence does not seem strong enough in the area of sex equality – in contrast to predestination, salvation, the family and other topics discussed above – to press for a close parallel.

Conclusion

This chapter has explored various resemblances between ideas associated with Galtonian intelligence and intelligence testing on the one hand, and puritan thinking on the other. There are similarities between the Calvinist notion of predestination and the idea that one's degree of innate intelligence may rule out for one the possibility of a professional career and with it a certain standard of living. There are similarities between the puritan concern with salvation on the one hand and the intelligence theorists' preoccupation with 'eminence', 'reputation', 'giftedness', 'rescuing' bright working-class youngsters through IQ tests and the scholarship system. Both groups were attached to the virtues of the work ethic and had no time for the idleness and moral looseness associated with the reprobate in the one case and those of low IQ in the other. Both saw the conjugal family as an important institution for the transmission of desirable features across generations: in the religious case, a presumption of salvation; and in the psychological, a presumption of high intelligence. Both favoured an intellectually demanding education for its favoured group; and both saw it as equipping its recipients for a worthwhile vocation. Views on the superiority in ability of white, especially Nordic, peoples were also common in both groups.

There do not seem to be close correspondences between religious and psychological views about sex differences in ability. But in the other cases there are clear parallels, echoes across the centuries which may, or may not, be coincidental. Chapters 3 and 4 present evidence that more than coincidence may be at work.

3   Origins

All the leading pioneers in the intelligence testing movement, including all the psychologists mentioned so far – as well as others, had puritan roots. So did Robert Morant, the architect of selective state education in England, for which intelligence testing provided a rationale for his dual system of schooling.

That these men were influenced by religion, let alone by the same branch of christianity, is not at first sight apparent in their writings and their deeds. The psychologists among them, in particular, made it very clear that they were *scientists*. They were extending the remit of the sciences to include the mental as well as the physical world. Their work was based not on subjective judgement, but on rigorous attention to empirical data and the application to it of statistical methods.

Such, at least, was the message they proclaimed – so successfully that in every introductory text on psychology the section on intelligence testing tells this same story. But the very self-consciousness about using a scientific approach that one finds in their writings, the very intensity of their attachment to new standards of objectivity, should make us dig deeper. These were men living at a time – the late nineteenth and early twentieth centuries – when Britain and the USA were still in large part religious societies. Darwin's *Origin of Species*, which did so much to undermine faith in later years, took time to have its effect. Its publication in 1859 preceded by only six years Galton's article in *Macmillan's Magazine* which brought into existence the new world of intelligence research. Although more and more people, including many of the psychologists of intelligence, came to find religious belief unacceptable, the increasingly secular thought-world within which they lived and worked was still permeated by ideas, or shadows of ideas, from the older religious culture. The new faith in mental science appears to be one such shadow. For an account of the religious roots of scientific psychology see Richards 2002: 284–9. Even as late as 1919, in his introduction to the British edition of Terman's *The Measurement of Intelligence*, Professor J.J. Findlay, writing about the progress of scientific psychology, could find it natural enough to write: 'The method of the confessional or of the Methodist class meeting, probing to the depths of motive and the springs of sentiment, are [sic] no longer confined to religious experience' (Terman 1919: ix).

It is time to substantiate in more detail the claim that the intelligence pioneers and their associates had puritan roots. I begin with Britons and then move on to Americans.

Francis Galton

Galton is an early example of someone whose religious faith was shaken by Darwin's *Origin of Species*. He said of his cousin's work that its effect

> was to demolish a multitude of dogmatic barriers by a single stroke, and to arouse a spirit of rebellion against all ancient authorities whose positive and unauthenticated statements were contradicted by modern science.
>
> (Galton 1907: 287, quoted in Fancher 2001: 5)

How far Galton's religious inclinations were as utterly destroyed as this comment may suggest is another question, given the remark at the end of his 1865 article that 'after myriads of years of barbarism, our race has but very recently grown to be civilized and religious' (Galton 1865: 327), as well as the comment at the end of *Hereditary Genius* that 'the constitution of the living Universe is a pure theism' (Galton 1978: 376).

At all events, until he read Darwin in 1859 or later Galton was a believing Anglican, who had married into an eminent Anglican family (Fancher 2001: 4). His father had also been an Anglican, having originated as a Quaker. Beyond that point, Galton's Quaker roots stretch back in impressive lineage to the early days of the movement in the mid-seventeenth century. Of Francis Galton's sixteen great-great-great grandparents on the paternal side, at least eleven and possibly thirteen were early members of the Society of Friends (Pearson 1914–30, Vol. I: 27). They include the influential seventeenth-century Scottish Quaker Robert Barclay, for whom salvation was dependent on obedience to the inner light in passive waiting on God (Watts 1978: 461). Other Barclays on that side of the family set up and developed Barclays Bank. By the eighteenth century the Galtons had interests in the manufacture of guns and in the slave trade. In 1795 Galton's grandfather, Samuel Galton FRS, was disowned by the Quakers for his gun-making activities, although he went on attending meetings until his death in 1832. He and his wife, Lucy Barclay, 'lived and died as Quakers' (Pearson 1914–30, Vol. I: 45). After being disowned he went into banking, as did Galton's father, Samuel Tertius Galton. The elder Samuel was a member of the celebrated Lunar Society of Birmingham, which devoted itself to scientific and technological advance. Here he was a colleague of Erasmus Darwin FRS, grandfather to Charles Darwin and also to Francis Galton, since the latter's father had married Erasmus Darwin's daughter.

How far did Francis Galton's Quaker ancestry influence his thinking about 'hereditary genius'? There is no incontrovertible evidence. There is nothing in Galton's works, to my knowledge, that says that assumptions on which his ideas rested derived from this source. But that is not surprising. Thinkers are often unaware of their own assumptions. This is true, not least, in a period of theoretical revolution, when, through their very attachment, those attached to the new find it difficult to see how the old still affects them. Many secular-minded philosophers of our own times, including myself, have experienced this with recent developments in ethics. It has become clearer to us that the ethics of rational rules and principles that we used to follow as the basis of a properly secular system still carried too much baggage from christian thinking. Principles-based ethics began to seem too close to the law-based ethics of the Ten Commandments. A different starting point was necessary; and Aristotle's discussions of the qualities human beings need in order to lead a flourishing life together seemed to many to provide it.

If, a century and more after Darwin, secular philosophers were unaware of the religious structuring of their own thought, how much harder must it have been for Darwin's contemporaries to see this. It would have been surprising indeed if Francis Galton had been able to detach himself completely from the two centuries of Quakerism which lay immediately behind him. His Quaker biographer, Karl Pearson, sometimes mentions its effect on his character, as in his reference to Galton's 'Quaker stubbornness' (Pearson 1914–30, Vol. I: 57). In his case it was no ordinary Quakerism. His ancestors were members of the Quaker commercial élite. The Quakers in Britain were an exclusive group in any case, as explained in Chapter 2, owing to their tight, bureaucratic organisation and prohibition against marriage to non-Quakers. Galton came from a rich and successful family within this close-knit community. It is hard to believe that this background had no effect on his view of the world. This is especially true in the light of Galton's own research. Its central claim is that high ability, or genius, is inherited; and its way of showing this is via the incidence of eminence among closely related members of the same élite families.

As we saw at the end of Chapter 1, the 1865 article in *Macmillan's Magazine* from which Galton's leading ideas derived does not have any obvious provenance apart from *The Origin of Species*. The article introduces to the world the notions that people are differently limited in the general intellectual ability that they have inherited; that a select group of gifted individuals should be encouraged to propagate so as to improve 'the breed of mankind'; that character as well as talent is inherited, also in different degrees, including 'the instinct of continuous steady labour' (Galton 1865: 325); that 'the lower classes of civilised man' (ibid.: 326) are in many ways close to barbarians; that ways can be found of reducing and eliminating society's 'refuse' (ibid.: 319); that mankind can evolve towards higher levels of civilisation and religion (ibid.: 327). These ideas cannot be derived from Darwin alone. If they were so derivable, then those of us who have accepted Darwin's main ideas should all accept them. But this is far from the case. Many of us would recoil from the view that one social group is to flourish while others languish: we are guided by a more egalitarian vision.

There has to be some further explanation of why Galton applied Darwinism, as he saw it, to human society in the way that he did – and also of how it is that this particular interpretation seems to have been *invented* around 1865 with no apparent intellectual forebears.

The standpoint from which both the 1865 article and *Hereditary Genius* are written is that of a comfortably off author who sees himself as belonging to a small, highly educated élite and who draws a sharp distinction between that élite and the shapeless, potentially dangerous mass below. He is someone who has a lot of time for achievement of a high order, for 'reputation'. These may be far from attitudes we associate with Quakerism today, but would not have been out of place in high Quaker circles in the early nineteenth century. As with other seventeenth-century dissenting groups, the very success of the early Quakers in devout fulfilment of the duties of their faith, including – not least – the duty of industriousness, meant that in the natural course of events they moved from small-scale business activity, especially in textile manufacture and mechanic trades, to successes in larger arenas (Watts 1978: 351). Quaker technologists like Abraham Darby and others were in the forefront of progress in the iron, lead and tin-plate industries in the eighteenth century. Friends were also bankers (Lloyds and Barclays), manufacturers of biscuits (Huntley and Palmers, Carr's) and chocolate (Fry, Rowntree, Cadbury). In a critique of his own community in 1859 John Rowntree

> revealed that what underpinned the Society of Friends was the assumption that the Quaker way of life was a route to [material] success. It comprised in effect an elite of preselected personal and social qualities which, while replenishing itself from generation to generation, had proved itself incapable of maintaining popular support. A wide base to the Society would have undermined that success.
>
> (Walvin 1997: 132)

The prohibition against marriage outside the Society caused a further reduction in the already tiny numbers in the Society: only about 20,000 in England and Wales in 1800 (Davidoff and Hall 1987: 86). Rowntree's analysis 'portrayed the Society as an unbending sect, tied to ideals and rituals of a long-lost era, and excluding the very people it had set out to help: the poor and deprived' (ibid.).

It is true that from the late eighteenth century more and more Quakers, like dissenters in general, began to devote themselves to humanitarian ends and became leaders in social reform, especially in the abolition of the slave trade and, later, in policies on poverty and peace. But older, more socially indifferent, attitudes still prevailed. While Friends, with their extended networks, were always ready to help their own, their benevolence often failed to extend to neediness beyond this circle. As employers during the industrial revolution, they shared the attitudes of other bosses, adopting a culture of long hours and low wages for their employees until late in the nineteenth century (Walvin 1997: 182).

After his father's death in 1844, Galton lived as a gentleman of independent means among the London intellectual élite. From an early age he was preoccupied by intellectual success. One advantage of his father's leaving the Quakers was that he was eligible to attend Oxford or Cambridge universities. The fact that Galton went to Cambridge and thus gained a passport to the London intellectual establishment was in line with the Quaker celebration of worldly achievement. As we saw in Chapter 1, Galton was bent on becoming a Wrangler in the final honours mathematics examination, but was thwarted by an emotional breakdown. More generally, the passage from *Hereditary Genius* which was quoted there reveals very clearly his Quaker-like concern with reputation: 'I look upon social and professional life as a continuous examination. All are candidates for the good opinions of others, and for success in their several professions' (Galton 1978: 6).

The notion of life as 'a continuous examination' is worth examining more closely. Today, the idea might well strike us as exaggerated, perhaps neurotic. Striving for recognition is still a feature of the culture, but few would see this in terms of examinations and examination candidates, let alone a never-ending examination. It makes immediate sense, however, against the background of a community of individuals ceaselessly concerned with how adequately in God's eyes they are responding to the inner light within. Galton's notion has every appearance of being a secularised version of this older belief, God's role having been taken over by that of an élite peer-group. Perhaps the latter was itself a secularised version of the small community of affluent Quakers, concerned not only with their own uprightness but with the probity of their fellows – the community which disowned Galton's grandfather for his gun-making.

A passage in Comenius (1907, ch. XXIV: section 6, section 9) – the seventeenth-century educationalist much influenced by radical protestant thinking (see also Chapter 5) – is interesting in connexion with Galton's notion of life as 'a continuous examination'. Drawing on Luther's notion that meditation, prayer and examination 'are essential to make a true Christian', Comenius writes:

> Examination is the continual testing of our progress in piety, and may come from ourselves or from others. Under this head come human, devilish, and divine temptations. For men should examine themselves to see if they are faithful, and do the will of God; and it is necessary that we should be tested by other men, by our friends, and by our enemies.
>
> (Comenius 1907: 219–220)

Another trait that Galton had in common with many of his Quaker forebears, and which was indeed deeply etched into the character of Old Dissent, was the desire to be socially useful. As we have seen, a central feature of the protestant Reformation, emerging most strongly in the puritan sects, was its attachment to everyday social and economic activity as the highest form of christian life. This meant fulfilling one's God-given vocation, as merchant, carpenter, minister, housewife. As the business activities of many British Old Dissenters flourished in the eighteenth century, scope for social utility widened from the local to the national. We have seen examples of this above, not least among Galton's ancestors. Galton himself was of the same cast of mind: he wanted to be 'of use in the world'. 'He was not simply content to sit back and enjoy the fruits of his wealth; he felt it was his duty in some way to benefit society' (Cowan 1977: 152–3). He pursued this end restlessly throughout his life. This often took the form of an extraordinary, and influential, inventiveness across a number of fields, including meteorology, statistics and the use of finger-printing in criminal or other investigations (Brookes 2004: 248). A minor and less illustrious example was his 'bicycle speedometer' of 1877. This consisted of:

nothing more than an egg-timer, which the cyclist was supposed to hold while counting the revolution of the pedals. The number of turns in the allotted time gave the speed in miles per hour. The size of the sand glass had to be calibrated to the diameter of the bicycle wheel for the system to work properly. Perhaps it wasn't much of a surprise that it never caught on.

(ibid.: 207)

Galton's social imaginativeness was displayed *par excellence* in his eugenic project. His search for 'useful work' was crowned with success on a grand scale in his visionary article of 1865. This utopian scheme 'provided him with a philanthropic cause that could engage all his altruistic and scientific impulses' (Cowan 1977: 153). I will come back to his eugenic mission in this connexion below.

Turning, meanwhile, to Galton's conception of natural ability, how far did this derive from his Quaker background? As we have seen, like Burt's notion of intelligence, it is describable as general intellectual ability which different individuals possess to different degrees, their ceilings being determined by innate factors. As we shall see in more detail in Chapter 4, the puritan movement as a whole placed great emphasis on the power of intellect. This is linked with a concern for personal salvation, since the eternal life is the life of the spirit. What continues in existence is that which is held to be least dependent on the world of sense-experience. Pure thought, as abstract as possible, and thus minimally enmeshed in the empirical world, best fits this specification. As we shall see in Chapter 4, logic – the most abstract of intellectual endeavours – was central to puritan thinking. Galton's own early attachment to pure mathematics, a bent of mind shared with many of the psychologists appearing in this chapter, is also in line with it. So is his preoccupation with that élite of pure mathematicians – which he strove so hard, but failed, to join – the Wranglers of Cambridge University. The latter group constitute his first example of hereditary genius in his book of that name.

The nature of the human mind – conceived in the wake of Cartesianism as a non-physical entity whose essence is thought – was an important topic in the puritan advanced curriculum of the eighteenth century because it was held to have affinities with the mind of God. The subject called 'pneumatology', the forerunner of modern psychology, was a staple of the Dissenting Academies, which Quakers among other groups attended, Galton's grandfather Samuel studying at Warrington Academy (Pearson 1914–30, Vol. I: 15). Pneumatology was taught as a two-part course beginning with the human mind and widening this to the divine mind.

Further details on all this will appear in Chapter 4. For present purposes, the account just given may throw some light on why Galton decided to investigate intellectual ability. Understanding one's own spiritual nature was an obligation on all puritan groups and must have been close to the heart of all his paternal forebears. It may well have helped to shape his own thinking.

A further reason why Quakers in particular among the puritan groups had reason to dwell on the nature of the human spirit/mind/soul comes from their notion of the 'inner light', mentioned above. From the start, Quakers differed from other puritan groups in believing that the kingdom of God was within us, that 'the indwelling of the Holy Spirit guaranteed perfection to the believer' (Watts 1978: 208). The identity of the human mind and the divine mind was particularly pronounced in their creed. With this in mind, the passage by now familiar to the reader, at the end of *Hereditary Genius*, may bear one further repetition:

> the constitution of the living Universe is a pure theism, and ... its form of activity is what may be described as cooperative ... all life is single in its essence, but various, ever varying, and interactive in its manifestations, and ... men and all other living animals are active workers and sharers in a vastly more extended system of cosmic action than any of ourselves, much less of them, can possibly comprehend ... they may contribute, more or less unconsciously, to the manifestation of a far higher life than our own, somewhat as – I do not propose to push the metaphor too far – the individual cells of one of the more complex animals contribute to the manifestation of its higher order of personality.
>
> (Galton 1978: 376)

The object of Galton's eugenic vision can be interpreted as the sifting away of the dross – the non-intellectual residue – that has accumulated in human and indeed animal minds across the ages so that ideally only pure intellect remains. We think of intellect as being in, or perhaps constituting, the minds of individuals; but individuals, as the passage suggests, are merely parts of 'a far higher life than our own'. This does look remarkably like a thesis of the identity of human and divine mind, with God now reconceptualised as living Nature.

The passage also suggests that the process of evolution is *directed*. There is a consciousness at work, working to a plan which is beyond our comprehension. God appears to be the architect of evolution. If this is so, then this teleological account of it is at odds with the standard post-Darwinian view that evolution is direction-less, the product of accident and circumstance.

The point just made, that God seems the architect of evolution on Galton's view, needs glossing. It may appear to contradict the whole eugenic project, because this assumes that human beings can interfere in the evolutionary process, helping it, as it were, on its way. But this need not be a problem for someone, like Galton, who believes in the identity of individual minds with supra-individual consciousness. It is, after all, only human beings of the highest intellect who are to direct the eugenic project, with a view to generating creatures of still higher abilities. These eugenic executives are closer to the divine consciousness than those of lesser ability. Although they do not by any means fully understand the overall plan for the universe, they have glimmerings sufficient for them to be, as it were, agents of Providence in realising it.

This interpretation is backed up by Galton's Quaker biographer Karl Pearson, who makes abundantly clear in a reference to Galton's *Inquiries into Human Faculty and its Development* the persistence of his religiosity after he had had his faith shaken by Darwin:

> It was a great revolution in thought that Galton was proposing and probably few grasped its extent in 1883. He had in mind a new religion, a religion which should not depend on revelation ... Man was to study the purpose of the universe in its past evolution, and by working to the same end, he was to make its progress less slow and less painful in the future ... If the purpose of the Deity be manifested in the development of the universe, then the aim of man should be, with such limited powers as he may at present possess, to facilitate the divine purpose.
>
> (Pearson 1914–30, Vol. II: 261)

Galton's new religion shared with that of his dissenting ancestors the notion that it is one's religious duty to be socially useful and thereby promote God's purposes. Was his vision, perhaps, a descendant of the puritans' 'New Jerusalem'? It was, at all events, an inspiration for the psychologists in the eugenic tradition who followed him, and whose puritan backgrounds are described below. Like Galton, they were all industrious contributors to social improvement, often, in their cases, as shapers of social and especially educational policy.

Support for Pearson's view of Galton's religiosity comes in the latter's statement in *Inquiries* that:

> Man has already furthered evolution very considerably, half unconsciously, and for his own personal advantages, but he has not yet risen to the conviction that it is his religious duty to do so deliberately and systematically.
>
> (Galton 1907: 198)

Further passages from Galton, which indicate religious intentions in his work, can be found in Fancher (2001: 3–4).

I suggested in Chapter 2 that the traditional notion of intelligence with its innately determined limitations is similar to the Calvinist notion of predestination. As we saw, Lippman thought likewise. But it is hard to claim that Galton himself derived from Quakerism any predestinatory element in his conception, for Quakers differed from Calvinist puritans like Congregationalists and Presbyterians precisely in their *rejection* of predestination. Quakers believed that salvation comes about not through God's antecedent decision, but through the individual's positive response to the inner light within – a life of virtue and industriousness instead of idleness and sin. On the other hand, the Quakers *were* salvationists. They were convinced that, given they followed the strict discipline within their tight community, they themselves would be saved; and the prohibition of marriage outside the Society reinforced the notion that Quaker blood was a passport to salvation. Each Quaker could therefore have a strong assurance that any child who might be born to him or her would, if well brought up, be among the saved. This is not predestination, but it is not far from it.

Given that by the eighteenth century the Quakers linked salvation in their own case both with birth and also with worldly success, it is understandable that Galton's theory of a link between eminence and inherited ability – a theory whose suddenness of appearance in 1865 is still in need of explanation (see Chapter 4) – may have partially derived from that source.

None of the arguments so far about the possible influence of his Quaker background on Galton has been clinching. But they show, I think, that such an influence is likely.

Cyril Burt

Cyril Burt was also of puritan stock, like Galton on his father's side. He tells us in his autobiographical sketch (Burt 1952: 55) that his mother was an Anglican and that his father, along with most of his, Cyril's, other male relatives, was a Congregationalist.

What evidence, if any, is there that Burt's views on intelligence and school selection were affected by his Congregationalist roots? Burt does not say that they are, but, as suggested above, we should not find that surprising. Although by no means hostile to religion, Burt saw himself very much as a scientist – and as a professional one, much more so than Galton. He saw his theoretical claims as rooted in hard empirical and statistical evidence, about the measured IQs of monozygotic twins reared apart, for instance, as compared with those of other siblings. I can testify from personal experience in the shape of the correspondence I conducted with him in 1970–1 that his – tenacious – arguments were at every point presented as those of a patient searcher after objective scientific truth (White 1970).

But not all psychological scientists of Burt's generation were drawn towards the particular investigations which attracted him. We need an explanation of why Burt took over the Galtonian notion of intelligence and applied it in the way that he did, especially to streaming and selection, within the state school system. How far does his Congregationalist background come into the story?

We know from Burt's autobiography that his childhood passed more directly under the influence of Congregationalism than Galton's did under that of Quakerism. Whereas Galton's father had become an Anglican, Burt's remained a Congregationalist. We know that he was in the medical profession, was working in London as chemist and surgeon during Burt's early childhood and moved to a Warwickshire village as a physician when Burt was 10. 'In his eyes', Burt tells us (Burt 1952: 55), 'I was, like my sister, unquestionably destined from birth to follow him as a doctor'. He was a keen classical scholar, who taught Burt 'the Latin declensions morning by morning while still in my cot, with stories from Livy or Nepos as a reward'. His grandfather on his father's side was also a Congregationalist. There is a record of his having been married in the Independent Chapel in Ramsgate in 1849 (personal communication from Norman Franke). He used to own a farm and quarry at Montacute in Somerset (Burt 1952: 54), and it seems later became a medical man like his son, having been first a surgeon and then a chemist/druggist (communication from Norman Franke). He was as keen on early learning as his son, since a few years later than the cot experience, 'my grandfather, who was a great admirer of German science and philosophy, made me learn the German declensions and recite the song from *Wilhelm Tell*' (Burt 1952: 55). Burt also tells us that 'on the bookshelves there were ancient medical tomes belonging to my great-grandfather' (ibid.: 54). Other researches show that the latter was called Edward Knuritt Burt. Like later Burts he was an apothecary. At the time of the 1851 census he was living in Montacute (Bevington n.d.).

As we shall see later, the Congregationalists, of all the puritan groups, had been traditionally the most committed to learning and teaching – across a broad range of subjects, not only in theology. This seems clearly reflected in Burt's own family. In addition to the facts laid out above, we know that the grandfather passed on to Burt 'all sorts of out-of-the-way scientific information which he, I think, gleaned mainly from his weekly copy of *Nature* or from the queer German publications that he picked up at Farringdon Market' (Burt 1952: 55). He was also connected with a 'ragged school'. Burt's father 'admired Milton, Raphael, Mozart, Christopher Wren', and modelled his prose style on that of Dr Johnson. When Burt went to school in Warwick:

> As the examinations drew near, my mother regularly related how my father had once won so many prizes at St. Saviour's Grammar School that a cab was necessary to cart them home, and I felt I should be disgraced if I did not bring back at least one prize.
>
> (ibid.: 56)

This is an interesting passage, because it not only supplies further evidence of the elder Burt's scholastic proclivities in general, but also shows the importance attached to examinations in Burt's household and that of his father. Again as we shall see in more detail in Chapter 5, examinations had a key place in the dissenting tradition, not least for Congregationalists. We know already from earlier material in this book the role they played in the life and thought of Galton, Burt's hero; and we know how Burt's professional career as an educational psychologist was built around scholastic testing and how his work contributed to the development of the 11+ exam after the Second World War. Burt himself passed an examination at the age of eleven which earned him a scholarship and free education at Christ's Hospital. He won several other scholarships at other points in his education. As he writes in his autobiography:

> Scholarships have thus played so indispensable a part in my life that, not unnaturally, one of my chief interests has been to widen, and if possible improve, the scholarship system and allied methods of examination and selection.
>
> (ibid.: 57, fn 2).

Mention of Galton recalls the passage in Chapter 1 describing how the latter first came to Burt's notice. It is interesting from the point of view of the present chapter that this happened via Burt's father. In his rounds as family doctor in rural Warwickshire, he used to visit the Galton family home at Claverdon at least once a week. Not surprisingly, Cyril Burt:

> ... heard more about Francis Galton than about anyone else. Next to Milton and Darwin, he was, I think, my father's supreme example of the Ideal Man ... On returning to school, I got from the library Galton's *Inquiries into Human Faculty*, and I still recollect a superstitious thrill when I noticed on the title-page that it first saw daylight in the same year that I was born.
>
> (ibid.: 59)

This, too, is an intriguing passage for two reasons. One is that, like the quotation about the cab-load of prizes, it shows how close Burt was to his father and ready to be influenced by him. The other is that it invites the question '*Why* did Burt's father see Galton as the Ideal Man?' Burt, unfortunately, does not tell us. Burt senior's two other paragons were a puritan sympathiser and a scientist. Was he attracted to Galton because he belonged to the same religious thought-world as himself (although not explicitly avowed as such in Galton's case)? Or because, also like himself, his work was in the field of biological science? Was Galton a model for him precisely because he brought the two ways of thinking, the religious and the scientific, together in the same person? Or was there some other reason?

Burt tells us that 'the last six generations have included six surgeons or physicians, three ministers of the church on the male side' (ibid.: 54). Connexions between science and religion thus go deep into his family past. It is important to remember that before Darwin, and indeed after him – as this book shows – the two were not always, by any means, seen as mutually threatening but often as mutually supporting. This is especially true of the Congregationalists, who were the leading organisers of Dissenting Academies from the seventeenth through to the nineteenth century. Science gained more and more prominence in their curricula as the eighteenth century progressed. Newtonian science was taught at his Northampton Academy between 1729 and 1751, along with theology and other subjects, by Philip Doddridge, one of the most celebrated of the academy teachers and a Congregationalist (Watts 1978: 369). Joseph Priestley, who studied at Daventry Academy, the successor to Northampton, promoted science at Warrington Academy after 1761. 'His *Theological and Miscellaneous Works* fill twenty-six volumes; he made an original contribution to chemistry, discovered ammonia, sulphur dioxide, and oxygen, and invented soda-water by impregnating water with carbon dioxide' (ibid.: 472). In general, 'the overriding purpose of the academies' courses on the natural sciences was to deduce arguments in favour of the wisdom and power of the Creator' (ibid.: 370).

How far was Burt himself interested in religion as well as science? He tells us that he was as a child. His Anglican mother 'secretly hoped I should enter the

Church. When I dressed up in surplice and hood, and preached her a sermon, she entered into the game' (Burt 1952: 55). At St Saviour's Grammar School in Warwick, spurred by his father's prize-winning at school, 'to make quite sure, I generally aimed at the Scripture prize, which nobody else seemed to covet' (ibid.: 56). He also won Scripture prizes at Christ's Hospital (ibid.: 59). There are, as far as I can see, no later references in his autobiographical essay to an interest in religion: science, in the shape of psychology, now dominates the story.

In the 21 years of his retirement from 1950 until 1971, however, theology became one of his three major non-professional interests, along with astronomy and music. He described himself as christian, as regards denomination 'Liberal Anglican', and as regards theology, Unitarian (Hearnshaw 1979: 207). He became quite proficient in Hebrew, read widely in theology and sketched out a book to be called 'The Pros and Cons of a Religious Metaphysic' (ibid.: 208). He also published several essays on psychical research, which by his last decade had become 'an integral part of his metaphysical system' (ibid.: 224). He was a dualist, holding that there are two types of consciousness, a passive form dependent on brain processes, and an active form – which he called 'psychon' – 'with a possibly infinite life-time'.

> Not only might the psychic fields of different individuals overlap, thus accounting for telepathic experiences, but there might well be a sort of 'oversoul' – 'a kind of group mind formed by the subconscious telepathic interaction of the minds of certain persons now living together perhaps with the psychic reservoir out of which the minds of individuals, now deceased, were formed, and into which they were re-absorbed on the death of their bodies'. This active 'psychon' was something that acted according to its own laws. Psychology was, therefore, a science in its own right, and not dependent on material data.
>
> (ibid.: 224–5)

Based on his view that 'psychon' could direct bodily action since voluntary choice could causally bring about changes in the brain, Burt believed, in his own words, 'in the supreme importance of consciousness in deciding the direction and furthering the progress of animal evolution' (quoted ibid.: 225).

Interestingly, Hearnshaw does not connect his discussion of these views on psychical research with what he wrote earlier in his biography about Burt's interest in theology: he treats them as belonging to the farther reaches of the latter's work in psychology. But should the science and the religion be kept apart?

That consciousness can outlast death into eternity is a standard christian notion. So is the idea of the identity of individual consciousness with something supra-individual. We have met this pattern of thought before, in Galton. He, too, thought that evolution was consciously directed, not accidental. It looks as if Burt took over from his mentor not only the conception of intelligence as innate, general intellectual ability, but also something of the wider metaphysical scheme into which that conception fitted and which supplied it with a rationale.

If this is right, then ultimately for Burt psychology and theology are mutually inextricable. Hearnshaw tells us that he believed psychology was 'a science in its own right, and not dependent on material data'. This is far from the thought that a secular thinker using these words might have: that just as chemistry and geology have crystallised into their own sub-domains of science over the last two centuries, psychology has joined them a little further down the road. What Burt appears to mean by its being a science in its own right and with its own laws is more grandiose. It is that the study of the human mind can give us glimpses of that trans-individual consciousness that governs the universe. Its laws are those of God himself. If this is right, Burt's view of psychology as an autonomous science locates it nearer to the Dissenters' pneumatology than to academic psychology today. (For more on pneumatology, see Chapter 4.)

Is this reading too much into Hearnshaw's description of Burt's interest in psychical research? Perhaps. Yet it is hard to take it, as it stands, in any less cosmic a way. Is it relevant that Burt's interest in these matters comes only at the end of his long life? Should we discount it as the freewheeling, somewhat soft-headed, thinking of a very old man? Is the real Burt the professional educational psychologist of his salaried years, at home in the minutiae of test results and statistical analyses?

Here we come back to the account of Burt the professional psychologist in Chapter 1. Burt's researches were set in the framework which he inherited from Galton. Burt took over from him not only the notion of innate, general intellectual ability, but also the eugenic project within which it was embedded. He was on the Consultative Council of the Eugenics Society in 1937 and 1957. His work in the school system on streaming and on selection, intended to promote giftedness and keep low intelligence in its place, was Galtonian eugenics in action. Given this, and given what we have already seen of the theological setting of Galton's own system, there is some evidence that Burt's grander religious inclinations were not the product of unbuttoned dotage, but were present, in the background, throughout his career.

Before we leave the relation between science and religion in his thinking, it may be relevant to come back to his notoriety since the 1970s for allegedly having cooked his research data. If Burt was above all a meticulous behavioural scientist, how could he possibly, one asks oneself, have *invented* his fictitious tally of fifty-three identical twins reared apart plus two female co-workers? We know that in his early years he was keen on academic success in the shape of competitive prizes. Hearnshaw writes of his slipperiness and unscrupulousness in debate. 'He would misrepresent his opponents and blur the issues. Beneath a polite exterior and apparent reasonableness was a steely determination to get the better of the argument, and to humiliate his opponents' (Hearnshaw 1979: 206). As someone who jousted with him on his conception of intelligence in his eighty-eighth year, I can corroborate this judgement. Did Burt invent data and colleagues because he just had to get the better of the argument about how far environmental factors can alter what has been innately predetermined? Was it that he had taken over his views on innate intelligence from Galton as a baseline belief, which in his eyes could not be false? If so, he emerges less as a scholar genuinely open to critique and more as a true believer. Is faith, after all, what motivated him rather than the open pursuit of truth? When he wrote in his autobiography – in unusual language for a scientist – about his 'disciples' (Burt 1952: 72), how did he conceive R.B. Cattell, H.J. Eysenck and the others he mentions? As academics whom he inducted into the objective standards of his craft, or as torchbearers who could keep the Galtonian faith alight through another generation?

All this is speculative and requires further investigation. Part of it, however is corroborated in Hearnshaw's comment that:

> He was never at heart a scientist. Much of the data he collected were [*sic*] hastily gathered and of doubtful quality. He was an able and ambitious man, who early came to regard the Galtonian tradition almost as gospel truth and himself as Galton's heir.
>
> (Hearnshaw 1987: 121)

This echoes Stephen Jay Gould's verdict that:

> The innateness of intelligence was Burt's idée fixe. When he turned his intellectual skills to other areas, he reasoned well, subtly, and often with great insight. When he considered the innateness of intelligence, blinders descended and his rational thinking evaporated before the hereditarian dogma that won his fame and eventually sealed his intellectual doom.
>
> (Gould 1981: 279)

I hope that enough has been brought out in the above discussion to show the significance of religious belief in Burt's life and work. Even so, it is patently *not* enough to clinch the argument that Congregationalism in particular was a significant influence on him. So far, we have seen a few possible pointers in that direction, no more. We know that Burt was close to his Congregationalist father and grandfather, that he shared their eclectic love of learning, as well as his father's desire for scholastic success. We know that the traditional duality of interest in his family in religion and in science was echoed in his own career. It was also a keynote of Congregationalist academic thinking in the eighteenth century, but we have seen no evidence that the latter impinged on Burt's ancestors.

We saw in Chapter 2 that Congregationalists were and are the direct descendants of the Calvinist puritans of the first Elizabeth's reign. Until the evangelical revival in the later eighteenth century caused some Congregationalists to move in a universalist direction, proclaiming that God predestined in such a way that all could be saved if they lived well (Jones 1962: 168–71), the traditional view within the group was that he predestined salvation only for his elect. In this, as has been said, they differed from the Quakers – although by the nineteenth century evangelical versions of Calvinism emphasised assurance of personal salvation through faith perhaps more than predestination (Bebbington 1989: 63–5). In other ways there are similarities between the two groups. Like the Quakers,

Congregationalists believed they belonged to the elect – dubbed by Chesterton 'the awful aristocracy of the elect' (Routley 1961: 63). They restricted membership of their church accordingly (Watts 1978: 169, 291); and like the Quakers, they traditionally tried to keep marriage within their faith (ibid.: 329–30). They also tended, again like the Quakers, to look after their own poor (ibid.: 337) while being indifferent to poverty in general, seeing it as part of the Providential plan (Jones 1962: 192). Socially, from the seventeenth century 'Congregationalism was very much the religion of the economically independent' (ibid.: 126), including merchants and tradesmen. Like the Quakers, they made up for their exclusion from much of public life by 'a fervent devotion to business' (ibid.: 127). They profited from and contributed to the rise of industry and commerce in the eighteenth century and by the nineteenth 'found themselves joining in the general adulation of worldly success' (ibid.: 288), being strong supporters of *laissez-faire* and competition. Like the Quakers, they produced wealthy entrepreneurs: men like Francis Crossley the carpet manufacturer, Titus Salt in the woollen industry, W.D.Wills in tobacco (ibid.: 289). It was the Congregationalists, the largest Christian group after the Anglicans and the Methodists, who became particularly associated with the defence of the 'Victorian virtues' of hard work, thrift, teetotalism, sabbatarianism, respect towards the family and suspicion of the theatre (ibid.: 290–4). An observer in 1902 wrote that their denomination was 'more than any other the Church of the middle classes, its membership being practically confined within the limits of the upper and lower sections of those included under that comprehensive title' (quoted in Bebbington 1989: 110).

We have already seen how the exclusionist attitudes of the Quakers – their inclination to see themselves as a religiously privileged group, sure of their own salvation – appear to be reflected in Galton's preoccupation with evolutionarily privileged people. It would not be surprising, if so, if Galton's eugenic vision also appealed to Congregationalists, with their own adulation of success and similar sense of innately given specialness.

We do not know whether Galton's work struck a chord in Burt's father partly for this sort of reason. Neither do we know why Burt himself became a Galtonian. There must have been some reason why he was attracted to this élitist application of Darwinism – and likewise some reason why he developed Galton's ideas in the way he did. There are several reasons to think he may have been influenced by his puritan roots. Some of these considerations we have already touched on and those will be mentioned only briefly.

1   The similarity between predestined, or at least assured, salvation on the one hand and the fact that a high, innately given, degree of intelligence fits one for selective schooling.
2   As a specification of [1], the similarity of the idea that one's calling is divinely given, and Burt's belief that one's innate intelligence is correlated with a range of occupations fitting one's intelligence level.
3   More generally, Burt's long-standing interest in vocational guidance and selection. In 1919 he was appointed the first head of the vocational section

of the new National Institute of Industrial Psychology (Burt 1952: 67). He explicitly structured his autobiographical sketch around his own choice of vocation as psychologist. This is why, as he says, in the essay he will 'keep mainly to the problem of "vocational selection" ' (ibid.: 53). Within his family, as we have seen, his own later choice of vocation was an important issue. 'It was generally assumed that I should eventually follow one of the callings that predominated in my father's family, and become either a parson or a doctor' (ibid.: 55). His mother hoped he would enter the Church, while his father saw him as 'unquestionably destined from birth to follow him as a doctor' (ibid). The phrase 'unquestionably destined' deserves emphasis.

4   Burt's interest in the different ranges of vocation of which individuals are capable or incapable connects with his use of intelligence tests to stratify the school population, both by streaming within the elementary school and by selection of the most gifted for secondary schools. Congregationalists, like Quakers, tended to hold to a broad stratification between their own elect group and the non-elect. This may be somewhere in the background of Burt's keenness on a selective school system. There is evidence, too, that Congregationalists were traditionally sensitive to more specific levels of social stratification, based not on election, but on wealth and status. 'The stratification of eighteenth-century society was reproduced in the meeting-house' (Jones 1962: 127), with the wealthy in pews hiding them from public view and seats closer or farther from the pulpit allocated according to occupational level.

   Burt's view that class differences in intelligence are largely innate, so that 'class differences become inevitable in any civilised society' (Burt 1969: 20) is in line with, and may have been influenced by, the nineteenth-century Congregationalist belief that 'society is providentially ordered to fulfil the divine purposes. Riches and poverty are not accidentally distributed, nor are social classes accidentally constituted' (Jones 1962: 192).

5   There is no general reason why psychologists interested in intelligence should focus on intellectual tasks rather than forms of practical intelligence. Yet Burt, like Galton, chose that orientation. We have discussed above the particular interest that puritans always took in intellectual matters, and the prominence of Congregationalists in particular in the academically-inclined Dissenting Academies. Burt's account of his extraordinary early academic education at the hands of his father and grandfather may reflect this Congregationalist bent. So may the fact that throughout his life Burt was an omnivorous digester of academic material across a huge number of fields (Hearnshaw 1979: 206).

As with Galton, and indeed as with all the other figures still to be discussed, there is no hard, undeniable evidence that Burt's puritan ancestry helped to shape his work as a psychologist. All sorts of people without puritan roots are involved in vocational training, or have eclectic intellectual interests, are élitists, favour social stratification, believe in eternal life and the individual's unity with God, or have joined eugenic societies. The considerations presented for a link with puritanism may be no more than coincidences. On the other hand, the concatenation of all these features in the same person may – or may not – incline one to think it non-accidental. So may the fact that virtually *all* the pioneers of intelligence testing and school selection came, as we shall see, from one branch or other of the puritan family. This may still be a coincidence, but if it is, it is an extraordinary one.

Other British psychologists

In his autobiographical sketch Burt mentions William McDougall (1871–1938) and Karl Pearson (1857–1936) as significant figures in his early training as a psychologist of the Galtonian school (Burt 1952: 60–2). It was through meeting William McDougall while an undergraduate at Oxford studying classics in 1904 or 1905 that Burt decided to take psychology with him as a special subject for his final examination. McDougall had been appointed Wilde Reader in Mental Philosophy at Oxford in 1904 and since 1900 had also held a part-time post at University College London. Knowing of Burt's interest in Galton's work, McDougall suggested as a research topic for him 'the standardisation of psychological tests for the anthropometric survey which a Committee of the British Association was planning at Galton's instigation. The scheme was to cover "all levels of the mental hierarchy"' (ibid.: 60). While at Oxford McDougall himself worked among other things on devising 'a series of mental tests that should be, as far as possible, independent of language and learning, and universally applicable' (McDougall 1930: 210). But his main work in psychology, as it developed through his career, was on the purposiveness embedded in innately given instincts. He was a eugenicist who, after emigrating to the USA at the beginning of the 1920s, wrote a book on national eugenics called *Is America Safe for Democracy?* which evoked hostility for its racist views (ibid.: 213). Like Burt, he was interested in psychical research, and although agnostic in religious matters, became increasingly inclined to believe in the reality of telepathy (ibid.: 220).

McDougall, like Burt, came from dissenting stock. His father, who ran a profitable chemical business, 'was successively a member of most of the leading Christian sects' (ibid.: 191). He shared the views of other northern manufacturers, who were 'class-conscious, conscious of power and of their peculiar interests', and attached to the Liberal party. McDougall remembered his paternal grandfather, who had founded the chemical business, as 'a stern and very pious old gentleman whose hobby was the writing of articles to show that the Bible miracles were compatible with the teachings of science' (ibid.: 191). He had been a pupil of John Dalton, the chemist and author of the atomic theory. Dalton was a Quaker, who had lectured in mathematics and science at the Manchester Academy from 1793 to 1800 (McLachlan 1931: 258) and was active at another dissenting academy in Blackburn in 1819 (ibid.: 272). It is not known where he taught McDougall's grandfather.

Karl Pearson was Galton's biographer and, like Burt, a devotee. He was a professor at University College London from 1884 until 1933, at first in applied mathematics and mechanics and then, from 1911 until 1933, as the first Galton Professor of Eugenics, a chair endowed by Galton, who died that year, in his will. In 1901 he joined Galton and a colleague from UCL in founding the journal *Biometrika*. He was 'an active socialist … But he was more a socialist in the abstract and, as an intellectual snob, believed that social progress would inevitably favour those who worked mainly with their brains rather than their hands' (Gillham 2001: 273).

When he turned to psychology at Oxford, Burt was impressed by work of Pearson's on anthropometry and soon met him personally, Pearson's son being among the group of schoolboys Burt was testing (Burt 1952: 60). Pearson was a main influence on Burt's early work on statistical aspects of mental testing (ibid.: 61, 62); and it was he who, along with Galton and others, drew up a scheme, finally accepted by the London County Council, for adding an educational psychologist to the inspectorate, the post which Burt was the first to occupy (ibid.: 63).

Karl Pearson, like Galton, was of Quaker stock on his father's side. His son and biographer mentions his many visits to the Yorkshire Dales, where 'he loved to mix more serious work at statistics with walks along the tracks and bridle-paths between the dale-side farms where his Quaker ancestors had lived and died' (Pearson 1938: 2).

Like Galton – and indeed like both men's Quaker ancestors – Pearson, despite his generally secular stance, saw science and religion fundamentally not as opponents but as collaborators. His section on 'eugenics as a religious faith' in Pearson (1914–30, Vol. IIIA: 87ff) not only describes Galton's views, but also expresses his own. Religion, he writes,

> from the earliest times has been the guardian of tribal custom in regard to marriage, birth and death. It has therefore concerned itself with matters which from our present knowledge of the laws of natural selection and heredity we recognise as bearing on human evolution. It is impossible – and this the Church is now beginning to recognise – to place the scientific doctrine of evolution and the moral conduct of man as inspired by religious belief in separate water-tight compartments.
>
> (ibid.: 88–9)

A few pages later, in his approving comments on Galton's idea of eugenics as a national religion, Pearson states that the application of the laws of heredity and environment:

> to the progressive evolution of the race will become the religion of each nation. Such is the goal of Galtonian teaching, the conversion of the Darwinian doctrine of evolution into a religious precept, a practical

philosophy of life. Is this more than saying that it must be the goal of every true patriot?

(ibid.: 93)

Charles Spearman (1863–1945) is the most famous of the British pioneers as yet unmentioned. The originator of factor analysis and the concept of general intelligence (g), he held chairs in psychology and philosophy of mind at University College London, from 1907 until 1931. He was a member of the Eugenics Society Council in 1916 and became a Fellow in 1938. The religious background of his family is uncertain. I have seen no evidence of nonconformity. Given his connexions with the army (he was a professional soldier before he became a psychologist), as well as the fact that his father, the Right Honourable Sir A.Y. Spearman, was a senior civil servant in the Treasury in the 1830s, his establishment background suggests Anglicanism, but I have no firmer evidence of this.

Is Spearman then a counter-example to the thesis that the intelligence pioneers had puritan links? If the thesis is interpreted broadly, probably yes. But if the focus is on those pioneers who were in the Galtonian eugenic tradition, the answer is less clear-cut. Norton (1980) suggests that the key to his thinking is to see it as a reaction to the prevailing associationism of academic philosophy in favour of the philosophical idealism of his old teacher Wilhelm Wundt. Spearman describes 'g' as a fund of 'mental energy' (Norton 1980: 61) and refers to 'the mind or soul as the agent in conduct' (ibid.: 64). His orientation was academic rather than practical. He appears to have lacked the puritan drive to be socially useful.

Like many scientists of his time, Spearman was not slow to draw attention to the eugenic potential of his work. But, when one examines the pattern of his productions and interests, one finds there nothing to indicate the presence of eugenic ideology as a driving force. There was none of the practical concern with mental testing and social organisation that characterised, say, a Cyril Burt. Spearman, first and last, wished to uncover the architecture of the mind – to show the principles according to which our mental contents are constructed.

(ibid.: 63)

More recent British psychologists in the Galtonian tradition, and also fellow-eugenicists, include Godfrey Thomson (1881–1955) and R.B. Cattell (1905–1998). Again, I have found no clear evidence of family religion, although the industrialist background in each case may point to nonconformity. Thomson's grandfather had helped to set up a chemical works with his cousin in Tyneside (Thomson 1969: 1–2); while Cattell's father and grandfather were both 'engineer designers running their own business in the English Midlands' and also liberal in politics (Cattell 1974: 61).

I turn now to the pioneers of intelligence testing in the USA.

US psychologists of intelligence: Goddard and Terman

Henry Herbert Goddard (1866–1957)

H.H. Goddard was introduced in Chapter 1 as America's first intelligence tester, a eugenicist, and author of *The Kallikak Family*.

He was born in New England of Quaker parents who could both trace their families back to English roots in the seventeenth century. His mother was related to the colonial governor of Plymouth Colony, Edward Winslow, who had come over in the *Mayflower* (Zenderland 1998: 16). Goddard's father had been a farmer but was reduced to being a day labourer. He died when Herbert was nine and 'were it not' he wrote, 'for the Society of Friends (Quakers) it would probably have gone hard with us … The Friends always take care of their poor' (ibid.: 17). His mother was a committed Quaker; and her commitment grew during Herbert's childhood in the wake of nation-wide Quaker revivalism in the 1870s which deeply affected their Maine community. The 'great change' which had been wrought in her caused the local Friends to recognise her 'gift in the ministry' (she preached in the local Congregational Church among other places). In the following years she felt 'called to visit Friends Meetings in distant communities', travelling widely for this purpose across Canada and the USA (ibid.: 19) and afterwards in Europe.

Goddard, meanwhile, was left at home with his married sister and was educated by the Quakers at Oak Grove Seminary, the Friends School in Providence and later at Haverford College. He resented the latter's reputation as, in his own words, 'a convenient way to keep sons of rich Philadelphia Quakers out of mischief' (ibid.: 20), and disliked its narrow, 'guarded', education. Despite this, he graduated from Haverford with a BA, followed by an MA in mathematics, and got married, his wife soon coming to share his Quaker faith (ibid.: 25). Goddard became principal of a Quaker school in Ohio and two years later principal of his old school, Oak Grove Seminary.

It was while at Oak Grove that Goddard heard an address to local teachers given by G. Stanley Hall, one of the first American psychologists and at that time president of Clark University in Worcester, Massachusetts (ibid.: 28). Goddard was inspired, as were many others, by Clark's child-centred, science-based approach to education and in 1896 went to Clark University to study with him, gaining a doctorate within three years. In an ethos of free enquiry, Hall inducted Goddard into scientific thinking, especially in evolutionary psychology.

> Despite the stark differences distinguishing Quaker from Clark pedagogy, Goddard's education in science remained surprisingly consistent. Like other Protestants, Goddard's Quaker teachers had taught a version of natural theology, in which the order found in the physical world illuminated God's orderly mind. Science, Goddard learned, meant discovering the laws of nature.
> (ibid.: 30)

Goddard's Quaker schooling in Providence had included classes in geology based on evolutionary ideas deriving from Darwin. This prepared him well for his later studies, 'for he evidently perceived no open warfare between his Christian heritage and his new career as a scientist studying evolutionary theory' (ibid.: 31).

The intellectual autonomy of Hall's regime did nothing to shake Goddard's faith, given that Hall himself, brought up on strict Congregationalist lines as a child, had recently returned to christianity and now saw himself as providing a psychological reinterpretation of christian ideals, supplying, as he put it, 'modern methods of studying the soul' (ibid.). The same application of a new science to old subject-matter appears in the topic which Goddard chose for his doctoral dissertation: 'The Effects of Mind on Body as Evidenced in Faith Cures' (ibid.: 33).

Goddard maintained close ties to the Quakers in the following years (ibid.: 39). His biographer writes that:

> he never fully abandoned the modes of thinking acquired in his childhood. In his later years, both his negative and his positive responses to his early Quaker experiences would be evident in his actions. For the rest of his life, this scientist would always despise rigid pedagogy and strict theological dogma. In a deeper sense, however, his religious background would become intertwined with his very understanding of what a psychologist was.
>
> (ibid.: 42)

She suggests that:

> By the time he graduated, Goddard had found his vocation. He left Clark in 1899 a disciple less of the church's version of the Gospels than of G.Stanley Hall's. Moreover, Goddard embraced his new psychological calling with an evangelical zeal which matched his mother's. He now believed in an evolutionary version of the faith of his fathers.
>
> (ibid.: 43)

Zenderland's biography shows abundant evidence of the further intertwining of Goddard's commitment to both science and religion in his early work as an educator, especially in his work in the child study movement (ibid.: 46–9). What is more pertinent to the present investigation is the tenacity of his belief in the eugenic significance of individual differences in intelligence and the zeal with which he developed and promoted intelligence testing. We have already encountered his belief in these tests as a way of identifying the 'feeble-minded', not least among immigrants arriving in America; his polarisation of the highly able virtuous and the moronic vicious in the Kallikak book; and his vision of a society in which everyone pursues his vocation at his own mental level.

Like Burt and Galton, Goddard came from a branch of puritanism – Quaker or Congregationalist – that took virtually for granted their own election. The social philosophy of all these men was premised on the nurturing of a small group of gifted individuals, the constraining of the least intelligent, and the stratification of callings according to mental ability. Each found his calling in science; each threw himself with a lifetime's passion into the eugenic mission.

Lewis Terman (1877–1956)

As we saw in Chapter 1, Lewis Terman was, like Goddard, a pupil of G. Stanley Hall at Clark University and a Galtonian. He developed and publicised the Stanford–Binet test, applied it to tracking systems in school, and worked for many years on the intellectually gifted. He, too, was a eugenicist with a polarised interest in producing leaders at one end of the ability spectrum and curtailing feeble-mindedness at the other.

Like the other psychologists who shared his social outlook, Terman came from protestant stock – although in Terman's case we know fewer details than in others'. He was born and brought up on a farm in Indiana. His father enjoyed reading the Bible although seldom attended church (Seacoe 1975; 2). Each side of his family could trace its roots in America to around 1700. The facts that his paternal grandfather John H. Tarman, was of Scotch-Irish descent, and had changed his name to John Bunyan Terman (Minton 1988: 3) point strongly to a puritan connexion. Terman's mother was of protestant ancestry on both sides of her family – German (Pennsylvanian 'Dutch') and French Huguenot. Along with her husband she was firm on protestant family virtues like order, discipline and hard work (Seacoe 1975: 3). In his late teens, as a young teacher, Lewis Terman lost all interest in organised religion and became increasingly agnostic (ibid.: 6).

It is harder with Terman than with the other major figures in this chapter, to point unequivocally to a puritan connexion in a narrower sense of this term. The fact, however, that Terman's paternal grandfather, born around 1790, came from a Scotch-Irish family, strongly suggests Ulster Presbyterianism.

Other American psychologists

G. Stanley Hall (1844–1924) was, as we have seen, the teacher of both Goddard and Terman when they studied at Clark University, of which Hall was the first president. He was a pioneer of American scientific psychology, having launched the first psychological laboratory in the USA, its first journal of psychology, and the American Psychological Association (Schultz and Schultz 2000: 203–4). His particular interest was in evolutionary theory especially as applied to child psychology. His most influential work is *Adolescence* (1904). This includes his famous 'recapitulation theory', that children's development repeats the life history of the human race, from near-savagery to civilisation.

Hall came from a devout Congregationalist family in Massachusetts, both his mother and his father being descendants of passengers in the *Mayflower* (Ross 1972: 3). His father was described as 'a Calvinist of the old school' (ibid.: 5). Hall studied for the ministry at Union Theological Seminary in New York

City, but was never ordained, his interests in evolution theory and physiology leading him to a career as a psychologist (Schultz and Schultz 2000: 202). He retained, however, his interest in religion, inaugurating both the Clark School of Religious Psychology and the *Journal of Religious Psychology* (ibid.: 204). He shared the practical bent of most of the other psychologists discussed in this book, being determined at an early age to 'do and be something in the world', and first making his name by applying psychology to education (ibid.: 201–3). For more on the historical significance of Hall's work in the transition, within American universities, from a religious interest in the mind to the scientific investigation of it, see Chapter 4.

James McKeen Cattell (1860–1944) was also a pupil of G.S. Hall – at Johns Hopkins University, before Hall went to Clark – and an early devotee of mental tests following his meeting with Galton, who inspired him to investigate individual differences. He later taught psychology at Columbia University from 1891 until 1917. Cattell's father was a Presbyterian minister and President of Lafayette College, an institution with Presbyterian connexions where Cattell himself studied.

As president of the American Psychological Association in 1916, **Robert M. Yerkes** (1876–1956) was the leading figure, working with Terman, Thorndike and Woodworth, in the introduction of Army Alpha test and Army Beta group tests of intelligence for US Army recruits. The dramatic effect of the army tests on the development of intelligence testing after World War I has been described in Chapter 2. Yerkes was a eugenicist and a member of the Eugenic Record Office's Committee on the inheritance of mental traits (Blum 1978: 57).

Yerkes's mother was the strongest influence in his early life (Yerkes 1932: 382). She 'wished me to enter the church. Almost certainly she would have become a foreign missionary had she been free to choose a career' (ibid.: 385). Before becoming a student at Harvard in 1898, from 1892 to 1897 Yerkes studied at Ursinus Academy, Pennsylvania, an institution associated at that time with the low church party in the German Reformed Church.

Other psychologists whose work lay partly in the psychology of intelligence include **E. L. Thorndike** (1874–1949). His interests in psychology were markedly practical: he held a chair in educational psychology for 40 years (Pastore 1949: 71). He was an innatist, a follower of Galton, writing in 1911 that 'on the whole, intellectual and moral individuality seems to be determined by the germs' (ibid.: 66). Politically he was to the right, arguing that the unemployed should be frugal during prosperous years so as to support themselves in the lean ones. Like Galton, he favoured an intellectual aristocracy for eugenic reasons, believing that 'the great bulk of the people do not wish to rule' (ibid.: 74). Like G.S. Hall, Thorndike came from old New England stock, both his parents being descended from English settlers from the 1630s (Jonçich 1968: 11, 15). His father was a Methodist minister; his mother was 'more than a resolute Victorian: she is confident that she "knows the way", and that a Puritan-like duty bids her keep her husband and children from error' (ibid.: 22). Thorndike himself attended Wesleyan University, a Methodist foundation.

L.L.Thurstone's parents were both Lutherans from Sweden; and in later life his father became a Lutheran minister (Thurstone 1952: 295). For generations all **R.S. Woodworth**'s ancestors had been New Englanders. His father was a Congregational minister, 'intensely and sternly religious' (Woodworth 1932: 359).

More recent psychologists in Britain and USA

How far should we expect to find echoes of the Old Dissenting/puritan world in more recent thinking about intelligence? It is now 140 years since Galton's article appeared in *Macmillan's Magazine*, and nearly a century since the beginnings of work by Terman, Goddard and Burt. Theirs was a more religious age than our own and it is likely that any echoes were more audible in their own age than in later times.

This is indeed how it seems to be. In the second half of the twentieth century evidence of radical protestant links among prominent intelligence researchers becomes thinner the closer we come to our own times. If the main hypothesis of this book is correct, one would expect to find many of the early pioneers attracted to work on intelligence because of affinities between this work and the cultural background with which they were familiar and which may have affected them despite themselves. By the mid-twentieth century, intelligence research had become an established branch of psychology with its own career paths. It was also a high-profile area, given its involvement in educational policy-making and its politically controversial nature. Increasingly, still following the main hypothesis, one would expect newly qualified psychologists to move into this area for a wide variety of overlapping reasons: career considerations, for instance, or a desire to work in an area of intense public interest, the influence of a favourite teacher. It would be less likely, perhaps, than with the early pioneers for cultural affinities to play a part.

Let us look forward, then, from around 1950, coming closer to our own times as we go. Two of the most prominent figures in British intelligence testing in the earlier period were Philip Vernon and Hans Eysenck.

Philip Vernon (1905–87), Professor of Psychology of Education at the Institute of Education in London from 1949 until 1968 and later at the University of Calgary in Canada, was a prominent member of the Eugenics Society between 1933 and 1961. He became in time the foremost critic of the claim that IQ remains constant, showed that coaching for the test can significantly increase one's score, and argued from a psychological perspective in favour of non-selective, comprehensive schools and against streaming. Like Galton and Burt, he was from a puritan family. He writes in an autobiographical sketch:

My grandfather was a Baptist minister in London, whose three eldest children all became medically qualified, including my father ... He [the father] was a puritanical, authoritarian figure, who seldom had any time for his children, and of whom I was thoroughly frightened; though I realise now that I resemble him in many ways and have been much influenced by him.

(Vernon 1978: 303)

It was Vernon's father – who gave up his lecturership in physiology at Oxford University in the First World War to do pioneer work in industrial psychology on the bad effects of long working hours – who advised Vernon and his sister to become psychologists (ibid.: 305–6). In a frank piece of self-reflection, Vernon tells us that, given his reclusive nature, 'it might be thought I was the last person to become absorbed in a profession depending on understanding of human personality and social interactions' (ibid.: 309). He suggests that he may have taken to psychology 'because of some underlying need for affiliation with people ... yet at the same time I avoid too much emotional entanglement by treating them nomothetically, and concentrating particularly on impersonal things like abilities and test scores' (ibid.: 309–10). This is an interesting remark. It prompts one to wonder whether any of the other psychologists of intelligence studied in this book were similarly motivated, given the low value that the puritan tradition has placed on emotional involvement with others.

Hans Eysenck (1916–97) studied psychology with Cyril Burt at University College London, and among his other interests, especially in personality theory, pugnaciously continued the Galton–Burt tradition of work on intelligence and its testing into our own age. Like Burt, he held that the IQ is reasonably constant and that individual differences in IQ are overwhelmingly due to innate causes. He was a Eugenics Society Fellow in 1947 and 1957. He was born in Berlin of parents who were not religious themselves, although his father came from Catholic stock and his mother from Lutheran. He was brought up by his maternal grandmother, Frau Werner, who had a firm belief in God (Eysenck 1990: 14), although he claimed that her Lutheranism had little influence on him (Gibson 1981: 17). His biographer suggests, however, that

It is just possible that [religion] has had more influence on him in certain respects than he realizes. Viewing his whole career in perspective, one wonders whether the ethos of Martin Luther's teachings has been entirely lost on him. Eysenck has performed the act of nailing his own principles to various church doors, in defiance of some established creeds, rather too often to make the supposition entirely without foundation.

(ibid.)

Eysenck, like Burt, was a frequent contributor to the *Black Papers* of the 1970s which paved the way for the Thatcher government's shift in educational policy between 1979 and 1990 away from comprehensive towards selective schooling based on parental choice, and towards a traditional school curriculum. His 1975 contribution, entitled 'Educational consequences of human inequality' (Eysenck 1975) continues the traditional eugenic theme in its statement that: 'We must conclude that in so far as our civilisation is based on education, it is in danger of suffering a serious blow through the consistent disregard of biological reality manifested by present-day educational theorists' (ibid.: 41) – and inveighs against the lack of choice open to parents who find that 'all they are offered are so-called "modern" comprehensive schools which have abandoned all pretence of teaching traditional subjects along traditional lines, maintaining discipline, and safeguarding academic standards' (ibid).

The most prominent American scholar in the field in the post-1950 period was Arthur Jensen (1923–), whose 1969 work on racial differences in IQ has already been mentioned. In the light of his claim that most of the average fifteen point IQ difference between American blacks and whites is genetically based, he held that education for blacks should be centred on rote-learning, as distinct from the conceptual learning appropriate for whites. Jensen was a disciple of Eysenck's, with whom he studied at the Institute of Psychiatry in London, and was later a member of the American Eugenics Society.

Jensen's mother was of Polish Jewish stock, while his father was the son of immigrants from Copenhagen. Frank Miele, in his study of Jensen's life and works, says:

> Early on, Jensen noted how the dour demeanour of his Danish relatives contrasted with the fun-loving atmosphere of his mother's side of the family.
> (Miele 2002: 8)

Miele also tells us that his mother had to leave Berlin, where she was living, because both families – his mother's and his father's – disapproved of marriage across religious lines (ibid.). From this, it is likely that Jensen's Danish relatives were practising Lutherans, but one cannot be certain of this.

Does Jensen's probable Lutheran background have any bearing on the direction of his research interests? Or should we put weight on the deep impression which his teacher Hans Eysenck made on him? There is certainly evidence for the latter, but none that I know for the former (unless one builds – fragilely – on the Lutheranism most probably present in both Eysenck's and Jensen's backgrounds).

Richard Herrnstein (1930–94) extended Jensen's analysis from race to class, arguing in Herrnstein (1971) for the genetic superiority of those who have risen in our open society into the meritocratic élite. The same thesis is argued for in his co-authored book *The Bell Curve* (1994), mentioned above. There is nothing in Herrnstein's background that, as far as I know, points to a protestant link. His father was Jewish and his mother, to whom he was particularly attached, was of Hungarian stock.

If we move from the 1960s and 1970s into the late twentieth century, there is no significant evidence that I know of ascetic protestant influences on intelligence researchers working within the IQ paradigm. (I am indebted to Christopher Brand, formerly of Edinburgh University, and Richard Lynn, Professor Emeritus of the University of Ulster, for help on this topic.)

Pastore's thesis and the question of counter-examples

In 1949 Nicholas Pastore published a book called *The Nature–Nurture Controversy* (Pastore 1949). In it he examined the writings of twenty-four scientists involved in this controversy 'to ascertain whether there was any significant relationship between their emphasis on nature or nurture and their particular socio-political orientation' (ibid.: 176). These scientists, who were drawn from biology and education as well as from psychology, include several people appearing in the present book: J.M. Cattell, Galton, Goddard, McDougall, Pearson, Terman and Thorndike. Pastore's conclusion on the group of twenty-four was that, with one or two exceptions, 'those emphasizing environmental factors tended towards liberalism or radicalism, those emphasizing hereditary factors tended towards conservatism' (ibid.: 176–7). Among the latter group were Galton, Goddard, McDougall, Pearson and Thorndike. Cattell was classified as environmentalist and liberal. Terman proved an anomaly: an innatist liberal.

There are problems – which we can largely bypass – about whether Cattell was always an environmentalist and Terman a liberal; in their early careers they belonged more on the other side of each of their fences, as, in Terman's case, quotations in Chapter 1 help to indicate. More broadly, Pastore's investigation is of interest to us for two reasons.

As one of the first scholars to take a group of leading psychologists of intelligence (among other scientists) and examine their ideological orientations, he does not refer to the common radical protestant background they all shared – although he is certainly not unaware of the continuity between religious and biological ideas in the nineteenth century:

> The breakdown of the dominant religious patterns of defense, which was partly due to the general acceptance of the controversial Darwinian doctrine, paved the way for the acceptance of similar thought-patterns which were accorded the prestige of science. The idea of religious predestination, for example, could be replaced by that of 'biological determinism'.
>
> (Pastore 1949: 10)

He goes on to mention a remark from a member of the audience at a lecture by William Bateson, the biologist: 'Sir, you are preaching scientific Calvinism!' And he follows this by remarks on the difficulty which Galton found in 'breaking away from religion'. But there is no further discussion of this link between religion and science in the main body of his text. True, he has his sights on a link of a different sort – between *politics* and science – so it is not surprising, perhaps, that his single-mindedness in exploring it should exclude other considerations.

This brings me to the second point. One might say that in its pursuit of the puritan origins of the intelligence pioneers this present book is as single-minded as Pastore's. How far is it as even-handed, testing for counter-examples as well as for positive instances? I am more than conscious of the danger of bias towards the latter, but hope I have avoided it. The clearest case of contrary evidence presented so far is the apparent absence of any dissenting connexion in Spearman. Thomson and R.B. Cattell may also be counter-examples: clinching evidence is still lacking.

What of possible American counter-examples? **John Dewey** (1859–1952) was prominent in the 'New Psychology' of the end of the nineteenth century. Like Goddard, J.M. Cattell and Terman, he was a student of G.S. Hall's, in Dewey's case at Johns Hopkins. Dewey's first foray into psychology, while still a graduate student there, closely followed Hall's work on the unity of interests between psychology and religion (Ryan 1995: 75), but Dewey soon turned his back on Hall's thinking (ibid.: 74). Unlike Goddard and Terman, Dewey became an outspoken critic of Galtonian intelligence and the uses to which it was put. In an essay in *The New Republic* called 'Mediocrity and individuality' (Dewey 1990: 289ff), he applauded Walter Lippman's recent critique of intelligence testing in the same journal (see Chapter 2, p. 31) and wrote feelingly of the newly discovered 'way of dividing our population into definite classes' (Dewey 1990: 289).

Dewey is important as a possible counter-example to the book's thesis, because he had been brought up in a New England Congregationalist family. He had been especially influenced by his mother Lucina, whose devoutness combined 'the older, conservative emphasis on individual introspection – being good and possessing a rigid personal morality – with a loose interpretation of scripture, an intense liberal emphasis on doing good through social welfare, and a reformist drive' (Martin 2002: 21). Dewey later reacted resentfully against his mother's piety, especially as it affected himself in her repeated query 'Are you right with Jesus?'

> His mother's efforts eventually alienated Dewey from all moralities that dealt in 'sin' and guilt and by the same token from all understandings of religion that separated the believer from his God in the way that traditional Calvinist Christianity did.
>
> (Ryan 1995: 47)

Dewey shows that not all the early psychologists of intelligence who had puritan backgrounds became attached to Galtonian intelligence testing. Why was Dewey different? Was the family ethos of the other psychologists less liberal, more accepting of the social status quo, than in Dewey's case? Perhaps connected with this, did Dewey's more intensively philosophical turn of mind cause him to question the assumptions of the Galtonian tradition while men like Galton himself, Pearson, Burt, McDougall, Goddard and Terman and others, whose interests tended towards statistics and eugenics, were content to work within them? Further investigations, outside this book, may cast light on this.

Another possible counter-example of a sort is **J.B. Watson** (1878–1958). Watson was not a psychologist of intelligence, but is well-known as the founder of behaviorism. He came from a fundamentalist Calvinist family. He is a counter-example to the extent that behaviorism tended to extreme environmentalism and the rejection of any role for heredity in explaining human abilities. Watson was from Baptist stock in South Carolina and had promised his mother that he would become a minister. The death of his mother while he was still a student released him from this vow and led him to study philosophy rather than theology at the University of Chicago – under Dewey among others. This led to an intellectual crisis whereby he rejected the notions of consciousness and introspection (as a psychological method) because of their association with the christian notions of the soul and of conscience. It seems that his pre-Chicago undergraduate studies at the Baptist-affiliated Furman University sowed the seeds of this rejection. There he had studied philosophy and psychology at a time when the christian psychology of the soul and its faculties traditionally taught in American colleges and universities by protestant ministers was coming to be seriously questioned. For more on the transition from religiously-based to scientifically based psychology in American universities, see Chapter 4. (And for these and other details of Watson's rejection of Calvinism, see Creelan 1974.)

Why Watson rejected the notions of consciousness, the mind or soul, and innate faculties while the intelligence pioneers, coming from a similar religious background, retained them, we do not know. As with Dewey, there is the same philosophical turn of mind – an interest in exploring basic assumptions rather than taking them on board. But no doubt the full story is much more complicated than this.

A different kind of counter-example is collective rather than individual. Britain and the USA are both countries with partly puritan roots. Are there any similar countries where eugenic notions of intelligence and intelligence testing failed to make much impact? Early-twentieth-century Netherlands appears to fit this bill. According to Mulder and Heyting (1998: 349), here 'intelligence testing has been pragmatic and has not generated the heated controversies found in other cultures'. Although there were eugenicist testers like Herderschee and Luning Prak, 'eugenics … never became more than marginal in Dutch society' (ibid.: 359). One reason for this was the 'relatively homogeneous composition of Dutch society, culturally as well as ethically' (ibid.). There was not the racial motive for stressing differences of intelligence that existed in the United States. Another reason was so-called 'pillarisation': the 'system of institutionalised segmentation' whereby each religious or quasi-religious group was subsidised by the state to create its own social world from nursery school upwards. The Calvinist minority was one such group, along with liberal protestants and Catholics and others (ibid.: 359–60). There was nothing in Holland parallel to the stratified position of the British Dissenters in the general class structure and attempts to improve their relative status through political action, not least education.

Jean Piaget

A word, finally, in this discussion of psychologists, on Jean Piaget (1896–1980). Although he is not in the Galtonian tradition, he is a psychologist of intelligence who began work in intelligence testing at the Simon–Binet laboratory in Paris, using tests devised by Cyril Burt. His writings have several features in common with work of the Galtonians: an element of predestinarianism in his biological notion of stages of mental development which cannot be attained until previous stages have been completed; and an interest in general, abstract-logical aspects of mental life. (I am grateful for this observation to Jane Green.) Piaget's mother, Rebecca, née Jackson, was of English origin. Her great-grandfather James Jackson (1772–1829), was from a Quaker family from Lancashire (Jackson 1893: 152), and ran a steelworks in Birmingham. He was invited by the French Government in 1814 to move to France and bring his industrial secrets and expertise with him. He set up a family steel-making business in Saint-Etienne (Barrelet and Perret-Clermont 1996: 42) and is judged to have been one of the pioneers of the French steel industry as a whole. I have not been able to find, either in the library at Friends House in Bloomsbury, or elsewhere, any record of his activities in England. I do not know whether this is connected with the fact that he became *persona non grata* in 1814, having been banished by the British government and his property confiscated.

Belonging to an upper-middle-class protestant family closely allied in marriage with the Peugeot family, which was also protestant – her grandfather would appear to have been James Jackson's eldest son and steel entrepreneur William – Rebecca herself was very devout (Piaget 1952: 239). She became a member of the free evangelical church of Neuchâtel (Barrelet and Perret-Clermont 1996: 23). She passed on her Christian Socialist ideas and activist orientation to her son. Jean Piaget was brought up in a rigorous protestant faith (ibid.: 112), which generated his earliest book *La mission de l'idée* in 1915 (ibid.: 112–13).

Robert Morant

This concludes the biographical accounts of psychologists. In this section I come back to the administrator Robert Morant. He was introduced in Chapter 1, along with Cyril Burt, as a central figure in English educational history in the first part of the twentieth century. In around 1904 he set up a selective system of state education, whose selective features Cyril Burt later developed still further and which were given a supposedly scientific rationale via Burt's theory of intelligence and intelligence testing.

Like Burt, Morant had at least one parent with Congregationalist roots. His father died when Morant was ten and I have found no record of his religious affiliation. But:

> There was in fact a strong vein of puritanism in the family blood. Robert's mother traced back her descent to one of the Puritan stalwarts, a certain Colonel James Berry, who had been Cromwell's Major-General for the county

of Shropshire, and among his ancestors the boy numbered more than one who had been an Independent minister in the Midland Counties.

(Allen 1934: 3–4)

His mother's father was also an Independent minister and had been headmaster of Mill Hill School, founded in 1807 by Congregationalists and other nonconformists as a grammar school for the sons of protestant Dissenters (Brett-James (n.d.): 9). It is a direct descendant of the Dissenting Academies. In the late eighteenth century these had lost ground – and importantly, staff – to new private schools set up for sons of merchants and manufacturers, following the passing of a 1779 law allowing Dissenters to become schoolteachers. 'A few of the academies that survived became Public Schools of the type of Mill Hill' (McLachlan 1931: 5). Mill Hill's first headmaster was John Atkinson, who until then had taught at Hoxton Independent Academy in London (ibid.: 239).

Morant's grandfather, the Rev. Henry Lea Berry, himself an old Mill Hill boy, was appointed headmaster in 1831 and held the post for four years, resigning through ill-health (Brett-James (n.d.): 106–7, 111, 117–18). His grandfather's father, the Rev. Joseph Berry, who was a member of the governing committee of the school and a prominent man in religious circles (ibid.: 64), made an address to his son during his induction ceremony as headmaster (ibid.: 109). Like Cyril Burt, then, Morant had a Congregationalist grandfather and great-grandfather; and as in Burt's case, these both followed the family calling, medicine in the one case, the ministry in the other.

Like Cyril Burt, too, Morant was close to his Congregationalist grandfather. In Morant's case, the bond must have been even closer, since after leaving Mill Hill the grandfather came to live near his daughter in Hampstead. A boy of Morant's own age who attended the same kindergarten wrote that 'the most gracious influence in his earliest years must, I am sure, have been grandparental, his mother's father being a winning personality, stooping from age but more often still from a heart full of kindness to us children' (Allen 1934: 5).

What Allen describes as a 'potent influence' on Morant's childhood was the evangelical vicar of Christ Church, Hampstead, the Rev. E.H. Bickersteth. It was Bickersteth who opened the kindergarten mentioned, in his vicarage garden. Morant's mother was 'a devoted adherent' of his and brought up Robert and his two sisters 'in the strictest traditions of a devout Victorian household' (ibid.: 3). Given the confluence of Congregationalism and evangelicalism in her belief system, she may well fit into the category of 'moderate Calvinism' which Bebbington (1989: 63–5) describes in his history of evangelicalism. He quotes an early-nineteenth-century source suggesting that'Calvinism should be, in our general religious instructions, like a lump of sugar in a cup of tea; all should taste of it, but it should not be met with in a separate form' (ibid.: 63). Moderate Calvinism soft-pedalled predestination in favour of faith as the pathway to salvation, as well as sound morality, including dutifulness within the family.

By the time he left Winchester for New College Oxford in 1881, Morant was enthusiastically preparing to enter the Anglican church as an evangelical minister.

He signed up for a course in Hebrew alongside his work in classics, and threw himself into evangelistic work with the Inter-collegiate Christian Union. He also held regular services in Marston village, formed a 'Brotherhood' in New College for theological study with a few kindred spirits, and taught a Sunday school class at Hinksey (Allen 1934: 16–19).

Although Morant lost his faith in 1884–5, 'he remained true to the high ideals of conduct which lay at the root of that Faith' (ibid.: 59). A letter to a friend which he sent while working for the King of Siam in 1889 speaks of 'a following of an ideal, a restraint of self for the sake of an ideal' (ibid.). By 1898, three years after beginning work in the Education Department's Branch of Special Enquiries and Reports, his secular ideal had crystallised into a vision of stratified post-primary schools, each stratum having a distinctive function in promoting national development. He had been influenced by investigations he had made into stratified post-primary schools in France and Switzerland. What particularly impressed him about the latter was 'the contrast between the extreme care which the Swiss devoted to fostering their secondary or higher schools and the neglected condition in which the corresponding institutions were left in England' (ibid.: 123). In an article he wrote in 1898, soon after completing his report on Switzerland, he suggested that the only hope for the continued existence of a democratic state was 'to be found in an increasing recognition, *by* the democracy, of the increasing need of voluntarily subjecting the impulses of the many ignorant to the guidance and control of the few wise' (ibid.: 125). Without this:

> scrupulous safeguarding of the 'guidance of brains' … the more surely will the democratic State be beaten, in the long run, in the international struggle for existence, conquered from without by the force of the concentrated directing brain power of the competing nations, shattered from within by the centrifugal forces of her own people's unrestrained individualism and disintegrated utterly by the blind impulses of mere numerical majorities.
>
> (ibid.: 126)

This stark dualism between 'the many ignorant' and 'the few wise' was soon to be incorporated in the curriculum decisions of 1904 which drew the sharp line between the content of secondary and elementary education described in Chapter 1.

Morant's social vision is reminiscent of Galton's. It looks to an intellectual élite, recipients of a liberal education in all the main branches of knowledge, to save the nation. As with Galton, Morant leaves us in no doubt that he is among this elect. He likewise has a low opinion of the non-selected, the ignorant majority with its unrestrained individualism and blind impulses. Although he does not explicitly say so in the passage quoted, it looks as if he thinks the amount of 'brain power' one has is innately given and unchangeable. Otherwise, if one takes it that most people are 'ignorant', it makes sense to look to the education system to do what it can to make these people more knowledgeable. But Morant does not take this line, either in this passage or in his new curriculum for the elementary school. In the latter, as explained in Chapter 1, the hard knowledge taught in secondary schools – science, mathematics, literature, foreign languages, history, geography – is watered down or absent. These children are to work not with their brains but with their hands and their curriculum reflects this. A key aim of the elementary school is to form and strengthen their character – to implant in them habits of industry, self-control, respect for duty, readiness for self-sacrifice and striving after purity and truth (Board of Education 1929: 9). In this way, perhaps, their blind impulses may be subject to some kind of control. There is no egalitarian thought here that every child should be as well-equipped as the next one for a fulfilling life as an individual and as a citizen. As with Galton, as with Burt, so with Morant: the nation is divided in two – the gifted élite for whom all things are possible and who must be groomed for success, and the rest who are not going anywhere. Three centuries of dualising puritan social philosophy lay behind Morant, as it did Galton and possibly Burt. It is hard to believe that it did not help to shape his thinking. This is all the more true in Morant's case because of the very fervour of his evangelical commitment in his early years. This, too, was based on a dualism – of the brotherhood of the saved, to which Morant thought he belonged; and the unsaved majority. Not that this social dichotomy was ever, in his thinking, absolute. Preaching to save souls in the villages around Oxford presupposes the thought that some may be rescued, for otherwise there is no point to it. In the same way, twenty years later in Morant's career, we find him writing in his introduction to the Elementary School Code that 'it will be an important though subsidiary object of the School to discover individual children who show promise of exceptional capacity, and to develop their special gifts ... so that they may be qualified at the proper age to pass into secondary schools' (Board of Education 1929: 9). In education as in religion, for exceptional souls there is a ladder to a higher place.

Conclusion

This chapter has produced plentiful evidence of the puritan/dissenting family backgrounds of the intelligence pioneers and associated figures. It has also shown how religious notions in these backgrounds have or may have influenced their psychological and educational work. The arguments for this are not conclusive and are more clear-cut in some cases, e.g. Goddard's, than in others. Even so, there is sufficient evidence to show that the idea should be taken seriously. The fact that *virtually all* the leading figures in early intelligence studies came from a similar thought-world, and a thought-world with plausible links with eugenic notions, bolsters this contention. I have taken counter-evidence into account, both in the shape of psychologists without apparent puritan/dissenting ancestry who were central figures in intelligence testing (Spearman); and psychologists who distanced themselves from one or other aspect of Galtonian thinking and who *were* from puritan stock (Dewey, Watson).

Investigation now has to go deeper. We need to look more closely at the way in which the intelligence pioneers tended to think of intelligence; and we need to explore the possible origins of their conceptualisations. This will take us into aspects of the history of puritan thinking and provide further support for the claim that this kind of psychology has to be understood against a specific religious background. All this will be explored in Chapter 4.

4   Logic and mind

Intelligence as abstract intellectual ability

The Galtonian account of intelligence is built around *intellectual* ability – and intellectual ability of a *general* rather than a specific sort. This conception has so influenced common understandings of intelligence that it may not strike one how peculiar it is. Intelligent behaviour, as we saw in Chapter 1, takes innumerable forms, from coping with difficult relationships within the family to skilfully playing the stock market. Intellectual ability is only one form of intelligence. It itself is multifarious, the powers displayed in mathematical calculations being very different from those found in historical research or in law.

Why were the pioneers of intelligence testing so interested in general intellectual ability – even though such a thing probably does not exist? And how did they conceive this? Since they took it as part of our innate equipment, it could not be sensitive to anything requiring cultural initiation but had to be maximally abstracted from this. What, if anything, could fit this bill? The most abstract forms of intellectual activity are logic, including logical operations on elements of one's native language, and mathematics. It is not surprising that these operations figure so prominently in intelligence tests. Take, for instance, the test which Yerkes devised for illiterate US army personnel in the First World War – the so-called Beta test. Its seven items covered: a maze puzzle, counting the number of cubes, completing a series involving 0 and X, translating from numbers to symbols, finding discrepancies in number pairs, spotting missing features of objects, breaking a square into component pieces (see Gould 1981: 208–9).

Linguistic operations are more evident in the earlier stages of Terman's Stanford–Binet tests from the same period in *The Measurement of Intelligence* (Terman 1916). These become more abstract the older the testee. Many of the tests for very young children, following Binet, demand knowledge of simple facts like one's name, the day of the week, the difference between right and left, etc. At the other end of the age range, tests for average adults include defining abstract terms, stating the number of boxes enclosed in a larger box, repeating six digits reversed, comprehending physical relationships, to do, for instance, with the path of a cannon ball (Terman 1916: ch. 19). All this fits Terman's statement in the same work, that an individual is intelligent in proportion as he is able to carry on abstract thinking.'It is in the very essence of the higher thought processes to be conceptual and abstract' (ibid.: 344). Cyril Burt's tests in his *Mental and Scholastic Tests* (Burt 1947) are more like Terman's than like Yerkes's Beta test.

The abstract-intellectual nature of Galtonian intelligence is well described in a Eugenics Society lecture by Godfrey Thomson in 1947:

> But although intelligence expresses itself in different forms, in its highest aspects it is always concerned with abstractions and concepts and relationships. Practical intelligence, as it is called, is of considerable importance in the world: but theoretical intelligence is of immeasurably greater importance. The clever garage mechanic may improve a motor-car engine. The student of thermodynamics or of atomic physics is much more likely to make the motor-car engine obsolete and replace it by a more efficient engine. And such men think in abstractions, often clothed no doubt in symbols of some sort or another, symbols which may be verbal, or mathematical, or, like Faraday's tubes of force, more mundane and materialistic, but symbols nevertheless, the real values with which these minds are operating being abstract relationships.
>
> (Thomson 1947: 17)

One might well ask why practical intelligence is exemplified here by the work of a car mechanic rather than that of a diplomat or politician. Why is the theoretical favoured over the practical, and why, even so, only the more abstract forms of the former? Why, more generally, did the pioneers latch on to so peculiar a conception of intelligence – one so abstract and so unanchored in reality as we would understand this today?

Where did Galtonianism come from?

Is there anything in the puritan background that could provide us with a clue? A concept central to christianity in general and to puritanism in particular is the soul. There is a case for arguing that the pioneers' notion of intelligence is closely associated with the christian notion of the soul.

This is a dramatic claim and at first sight may appear ludicrous. We often think of intelligence testing today in a more matter-of-fact way, to do merely with things like occupational selection, diagnostic assessment of pupils and their allocation to parts of the educational system. But we are living a century and more since the first tests. New ways of conceiving intelligence testing have gathered power over the years. The predominantly religious culture found on both sides of the Atlantic in 1880 has given way, less in heartland America than elsewhere, to secular attitudes. Theological connotations of that culture's concepts have gradually withered, even though the words used to express those concepts have remained. In the early part of this period, the vehicle which carried forward the religious notion of intelligence was the eugenic movement. The movement lost its impetus with revelations about Nazi atrocities. The testers themselves disowned eugenics but still carried on their daily work, contributing thus to the lower-key, matter-of-fact associations which the terms 'intelligence' and 'intelligence tests' have now.

I said in Chapter 1 that the Galtonian notion of intelligence can be traced back to Galton's 1865 article which preceded his *Hereditary Genius* of 1869, and that there the trail stops. The origins of Galton's psychological theory cannot be found in the prevailing academic psychology of his time. The latter was still located within philosophy, where it had come to be labelled 'associationism'. A radically empiricist theory with origins in John Locke, this held that ideas in the mind – together with the mental operations that depend on them like reasoning – are not innate but derive from sensations, ideas being associated together by contiguity and other principles. In Galton's age, James Mill, John Stuart Mill and Alexander Bain had continued the associationist tradition originating with David Hartley and David Hume in the eighteenth century. Galton's notion that intellectual ability is innate is fundamentally at odds with this empiricism. Its origins must lie elsewhere. So must his view that there are individual differences in the amount of intellectual ability with which one is endowed. There is, as far as I know, no trace of this notion in the mainstream psychology of his day.

Another difference between the psychological tradition which Galton initiated and this associationist mainstream is the former's closer connexion with practical affairs. The associationist school was a form of 'pure' or 'general' psychology: that is, its objective was an accurate account of psychological data for its own sake. In that way it was the direct ancestor of the general scientific psychology of the late-nineteenth and twentieth centuries. This happened partly by its generating opposing theories, but within the same non-practical, wholly theoretical, paradigm. Spearman's work is an example of this. Galtonianism was from the start what we should now call 'applied' psychology. The pioneers of intelligence testing were, as we have seen, centrally concerned with policies in education, mental health, employment and immigration, as well as with the wider eugenic project into which these policies fitted. We will come back to the 'applied' nature of Galtonianism later.

To return, meanwhile, to the Galtonian idea of innate intelligence. For influential innatist accounts of the mind and its abilities we have to go back, before associationism, at least to the seventeenth century. Descartes' philosophy is the most celebrated example. Like other thinkers of his age also working within a Christian framework, Descartes held that the mind – or soul – is capable of existence in the absence of the body and possesses innate powers of judgement and reasoning, as well as innate ideas themselves, which enable it to process data coming to it from the senses. Although Descartes' theory of mind is the most well-known of the psychologies which flourished in the sixteenth and seventeenth centuries, there is no reason to think that it is especially important in the ancestry of Galtonianism. There is another possible influence from this period, as we shall now see.

The Galtonian tradition sees intellectual abilities as innate, not tied to particular subject matter, but abstract and general, and as most powerful among a gifted élite. With this in mind, consider this passage from Perry Miller's book *The*

New England Mind. Writing of social arrangements in seventeenth-century New England, Miller is discussing the generally held belief that the division of society into different classes is part of God's design and that, in the words of a contemporary, 'whoever is for a parity in any Society, will in the end reduce things into an heap of confusion'. Miller goes on:

> Whether arguing from right reason or from the law of Scripture, Puritan leaders came to the same conclusion, to an authoritarian state, a society of distinct classes, ruled by a few basic laws administered by the wise and learned of the upper class through their mastery of logic, their deductions from the basic laws being as valid as the laws themselves, and resistance to their conclusions being the most exorbitant sin of which the lower classes were capable.
>
> (Miller 1939: 429)

What stands out here is the reference to 'a mastery of logic'. To modern readers, at least to those not caught up in Galtonian eugenics, this looks odd in the extreme. Why should logic, that most abstract of intellectual fields, be so socially important?

To understand this, we have to grasp the crucial importance of logic in the puritan world view. The origins of this are in the sixteenth century, but 'the reign of logic … continued unbroken' until the nineteenth (ibid.: 115).

Harriet Beecher Stowe, writing in 1869 about an older generation of New Englanders, says:

> If there is a golden calf worshipped in our sanctified New England, its name is Logic; and my good friend the parson burns incense before it with a most sacred innocence of intention. He believes that sinners can be converted by logic, and that, if he could once get me into one of these neat little traps aforesaid, the salvation of my soul would be assured. He has caught numbers of the shrewdest infidel foxes among the farmers around, and I must say that there is no trap for the Yankee like the logic trap.
>
> (Stowe 1869: 224, quoted in Miller 1939: 115)

Ramist logic and the puritan mind

According to Miller, logic was important from the earliest days of puritanism as the key to understanding the nature of God and of the world he created. It was thereby also the key to acting well. A central intellectual influence on early puritanism was the mid-sixteenth century French logician Pierre de la Ramée or Petrus Ramus (1517–72), whose compact manual *Dialecticae Libri Duo* of 1556 (Ramus 1969) was 'one of the three or four outstanding books of the age' (Miller 1939: 116). Miller also tells us that 'it is not too much to say that, while Augustine and Calvin have been widely recognised as the sources of Puritanism, upon New England Puritans the logic of Petrus Ramus exerted fully as great an influence as did either of the theologians' (ibid.).

Given the common origins of British and New English puritans, it is not surprising to learn that Ramus was highly influential among the former as well as among the latter. In the mid-sixteenth century Ramist logic had come to Scotland from Paris; and in the 1570s it had reached Cambridge University, where it dominated the teaching of logic through Alexander Richardson and other commentators. 'In England the teaching prospered along with Puritanism, with which, by the beginning of the seventeenth century, it became almost synonymous' (ibid.: 117).

What was it about Ramus and his ideas that made them so popular in radical Protestant circles? Briefly, in *Dialecticae Libri Duo* and other works he provided a systematic map of the whole range of human knowledge and detailed guidance on how the items that constitute it can be transmitted from teacher to learner. Both of these were appealing to the puritan since they helped to meet a central spiritual need. The individual's soul had to be appropriately equipped for salvation. In distinction from the Catholic tradition, this meant that one's understanding of the nature of God and of his created world, as well as the moral virtues which were held to rest on this, were not dependent on the authority of a priestly hierarchy, but more reliant on one's own God-given intellectual powers. Ramus's systematic account of the created world and of the divine mind behind it, an account based ostensibly on logical deduction, fitted the puritan bill exactly. So did his methodological prescriptions about how this knowledge should be taught. Parents, as we saw in Chapter 2, were preoccupied by their children's salvation as well as their own; and a step-by-step, easily assimilable way of filling their minds with the knowledge they needed met this requirement well.

So what was Ramus's system? It was more Platonic than Aristotelian: indeed Ramus had set up his own logical system in deliberate opposition to Aristotle's, then dominant in European universities. Plato had held that for a proper understanding of the world one has to get behind what one can see, hear, smell and touch to reach the invisible structure underlying these phenomena. This is accessible not by the senses, but by the intellect alone. It takes the form of concepts, sometimes called 'ideas' or 'forms', organised within a hierarchy of concepts which becomes more general and abstract the farther one distances oneself from the world of sense-perception. At the apex of the scheme is the concept, or form, of the Good, in terms of which all the subordinate concepts and all their manifestations in the world of the senses are explained and made intelligible.

Ramus's logical system had much of the same shape, except that it was simpler and more mechanical. 'Ramus' in Latin means 'branch'. The link between surname and system must, I suppose, be coincidental, but it is helpful to think of Ramus's scheme as a ramifying structure, a more and more complex branching outwards from a single source. It has two key features, the first of which is shared by Plato. Ramus's scheme begins from the most abstract and general, and terminates in the concrete, particular phenomena of the world of sense-experience. The items in Ramus's branching structure, called 'arguments', included linguistic terms, concepts and things themselves (Miller 1939: 124). The other key feature, not shared by Plato, is that successive branchings from the original source take place by a repeated process of *dichotomising*.

The first dichotomy is between [a] the arrangement of individual 'arguments' and [b] judgements necessary for relating these arguments together. Through successive dichotomisings, both a complete scheme of arguments can be generated, as well as a complete account of methods of relating them. The dichotomisings end once one reaches terms or entities which are indivisible.

An attractive feature of later versions of Ramus's books to their puritan audience in these early days of typography was the spatial presentation of their ramifications in an immediately accessible form. Figure 4.1 is an example showing the most basic dichotomies branching from [a] and [b].

When put to use, the system was usually operated in reverse, as it were, beginning from a specific judgement like 'fire causes heat' and relating the elements of this to wider and wider dichotomous categories under which it falls (ibid.: 127). This enabled one to understand the particular in the light of the simpler and more abstract 'arguments' which provided a more general framework for it.

Crucial to Ramist logic is the Platonist assumption that in the arguments arranged within the system concepts are not distinguishable from things, their properties and relations. This was a main reason why the puritans took it so seriously. It appeared to provide a simple method, by moving in thought alone from general to particular and back from particular to general, of revealing in a clear and systematic way the features of the world that God created. It thus had a utility which the Aristotelian logic of the schoolmen lacked: rather than getting lost in fruitless disputations, it could be employed in the service of discovering ultimate truth (ibid.: 141–4).

In all this, Ramist logic posits an intimate connexion between the nature of reality and the nature of the human mind. 'The basic contention of the system was that logic should be derived both from the natural processes of the mind and from the natural order of the universe … Ramus taught that logic is the formalized or regularized version of the natural intelligence' (ibid.: 144).

In other words, human beings naturally think in a Ramist-like way. Their minds are attuned by nature to be revelatory instruments, able to lead their possessors, through reason, to an understanding of God and of God's world. The logic systematises this common ability, producing a higher-order, theoretical manifestation of what operates at an instinctive level. I come back to this below.

Not only the nature of the *human* mind can be read off the branching, abstract to concrete, structure of phenomena in the world. That world is, after all, God's creation. Its structure reflects, too, something of the way in which the *divine* mind operates (Morgan 1986: 107), human mentality being a microcosm of the latter.

It is easy to understand the appeal of such a system to a devout people for whom personal salvation was all-important. It enabled them to make sense of the whole of which their own individual experience was part. Miller again:

> … the appeal of this logic to the Puritan mind resulted from its satisfying one of the deepest desires of that mind. A world made up of concrete entities which conformed to no collective terms, to no rules conceived by men, could never serve as the scene for the drama of salvation.
>
> (Miller 1939: 147)

P. RAMI DIALECTICA.
TABVLA GENERALIS.

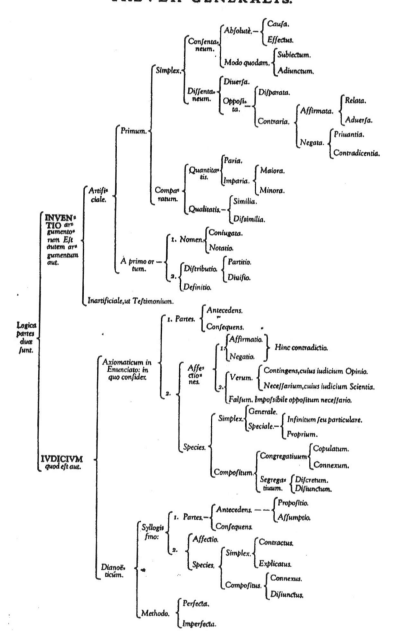

Figure 4.1 Ramus's logic

Source: Miller (1939: 126).

Ramist logic preceded the scientific revolution of the seventeenth century. To an age like our own, which takes that revolution for granted, the idea that one can rationally deduce the structure of reality without the aid of scientifically disciplined empirical observation belongs to an age of myth. To the early puritans it made perfect sense. The world had to be understood beneath a mesh of classifying terms and inferences, priority going, as with Plato, to the more abstract and general.

It is with these early puritans that the term '*intelligentia*' entered the discourse of Ramism. We owe it to Alexander Richardson, the Cambridge logician of the later sixteenth century, mentioned above. He used it to label the capability behind Ramus's first act of the mind, to 'see the simples in things', that is to see how specific phenomena are to be grasped in terms of the more general 'arguments' under which they fit. Richardson's '*intelligentia*' formed part of a larger system of terms used to explain the Ramist logic and its transmission. These also included among others '*scientia*' – the ability to join the simples in axioms, '*doctrina*' – the completed body of axioms as taught to others, and '*disciplina*' – the learning of these axioms. The complete set of terms 'continued in general usage for over a hundred years in New England' (ibid.: 169).

This account of the Ramism among early puritans makes it very clear why they saw no opposition between faith on the one hand and reliance on reason and the acquisition of knowledge on the other. Having faith depended, for the protestant, on the individual's unmediated understanding of his or her relationship to God and place in the divine scheme. Ramist logic was the key to this understanding. It showed how individual items of knowledge about the world could be plotted on an all-encompassing map. It linked detail to totality. Puritans took it for granted that anything they observed or discovered in the world could be fitted into such a scheme.

This included not only observable data about the workings of nature, but also, among other things, disciplines and sub-disciplines of enquiry itself (more details of which occur in Chapter 5, see pp. 115–16), as well as objects of knowledge within works of literature (Miller 1939: 145–6). The common perception that puritans have always been antithetical to the arts is not well-founded. It is true that more purely aesthetic considerations have weighed little with them, being too closely tied to the sensuous and the non-eternal; and that they have not been much drawn to imaginativeness, which, like the sensuous, has been a site for deviation from righteousness. But mining literature and other arts for the truths they can reveal is an entirely different enterprise (see also Chapter 5, p. 112 and p. 126).

More generally, then, logic pertains, as Ramus says above, 'to all things we wish to teach'. The percolation of that logic from puritan divines down into the rank and file had been extensive in the late sixteenth and early seventeenth centuries. Miller tells us that:

> the clergy were so far successful that by the time of the Civil Wars the mass
> of those who had come under Puritan influences were generally familiar with
> a marvelously large body of thought. The ability of Cromwell's soldiers to

debate intricate theological issues around their campfires was a wonder to all beholders; so in later times the proficiency of New England farm hands in threading the mazes of freewill, foreordination, and fate around the kitchen fire was a never-ending source of admiration to visitors. The evidence would seem to be that whenever a people were taught for any length of time by a Puritan ministry the level of their information was definitely raised. Leaving aside whether the sort of knowledge was worth while, or whether the people were more harmed than benefited by their acquisitions, the fact remains that for better or worse the people were instructed. By the light of history, it might seem that the chief function of Puritanism in the development of modern civilisation was the education it gave to a segment of the British public. In New England this function was the more assiduously performed because there the people were relatively uncontaminated by non-Puritanical influences ... Puritan education did not intend that students think for themselves, but it did intend that they should take in the vast quantity of received and orthodox information.

(Miller 1939: 86–7)

Logic in the Dissenting Academies

It is tempting to relate this early puritan attachment to logic and its transmission through education to what we know of the intelligence pioneers. Does the predilection of the latter for logic-based items in their tests have its ancestry partly in Ramist logic? Is Richardson's notion of *'intelligentia'* as the ability to see the simples in things linked historically, and not merely verbally, with modern conceptions of intelligence as the capacity for abstract reasoning? Has the marked interest of the pioneers in research which is to be put to practical use any connexion with the equally utilitarian attitudes of the Ramists towards their logic – as a vehicle for revealing the nature of God and his universe and thereby as an aid to salvation? Is there any link between the interest of the early puritans in amassing knowledge from any quarter and the intellectual eclecticism found in both Galton and in Burt and his family? Could the line of farmers from whom Lewis Terman descended have been imbued with something of the intellectual fervour found in the New England farm hands whom visitors so admired?

One reason for scepticism about such matters is the long time gap between the early puritans and the intelligence researchers. Ramus flourished in the middle and late sixteenth century; Galton, Goddard, Burt and the rest from the middle nineteenth to the early twentieth centuries. On the other hand, even though the budding of the puritan intellectual system goes back to the mid-sixteenth century and before, its full flowering is not until the seventeenth and eighteenth centuries, both in New England, as Miller's account makes plain, and in Britain, as we shall soon see. It did not remain unchanged, but accommodated itself – with more ease than one might expect – to the scientific revolution of that period, with its basis in empirical discovery rather than *a priori* deduction. In the rest of this chapter we see how the puritan notion of the soul as an entity designed for abstract thinking lived on through the eighteenth and nineteenth centuries and played a part – not a unique part, to be sure – in the early history of psychology as a scientific discipline. It should come as no surprise, in the light of this story, that the earliest psychologists of intelligence were from this same thought-world. Neither should it be surprising to discover that their puritan roots were an influence – not the sole influence, certainly – on their theories and their practices.

In Britain a key part in the transmission of the puritan notion of logic and of the world view which depended on it was played in England by the Dissenting Academies and in Scotland and America by universities and colleges.

To begin with the Dissenting Academies. Chapter 3 included a little about them, but we now need a fuller account. They originated with the Act of Uniformity in 1662, soon after the end of the puritan interregnum and the restoration of the monarchy in 1660. The act required conformity to the established church of every clergyman as well as of every university fellow, schoolmaster and private tutor (Watts 1978: 218–19). This effectively excluded dissenters from Oxford and Cambridge. The act imposed a penalty of £40 on any dissenter who tried to earn his living by teaching. Despite this, at least twenty ejected ministers established academies in order to provide higher education for the sons of dissenters (ibid.: 367), including those intending to enter the ministry, but others as well. The Toleration Act of 1689, which gave most dissenters freedom to worship in their own way, promoted the further growth of the academies. In the eighteenth century some of them were able to provide a higher education much superior to that of Oxford and Cambridge, encouraging a critical spirit in their students and introducing them to new developments in the natural sciences. Joseph Priestley's work at Warrington Academy after 1761 has already been mentioned (p. 64 above). The academies were supported financially by the various nonconformist sects, among whom the Presbyterians and especially the Congregationalists were most prominent. In the later eighteenth century the academies began to decline, concentrating increasingly on training candidates for the ministry and less on providing a general education. A few of them continued into the middle of the nineteenth century, by which time the founding of university colleges outside Oxbridge, in London, Manchester and elsewhere, enabled nonconformist laymen to acquire a university education.

The Dissenting Academies carried on the intellectual and educative work of the early puritans. In the best of them, like the Congregationalist Philip Doddridge's Northampton Academy, opened in 1729, there was a broad curriculum going far beyond the classics to which the inadequate teaching at Oxford and Cambridge was restricted. Teaching was in English, not Latin or Greek. The first and second years of the four-year course at Northampton were devoted to

First Year: logic, rhetoric, geography, metaphysics, geometry, algebra

Second Year: trigonometry, conic sections, celestial mechanics, natural and experimental philosophy, divinity, orations.

(McLachlan 1931: 147)

In the third and fourth years anatomy, history and civil law were also included, along with theological subjects. French was an optional subject and the classical languages also had a minor place.

In this scheme we see more than an echo of the Ramist philosophy. With some exceptions, we can detect a progression from more abstract studies to more concrete ones. Logic, the most abstract of all, comes first – with branches of mathematics and natural philosophy (science) close behind it – providing the overall framework into which more specific subjects like anatomy and history will later fit.

The prominence of logic in this curriculum was by no means a feature peculiar to Northampton. The five-year course at the first Manchester Academy (1699–1713) was described as including '"the usual" subjects of "Logick, Metaphysics, Somatology, Pneumatology, Natural Philosophy, Divinity, and Chronology" among others' (ibid.: 116). Of thirty-six books of reference used at Rathmell Academy (1669–98), nine were in logic (ibid.: 68). Ramus was frequently studied in the early academies (ibid.: 300), while in the eighteenth century the most widely used logic textbook became the Congregationalist Isaac Watts's treatise on *Logic* (Watts 1996). This was first published in 1724 and generated nine editions by 1800 and many more later (McLachlan 1931: 306).

The fading out of Ramus and his replacement by Watts reflects the increasing impossibility of keeping the early puritan world view intact with the new advances in science and philosophy. Natural science, backed by the empiricist philosophy of Locke and others, became an undeniably surer guide to the nature of the world than Ramist dichotomisings. Watts's *Logic* drops the Ramist opposition to Aristotle and has a recognisably modern look to it. It moves from perception and concepts to judgements and propositions and thence to reasoning and syllogism. It speaks favourably of Bacon, Copernicus, Newton, Locke and Boyle (Watts 1996: 203).

In some ways it is reminiscent of a modern book on clear thinking. Its subtitle speaks of 'the Right Use of Reason in the Inquiry after Truth. A variety of rules to guard against error in the affairs of religion and human life, as well as in the sciences'. The focus is on intellectual virtue and the avoidance of intellectual vice. Among the 'errors' discussed, for instance, are those deriving from attachment to custom and fashion (ibid.: 195), and the authority of men (ibid.: 199). 'Imagination is another fruitful spring of false judgments' (ibid.: 181).

Reason, Watts tells us:

> is the glory of human nature, and one of the chief eminencies whereby we are raised above our fellow-creatures, the brutes, in this lower world. Reason, as to the *power* and *principles* of it, is the common gift of God to all men; though all are not favoured with it by nature in an equal degree. But the *acquired improvement* of it, in different men, makes a much greater distinction between them than nature has made. I could even venture to say, that the *improvement of reason* hath raised the learned and the prudent, in the European world, almost as much above the *Hottentots*, and other savages of *Africa*, as those savages are by nature superior to the birds, the beasts and the fishes.
>
> (ibid.: 1, italics in original)

The ideas here remind us of Galton. Reason, that is, intellectual ability in general, is something with which all men are born, but they possess it by nature to different degrees. Educated Europeans have come to possess more of this ability than others, these others including members of savage races between educated Europeans and other animals, and, by implication, Europeans who are not 'learned and prudent'. On the comparison between educated Europeans and others, compare Galton's 1865 statement that, as human beings, 'our forefathers were utter savages from the beginning; and ... after myriads of years of barbarism, our race has but very recently grown to be civilized and religious' (Galton 1865: 327).

The chief difference from Galton seems to lie in Watts's belief in 'acquired improvement'. He is clearly thinking of the power of education. But whether he was what would now be labelled an 'environmentalist' is uncertain. His focus, like Galton's, is on educated Europeans, those whom he sees as at the acme of intellectual achievement. It is compatible with his stated position that the natural gifts of these people are such that, with a good education, they can attain the heights; and that the natural gifts of others less favoured are not enough to be able to benefit by such an education. How near or far he is from Galton is not clear.

If we try now to sum up the place of logic in the puritan heritage in England, we have seen that, despite the new turn it took in the eighteenth century, from the sixteenth century the subject itself had had a prominent position in the puritan intellectual and educational system and retained this until the nineteenth century. But we have also seen that logic, as originally conceived by Ramus, was not just the innate, God-given, power to pursue truth, to which, in the shape of 'reason', Ramist logic had been reduced by the time of Watts – given the increasing inadequacy of the Ramist dichotomies to capture the nature of empirical reality. Originally, Ramism was in addition a system for understanding the structure of God's world, a system that put most weight on the most abstract categories and forms of thought. This is where puritan logic was more easily able to accommodate itself to the scientific revolution, with its revelation under Newton and others of the mathematical structure of the physical world. The centrality of logic, mathematics and natural philosophy to the eighteenth-century dissenters' curriculum is a manifestation of this. As we shall see in Chapter 5, these abstract subjects, especially mathematics and science, continued to be influential in school curricula throughout the nineteenth and twentieth centuries and into our own age, where science and mathematics constitute two of the three core subjects, along with English, in the National Curriculum for England.

The early psychologists of intelligence built their tests around abstract thinking of a logical and mathematical kind. They thought of intelligence as abstract general ability. Their own intellectual background and predilections were usually mathematical. One thinks of Galton's early desire to join the Cambridge wranglers and of the prime place he gave this group in studying the eminent; and, more generally, of the attachment to statistics common to all the English pioneers, from Galton himself to Pearson, Burt and others. All this falls into place once one understands the intellectual heritage of the puritan communities from which their families came.

On a related topic, the abstract tendency of puritan thinking is also found in its interest in classification. This, too, emanated from Ramus and his dichotomously branching categories. Although under pressure of empirical discoveries in chemistry and biology dichotomising was shown to have limited application, a more general interest in classifying and collecting phenomena persisted in the psyche of radical protestantism. One sees it in botany in the Lutheran Linnaeus; in chemistry in the Congregationalist and later Unitarian Priestley; and in an eclectic multitude of fields in the Quaker-descended Galton. This is not, of course, to claim that only Old Dissenters and other radical protestants were classifiers: Charles Darwin, from an Anglican background, is an obvious exception. But an interest in bringing into systematic order the manifold variety of God's creation was, as we have seen, especially marked in the former group. It is the extension of classification from the non-human biological world to types of human intellect that hallmarks the work of the intelligence psychologists. This is true on the macro-level of a hierarchy between different so-called 'races'; and also, within particular societies, in distinctions made between the 'gifted', the 'average', the 'backward', the 'feeble-minded' and the like; as well as in micro-classifications of ability at the level of individual IQ scores. Once again, given the puritan backgrounds of nearly all the pioneers, it is not surprising that they were drawn to studies of this kind. In addition, the dichotomising tendency of much of their eugenics, between good (bright, virtuous, industrious) stock and bad (moronic, vicious, idle) could be at least partly rooted in the dualising thought style that had percolated into puritan communities since the days of Ramus (for more on dualism, see comments on Dewey in Chapter 5, p. 135).

Pneumatology in the Dissenting Academies

We have seen that Ramist logic was as much about the nature of the human mind as about the nature of reality. Human beings naturally think in a way that reflects that logic's ramifying structure, from abstract to concrete. They are programmed by God with the ability to think in abstract categories and apply them to the world. We also saw how this psychological side of Ramism outlived it as a system of knowledge. 'Reason was no longer a systematic logic applied to the world, but instead an innate ability to see the self-evident truth for oneself' (McKnight 2003: 57).

Closely linked with logic in the Dissenting Academies was, as we saw from the list of 'usual' subjects above, 'pneumatology'. The main textbook was a posthumous work of Philip Doddridge, his 1763 *Lectures on Pneumatology, Ethics and Theology* (McLachlan 1931: 303–4). This ran to a fourth edition by 1799 and was reprinted in the year of Galton's birth, 1822.

Doddridge's lectures on pneumatology (in Doddridge 1803: 299–413) are divided into two parts:

Part 1 Of the Powers and Faculties of the Human Mind, and the Instinct of Brutes

Part 2 Of the Being of God, and his natural Perfections

Goddard's Quaker schooling in Providence had included classes in geology based on evolutionary ideas deriving from Darwin. This prepared him well for his later studies, 'for he evidently perceived no open warfare between his Christian heritage and his new career as a scientist studying evolutionary theory' (ibid.: 31).

The intellectual autonomy of Hall's regime did nothing to shake Goddard's faith, given that Hall himself, brought up on strict Congregationalist lines as a child, had recently returned to christianity and now saw himself as providing a psychological reinterpretation of christian ideals, supplying, as he put it, 'modern methods of studying the soul' (ibid.). The same application of a new science to old subject-matter appears in the topic which Goddard chose for his doctoral dissertation: 'The Effects of Mind on Body as Evidenced in Faith Cures' (ibid.: 33).

Goddard maintained close ties to the Quakers in the following years (ibid.: 39). His biographer writes that:

> he never fully abandoned the modes of thinking acquired in his childhood. In his later years, both his negative and his positive responses to his early Quaker experiences would be evident in his actions. For the rest of his life, this scientist would always despise rigid pedagogy and strict theological dogma. In a deeper sense, however, his religious background would become intertwined with his very understanding of what a psychologist was.
>
> (ibid.: 42)

She suggests that:

> By the time he graduated, Goddard had found his vocation. He left Clark in 1899 a disciple less of the church's version of the Gospels than of G.Stanley Hall's. Moreover, Goddard embraced his new psychological calling with an evangelical zeal which matched his mother's. He now believed in an evolutionary version of the faith of his fathers.
>
> (ibid.: 43)

Zenderland's biography shows abundant evidence of the further intertwining of Goddard's commitment to both science and religion in his early work as an educator, especially in his work in the child study movement (ibid.: 46–9). What is more pertinent to the present investigation is the tenacity of his belief in the eugenic significance of individual differences in intelligence and the zeal with which he developed and promoted intelligence testing. We have already encountered his belief in these tests as a way of identifying the 'feeble-minded', not least among immigrants arriving in America; his polarisation of the highly able virtuous and the moronic vicious in the Kallikak book; and his vision of a society in which everyone pursues his vocation at his own mental level.

Like Burt and Galton, Goddard came from a branch of puritanism – Quaker or Congregationalist – that took virtually for granted their own election. The social

US psychologists of intelligence: Goddard and Terman

Henry Herbert Goddard (1866–1957)

H.H. Goddard was introduced in Chapter 1 as America's first intelligence tester, a eugenicist, and author of *The Kallikak Family*.

He was born in New England of Quaker parents who could both trace their families back to English roots in the seventeenth century. His mother was related to the colonial governor of Plymouth Colony, Edward Winslow, who had come over in the *Mayflower* (Zenderland 1998: 16). Goddard's father had been a farmer but was reduced to being a day labourer. He died when Herbert was nine and 'were it not' he wrote, 'for the Society of Friends (Quakers) it would probably have gone hard with us ... The Friends always take care of their poor' (ibid.: 17). His mother was a committed Quaker; and her commitment grew during Herbert's childhood in the wake of nation-wide Quaker revivalism in the 1870s which deeply affected their Maine community. The 'great change' which had been wrought in her caused the local Friends to recognise her 'gift in the ministry' (she preached in the local Congregational Church among other places). In the following years she felt 'called to visit Friends Meetings in distant communities', travelling widely for this purpose across Canada and the USA (ibid.: 19) and afterwards in Europe.

Goddard, meanwhile, was left at home with his married sister and was educated by the Quakers at Oak Grove Seminary, the Friends School in Providence and later at Haverford College. He resented the latter's reputation as, in his own words, 'a convenient way to keep sons of rich Philadelphia Quakers out of mischief' (ibid.: 20), and disliked its narrow, 'guarded', education. Despite this, he graduated from Haverford with a BA, followed by an MA in mathematics, and got married, his wife soon coming to share his Quaker faith (ibid.: 25). Goddard became principal of a Quaker school in Ohio and two years later principal of his old school, Oak Grove Seminary.

It was while at Oak Grove that Goddard heard an address to local teachers given by G. Stanley Hall, one of the first American psychologists and at that time president of Clark University in Worcester, Massachusetts (ibid.: 28). Goddard was inspired, as were many others, by Clark's child-centred, science-based approach to education and in 1896 went to Clark University to study with him, gaining a doctorate within three years. In an ethos of free enquiry, Hall inducted Goddard into scientific thinking, especially in evolutionary psychology.

> Despite the stark differences distinguishing Quaker from Clark pedagogy, Goddard's education in science remained surprisingly consistent. Like other Protestants, Goddard's Quaker teachers had taught a version of natural theology, in which the order found in the physical world illuminated God's orderly mind. Science, Goddard learned, meant discovering the laws of nature.
>
> (ibid.: 30)

As Anderson (1983: 30) points out, in a discussion of Scottish universities in the early nineteenth century, 'logic [as in 1700] was taken in the second year, and formed an introduction to the philosophical subjects'. This, too, was in line with the tradition of puritan thinking since Ramus, always beginning with the most abstract of enquiries.

The insistence on logic as one of the compulsory subjects was reaffirmed in the mid-nineteenth century: as a result of the Universities (Scotland) Act of 1858 one year's attendance at logic classes was made a prescribed part of the remodelled MA course (Knox 1953: 93).

Not everyone was attached to logic, however. A witness to the Royal Commission on Scottish Universities in 1876, John Shairp, an anglophile professor at St Andrews, spoke favourably of history as a subject

> 'particularly necessary to give something of the concrete to the Scottish mind, which is so tremendously apt to run off into abstractions, metaphysics and logic' ... Shairp would retain logic as part of 'a preliminary basis of disciplinary study' for all students, but would define it more strictly: 'At present all our logic classes are full of psychology, if not metaphysics, but I would knock off all that; I think we have terribly overdone it in Scotland, – cramming metaphysics upon raw minds'.
>
> (Anderson 1983: 94)

In pneumatology as distinct from logic, the most important figure in eighteenth century Scottish philosophy was Thomas Reid (1710–96). Reid was a Presbyterian minister for fourteen years before teaching philosophy at Aberdeen University and becoming Professor of Moral Philosophy at Glasgow. In the preface to his most celebrated work, still important in the philosophy of perception today, his *Essays on the Intellectual Powers of Man* (Reid 1785), Reid contrasts the material world with the intellectual: 'the whole system of minds, from the infinite Creator, to the meanest creature endowed with thought may be called the Intellectual World' (ibid.: xxxiii).

He tells us that 'the branch [of philosophy] which treats of the nature and operations of minds has by some been called Pneumatology' (ibid.: xxxv); and that his book is about the human mind in particular because 'the mind of man is the noblest work of God which reason discovers to us, and therefore, on account of its dignity, deserves our study' (ibid.). The preface, interestingly, also several times uses the term 'intelligence', as in 'We have no reason to ascribe intelligence, or even sensation, to plants' (ibid.: xxxiv).

Here the term appears to refer to those mental operations which, unlike a feeling like pain, involve the use of concepts. In his dedication, which precedes the preface, Reid mentions his exclusion from the book of various repetitions and illustrations in the lectures on which the book was based. He writes, 'I am afraid, indeed, that the more intelligent reader, who is conversant in such abstract subjects, may think that there are repetitions still left, which might be spared' (ibid.: xxxi). It is interesting to see here another apparent example of a link between intelligence and abstract thinking.

Reid also states that:

> It is nature undoubtedly that gives us the capacity of reasoning. When this is wanting, no art nor education can supply it. But this capacity may be dormant through life, like the seed of a plant, which, for want of heat and moisture, never vegetates. This is probably the case of some savages.

(ibid.: 712)

Reid thus believes in innate intellectual ability – as a gift of nature, i.e. God (elsewhere he writes of 'the faculties that God hath given us' (ibid.: xxxiv)). He also thinks it likely that there are individual differences in this ability. 'Although the capacity be purely the gift of Nature, and probably given in very different degrees to different persons; yet the power of reasoning seems to be got by habit, as much as the power of walking or running' (ibid.: 712).

Logic and mind in America

In Britain after 1865 the 'common sense' faculty psychology of the 'Scottish school' under Reid and others did not recover from the blow dealt by J.S. Mill's criticisms of it (Passmore 1957: 28); but it became influential in America, where it 'came to dominate the indigenous American "Mental and Moral Philosophy" tradition of the nineteenth century'. 'In many respects the work of this school anticipated that of modern psychology' more than associationism and rationalism, its two other contributing traditions (Richards 2002: 22). James McCosh (1811–94) was an important figure in this development. He was a Scottish philosopher, educated at Glasgow and Edinburgh, who became president of Princeton University from 1868 to 1888 (Reid 1785, introduction by B.S. Brody: xxv). Scottish common sense philosophy was in the direct line of descent from the early puritans' interest in logic and the mind through to the intelligence pioneers of the late nineteenth century.

We saw above Miller's contention that 'the reign of logic ... continued unbroken' until the nineteenth century. It was a staple subject in the religiously-affiliated colleges of the eighteenth and nineteenth centuries (e.g. at the College of William and Mary, Virginia, in 1727 (Hofstadter and Smith 1961: 44), and at the University of Virginia in 1824 (ibid.: 231)).

The traditional puritan preoccupation with the soul or mind was carried through, via the Scottish connexion, into the mental and moral philosophy curriculum. This had become a compulsory course in American universities and colleges in the early nineteenth century. 'The reason for this was that these institutions (invariably having denominational affiliations, most frequently Presbyterian) felt it necessary to counter the materialist and atheist arguments of many leading European thinkers by demonstrating the consistency of Christianity with philosophy and logic' (Richards 2002: 53).

It was the responsibility of the college presidents, like McCosh at Princeton, to deliver the mental and moral philosophy course to senior students. According to Rudolph (1962: 141):

> Preconceived theological views and evangelistic purposes combined to deprive the course of anything resembling earnest philosophical investigation. One student described the course as embracing 'man in his unity, and God in his sovereignty', and he was not exaggerating.

Mark Hopkins, president of Williams College, described his course to a gathering of alumni as beginning with the physical man and leading, in Rudolph's words (ibid.) 'through the byways of mental faculties, grounds of belief, logic, and emotion, to the ultimate destination, the moral government of God'.

The pioneers of the scientifically-orientated 'new psychology' in America after 1880 have been cast as 'breaking the stranglehold of this sterile force' (Richards 2002: 53), but it seems from recent research that the continuities are as important as the divergences:

> My own view is that, while Psychology established itself as a replacement for Mental and Moral Philosophy …, there were some important respects in which it continued to play a similar 'moral education' role. Furthermore, many textbooks published as 'Psychology' between 1880 and 1900 closely resemble their predecessors in agenda and structure, even if they are more secular in approach and more 'scientific' in tone. In other words, there were fairly high levels of continuity between old and new, and the New Psychology's revolutionary rhetoric was frequently more an expression of aspiration than achievement: not until the following century was any 'revolution' really accomplished.
>
> (ibid.: 54)

A key figure in this transition from the old to the new was the Congregationalist G. Stanley Hall, whose influence on Goddard, Terman, J.M. Cattell and Dewey was mentioned in Chapter 3. Hall became first president of Clark University in 1888 and also served as professor of psychology. Details of his achievements in the latter field were given on p. 75. Richards (ibid.: 55) describes him as

> a highly effective political animal in promoting Psychology's interests between 1880 and 1910, capable of trimming his sails to the prevailing wind when necessary (e.g. variously claiming Psychology was entirely secular or affirming its doctrinal respectability according to the audience being addressed).

Psychology was not the only human science in America to emerge from native protestant roots. A collection of autobiographical sketches by sociologists collected in the 1920s and 1930s reveals the role of evangelical protestantism in *its* early history. The backgrounds from which the respondents overwhelmingly came, in decreasing order of numbers of replies, were Baptist, Methodist, Presbyterian or Congregationalist (Henking 1992: 326).

Back to Galton

A further – and last – word about Galton's 1865 article and the mystery of where his ideas on intellectual ability expressed there originated. There are two separable notions here: one, that intellectual ability is innate; two, that there are individual differences in it which are also innate. We have seen that these were at odds with the dominant psychology of the day, associationism, so their source or sources must lie elsewhere. Chapter 1 affirmed that Darwin's 1859 theory of evolution was a major influence. The idea of innate individual differences among attributes of organisms is contained within it. This is not to say, however, that Darwin was the sole influence here. What is not in Darwin is the idea of innate *intellectual* ability in human beings, or, consequently, the idea that there are innate individual differences in *this* attribute. These appear to be original to Galton.

Or were they? Both these ideas are locatable in the works of influential Old Dissenters in the eighteenth and early nineteenth centuries. We saw above Isaac Watts's comment in 1724 that 'reason is the common gift of God to all men' (Watts 1996: 1) and also that, in this respect, 'all are not favoured with it by nature in an equal degree' (ibid.). And we have also seen similar views expressed by Thomas Reid some sixty years later. In both writers, one Congregationalist, the other Presbyterian, the notion of innate individual differences in reasoning ability is most obviously to be explained by the traditional emphasis on the varied gifts from God which underlie different individuals' callings. The idea of innate individual differences in intellectual and other qualities is central to the puritan notion of vocation.

Forty years on again, in 1828 and indeed in Galton's own lifetime, a much fuller presentation of these ideas appears in a work by George Combe, called *The Constitution of Man* (Combe 1828). George Combe (1788–1858), a solicitor born into a Calvinist Edinburgh brewing family (Gibbon 1878, Vol. I: 40–2; Cooter 1984: 102–6), who went from high school to Edinburgh University, was a pioneer of phrenology in Britain. This 'claimed that brain functions were highly localised in different "cerebral organs", the relative sizes of which indicated an individual's character ... Phrenology enjoyed a particularly sympathetic reception in Scotland where its list of functions closely matched the Reidians' "powers"' (Richards 2002: 24). Combe's *Constitution of Man* was not, however, a predominantly phrenological work. It argued for a harmonious system of 'natural', i.e. divine, laws – organic, moral and intellectual – which, if generally obeyed, would greatly improve social and individual well-being and bring people nearer to God. The book was a huge best-seller, its sales reaching some 300,000 copies by 1860 (Cooter 1984: 120).

In a section called 'hereditary transmission of qualities', Combe argued, allegedly partly on the basis of the size of various 'moral and intellectual organs' in the brains of parents and their children, that the good and bad qualities transmitted from the former to the latter, are dependent not solely on the inherited qualities found in the parents, but on how far they have improved them or allowed them to degenerate up to the time of conception. 'Parents', for instance, 'in whom the moral and intellectual organs exist in supreme vigour, will transmit these in greatest perfection' (Combe 1828: 161). He also writes:

> According to this rule [of the 'hereditary transmission of qualities'], the children of the individuals who have obeyed the organic, the moral and the intellectual laws, will not only start from the highest level of their parents in acquired knowledge, but will inherit an enlarged development of the moral and intellectual organs, and thereby enjoy an increasing capability of discovering and obeying the institutions of the Creator.
>
> (ibid.: 167)

Although Combe's Lamarckian view of heredity was opposed to Galton's Darwinian conception of it, they shared a belief in innate intellectual powers and in individual differences in these. What this shows, at the very least, and given the popularity of Combe's book, is that these notions were in wide circulation by the time Galton wrote his article in 1865. If we are looking for the origins of Galton's ideas here, it may be that they are found in the way of thinking which – in general terms, not in the phrenological and other detail – Combe shared with others in the dissenting tradition, including not only the notion of innate intellectual differences between individuals, but also that of the importance of discovering the structure of God's world.

Could there be a closer connexion between the 1865 article and Combe's book? Could Galton have been affected by the latter after reading *The Origin of Species* in or after 1859? Could Combe's theory have been a catalyst for his own? Could it be that, in the light of Darwin, Galton rejected Combe's account of heredity but kept hold of the idea of the hereditary transmission of intellectual abilities and the cosmic progress that could follow from the proper management of these?

There is, so far as I know, no direct evidence of this, but the thought that there might be this closer connexion has been prompted by several affinities between the two works. These range from specific to general.

A specific similarity is in the interest both authors have in formalising marriage arrangements so as to maximise the benefits of hereditary transmission. For Combe, later marriage is desirable because the spouses will then be more mature. He is attracted by the law in force in Wurtemburg, that men cannot marry before 25 and have to prove to the authorities that they are able to look after a wife and family (Combe 1828: 165–6). Galton, as we saw in Chapter 1, imagines a utopia in which young men of 25, who have passed a competitive examination on their suitability as fathers, are encouraged at a public ceremony, by financial and other inducements, to marry particular young women whose qualities have been matched with theirs (Galton 1865: 165–6).

More generally, both writers are attracted by the possibility of improving human intellectual and moral stock by selective breeding and write about its benefits in high-flown terms. Combe envisages a continuous amelioration as each generation of mature individuals of good stock adds value to the preceding one (Combe 1828: 164). At the same time, marriages of unsuitable partners – the immature, or those constitutionally enfeebled, mentally or physically – are to be discouraged or prevented (ibid.: 164–5). Galton, as we saw earlier, also favours a differential marriage policy, of encouraging the gifted and eliminating the 'refuse'(Galton 1865: 165–6). He, too, foresees continuous improvement, but not via a 'value added' route.

Combe gives an account of his vision as follows:

> If it be true that this lower world is arranged in harmony with the supremacy of the higher faculties, what a noble prospect would this law open up, of the possibility of man ultimately becoming capable of placing himself more fully in accordance with the Divine institutions than he has hitherto been able to do, and, in consequence, of reaping numberless enjoyments that appeared destined for him by his Creator, and avoiding thousands of miseries that now render life too often only a series of calamities!
>
> (Combe 1828: 162)

Galton writes equally lyrically, although not here in the religious framework he sometimes uses elsewhere:

> If a twentieth part of the cost and pains were spent in measures for the improvement of the human race that is spent on the improvement of the breed of horses and cattle, what a galaxy of genius might we not create! We might introduce prophets and high priests of our civilization into a world as surely as we can propagate idiots by mating *crétins*. Men and women of the present day are, to those we might hope to bring into existence, what the pariah dogs of the streets of an Eastern town are to our own highly bred varieties.
>
> (Galton 1865: 165–6)

In one passage, Combe assesses the alternative theory to his own, which supposes that 'the natural qualities of each individual of the race to be conferred at birth, without the slightest reference to what his parents might have done'. His view is that this rules out the possibility of any improvement in the race, given that 'every phrenologist knows that the brains of New Hollanders, Caribs and other savage tribes are distinguished by great deficiencies in the moral and intellectual organs' (Combe 1828: 166): it is impossible to see, therefore, how civilised peoples could have emerged from savagery. Since Galton held the theory Combe is attacking, could he have taken Combe's position as a challenge, to which his own Darwinism was a response? I should reiterate that I know of no direct evidence that Galton read, or was influenced by, Combe. But the affinities described make this at least a possibility.

This concludes the evidence, such as it is, that, although Galton's ideas on innate abilities were out of kilter with the prevailing associationist psychology of his day, there is another line of thought, connected with the dissenting tradition, into which they fit more comfortably. There is a still more ancient tradition of innate intellectual powers and individual differences among them: that of Plato in such dialogues as *Republic* and *Meno*. Learning, for Plato, is a matter of coming, often with some difficulty, to remember ideas already present in us at birth. He tells us in his myth of the rulers that some people, the future rulers of his ideal state, are constitutionally better-endowed intellectually than the military class, who in turn outstrip the common people (*Republic* 414 D ff). When the tripartite system of schooling introduced in England after 1944 was under attack in the 1960s, partly for its basis in Galtonian theory as filtered through Cyril Burt, comparisons were often made with Plato's three-class system in his *Republic* (Books 2–4) and its foundation in innate differences (for a later reference see Kleinig 1982: 132). At that time, I thought that the two theories were coincidentally similar, with no historical thread linking them. Now, I wonder.

If the line from Burt back to Galton to the dissenting tradition is more than a fiction, it may be traced back further, as we have seen, to Ramism and Ramus himself. Comenius (1907: XVI, 45) states that 'the subjects learned should be arranged in such a manner that the studies that come later introduce nothing new, but only expand the elements of knowledge that the boy has already mastered'.

This looks as though it derives from Ramus's notion of branching dichotomies, proliferating from the most general ideas towards the most particular. It prompts the question: how do pupils acquire the most general ideas? Plato's answer is that these – the 'forms' – are innate. While, according to Miller (1939: 177), 'Ramus would not admit outright the existence of innate ideas', he and his followers, not least in New England, were indebted to Plato for their notion that general concepts are features of supersensuous reality – an idea that is hard to separate from innatism (ibid.: 147, 177).

As far as I know there is no indication in Ramus himself of individual differences in innate abilities, so this other aspect of Plato's theory does not carry through to Ramism. To find the origin of this idea, familiarised by the intelligence testers, we have to look, perhaps, to the combination of Ramism with the puritan notion of innate gifts linked to vocation.

Conclusion

This chapter throws further historical light on the thinking of the intelligence pioneers. It connects their work with the thought-world of their family ancestry and suggests that the cast of mind which so many of them possessed – an inclination towards abstract, especially logico-mathematical, thinking; a penchant for neat and sometimes dichotomised classification of the phenomena of human ability; a commitment to social improvement but not in an egalitarian direction; as well as in many cases a lingering religiosity – may be at least partially understood by reference to their shared puritan background.

This all but concludes the psychological section of the book – except, that is, for a section in Chapter 5 on examining and testing; and sections in Chapter 6 on contemporary work on intelligence and on the British government's programme for Gifted and Talented Youth. But this is not all there is to say about puritanism and its legacy. The more I studied this in connexion with intelligence, the more I came to see how important it also is in the history of the school curriculum, specifically the broad curriculum of discrete academic subjects, which in England has now become an entrenched educational institution. Not that it is possible to keep in separate compartments the history of the subject-based curriculum and the history of intelligence testing. As we saw at the beginning of the book, for instance, Morant's work on school curricula and that of Burt on testing and tracking fitted together hand in glove. This said, Chapter 5 will take us largely away from the intelligence story and centrally into the curriculum story.

5 Knowledge and the curriculum

In the first half of the twentieth century the history of the Galtonian notion of intelligence became intertwined, in Britain, with the history of the school curriculum. We saw in Chapter 1 how the work of Cyril Burt and Robert Morant in their respective fields helped to shape government policy over this period. Morant's post-1904 secondary schools were the forerunners of the post-1944 grammar schools for which children were selected at 11+ partly on the basis of their superior IQs. The secondary curriculum was very different from the less academic diet prescribed for the elementary school. It consisted of 'English language and literature, at least one language other than English, geography, history, mathematics, science, drawing, manual instruction (boys), domestic subjects (girls), physical exercise and organised games' (Maclure 1965: 159).

Morant's curriculum has been of especial interest to educationalists since the National Curriculum was introduced in1988, since, as Richard Aldrich (1988: 22) has pointed out, the latter's new statutory subjects were almost identical to those just detailed. I will come back in Chapter 6 to the significance this has for us today. Meanwhile, in this chapter, I look backward rather than forward and examine the origins of this academic subject-based curriculum which has proved so resilient over the past century.

The Dissenting Academies and the roots of the traditional academic curriculum

In the context of this book, the interest in exploring these origins lies in the claim that has often been made that they are to be found in puritanism and dissent. The Dissenting Academies, mentioned in connexion with the teaching of logic and pneumatology in Chapter 4, have an especially prominent role in this story. How far the story is reliable is a main theme of the present chapter.

In *The Long Revolution* Raymond Williams (1961: 133–4) writes of the Dissenting Academies:

> These varied considerably in quality, but it can fairly be claimed that in the best of them, in the eighteenth century, a new definition of the content of a general education was worked out and put into practice. Here, for the first

time, the curriculum begins to take its modern shape, with the addition of mathematics, geography, modern languages, and crucially the physical sciences.

We know from the history of the Academies that, as well as preparing students for the ministry, they also provided a general higher education – in our terms an upper secondary/university education – for sons of dissenters prevented by law after 1662 from attending universities. Boys usually began to attend the Academies at 15, 16 or 17, staying for four or five years (McLachlan 1931: 26). As many of the English dissenters grew richer through commerce and industry throughout the eighteenth century, more and more of them must have had the wealth needed to prolong their sons' general education in this way, enabling them later to choose some 'liberal', non-manual, calling on the basis of a wider knowledge of God's world and of their own capabilities.

Chapter 4 introduced us to some of the evidence which could be used to support Williams's claim about the broadening of the Academies' curriculum beyond the classics. The early Academies, which had to rely on teachers from Oxford and Cambridge, followed the traditional classical curriculum of those universities. With the founding of Philip Doddridge's Academy at Northampton in 1729 English finally replaced Latin as the medium of instruction. Without this, the new subjects which began to appear on the curriculum would have been far more difficult to teach. At Northampton the full list of subjects of study for the four-year course was, as we partly saw in Chapter 4, as follows:

First Year: logic, rhetoric, geography, metaphysics, geometry, algebra

Second Year: trigonometry, conic sections, celestial mechanics, natural and experimental philosophy, divinity, orations

Third Year: natural and civil history, anatomy, Jewish antiquities, divinity, orations

Fourth Year: civil law, mythology and hieroglyphics, English history, history of nonconformity, divinity, preaching and pastoral care

In addition, French was an optional subject and Hebrew, Greek and Latin, besides being used in prayers, were also taught in evening tutorials. In the first two years there were also required disputations in Latin and English (McLachlan 1931: 147). A similar pattern of subjects, with some variations, spread from Northampton to other Academies as the eighteenth century progressed.

A word about English. Its only mention in the 1729 account is in connexion with required disputations in the first two years. In addition, divinity courses at the Academies standardly included practice in sermon writing; and according to McLachlan (ibid.: 28), this marked the origin of the English composition which has since become a staple of English lessons. In some later academies English began to become a subject in itself, as at the end of the eighteenth century did 'belles lettres', in which literary works were studied, largely for the truths they contained (ibid.).

Art, with the aesthetic connotations the term has for us today, had little or no place in the Academies, their emphasis being on knowledge. The early puritan belief in the need to acquire it as a requisite of salvation had persisted into the age of the Academies. As we saw in Chapter 4, there was no tension in puritan thinking between acquiring knowledge on the one hand and faith on the other: philosophy, science, mathematics, history, geography and other subjects were held to be vehicles of the latter as they revealed the varied features of God's created world. Imagination and emotion, however, the sources of so much art, were thought of – in Watts's *Logic*, for instance – as tempters into error, as a 'fruitful source of false judgments' (above, p. 98). The pursuit of truth was the all-encompassing aim.

Others besides Raymond Williams have noticed, or thought they have noticed, the revolutionary importance of the Academies for the content of education. Some years before Williams the educationalist Fred Clarke, for instance, wrote:

> The Dissenting Academies are thus of importance in English educational history as representing a vigorous and sustained effort to think out a 'modern' curriculum and apply it in practice. While not departing from the dominant idea of education for culture, and while remaining thoroughly English in temper, they cut loose from the prevailing tradition of classical training and aristocratic accomplishments, looked at their own actual world with open eyes, and worked out a curriculum which would prepare for effective living in such a world. In it, as it developed, classics and the customary linguistic studies had no great place; instead, we find English, history and modern languages with a good deal of mathematics and science.
>
> (Clarke 1940: 16)

Although Clarke's last sentence, like Williams' own account, may exaggerate the extent of the change – modern languages, for instance, being optional and so more peripheral than he implies – his reference to 'the dominant idea of education for culture' touches something really important. The dissenters' curriculum was not intended to provide specialist training. Here and there it included 'commerce' (McLachlan 1931: 331), but overwhelmingly its interest was in pure rather than applied knowledge. Theoretical rationality rather than practical was the substance. We know that alumni of the Academies went on to apply what they had learnt to build the new industrial and commercial England of the late eighteenth and early nineteenth centuries. And it is true that if such items as mechanics and trigonometry and chemistry and hydrostatics had not been part of their programme they could never have used them to create the new world. But the main purpose of teaching them was not to help on the process of industrialisation, but to reveal the world as it truly is. At a higher-order level, this still had a practical purpose behind it in the shape of a religious, salvationist, aim – perhaps something of the same religious aim as Fred Clarke himself believed in, when he wrote in an earlier work that 'the ultimate reason for teaching Long Division to little Johnny is that he is an immortal soul' (Clarke 1923: 2).

How accurate is the picture of the Dissenting Academies as catalysts of curricular revolution that we find in Clarke and Williams, as well as in full-length academic works on the Academies published by Parker (1914) and McLachlan (1931) earlier last century? There are things to be said on the other side. Hans (1951) provides a more global account of 'new trends in education in the eighteenth century', and, while not denying the contribution that the Academies made, locates them as just one of several types of institution responsible for curricular modernisation. These included Oxford and Cambridge, grammar schools and private academies. Mercer (2001) also claims that Parker and McLachlan exaggerated the role played by the Academies in providing a progressive education for lay students. Although this was true of a handful of liberal Academies like Warrington, Manchester College and Hackney New College, 'after 1750 the vast majority of academies were small orthodox seminaries for the training of Nonconformist ministers' (ibid.: 35).

These doubts would appear to count against the bold thesis that the Dissenting Academies originated the modern subject-based curriculum that we find in English schools today. At the very least, this may require considerable qualification. A more circumspect claim would be the broader one, that puritan/dissenting educational ideas and practices had a major, if not the only, role in the story.

This latter thesis broadens horizons beyond the Academies and enables us to take into account other dissenting institutions and ways of thinking. These include, in England, schools set up for dissenters from the end of the eighteenth century, and in eighteenth century Scotland both grammar schools and universities. The more accommodating thesis also allows us to go back to the world of puritan education in the sixteenth and seventeenth centuries, before the first Academies appeared towards the end of the latter.

Ramus and the puritan curriculum

In Chapter 4 we looked at the part played by Ramus in the late sixteenth century in forming the puritans' attachment to logic. He has also been seen as a major figure in the history of the curriculum more generally. This comes out forcibly in David Hamilton's (1990) book *Curriculum History*. As we saw in Chapter 4, Ramus's logic consisted of a branching scheme of dichotomies, from the most general categories to the most specific, within which the heterogeneity of God's created world could be systematically arranged. Following Plato, Ramus held that this world was to be understood as a 'material counterpart of an ordered series of ideas existing in the mind of God' (quoted in Morgan 1986: 107). Hamilton relates Ramus to a wider group of humanist educationalists who preceded him and who were preoccupied with how teaching could best be organised. He quotes from Grafton and Jardine (1986: 124):

'Method' was the catchword of promoters of humanist education from the 1510s onwards. This practical emphasis on procedure signals a shift in intellectual focus on the part of pedagogical reformers, from the ideal end-product of a classical education (the perfect orator …) to classroom aids (textbooks, manuals and teaching drills).

Ramus was, in Hamilton's words (1990: 23), 'the high priest of method'. His logical maps were about both what to teach and how to teach it (ibid.: 26). They enabled the content of learning to be systematically arranged in discrete – non-overlapping – branches of knowledge; and they gave teachers clear routes through the material, moving especially from more abstract to less abstract, experience-related components, but also vice versa. It is easy to understand the attractiveness of Ramist method to puritan or allied sect preachers, schoolmasters and textbook writers in the late sixteenth and early seventeenth centuries – Comenius (1592–1670), for instance (Triche and McKnight 2004: 53) – given their interest, mentioned in Chapter 4 (see p. 96) in transmitting to their audiences huge quantities of orthodox information rather than encouraging them to think for themselves. (See Comenius (1907) on the possibility of mass education once one finds the one right method for teaching any subject matter (XIII: 15; XIX: 14–54); on teaching from the abstract and general towards the concrete and detailed (XVI: 38–45; XX: 19); on items learnt forming an encyclopaedic whole (XVIII: 34–5; XIX: 6).) In addition – and it is hard to know how much weight to put on the point – Ramist maps contain, according to Hamilton, the first recorded use of the word 'curriculum' in an academic context. Hamilton suggests that it might be linked with the Calvinist predilection for the use of the term in the phrase '*vitae curriculum*', allied with the common presentation of human life as an obstacle course on the way to salvation (Hamilton 1990: 26–8). Certainly, Ramist learning was far from detached from everyday preoccupations. It provided spiritual security.

> Uncertainty was the bane of Puritan existence, as in the well-reported psychological anxiety produced by nagging doubt of whether one was to undergo conversion or not. Ramist method provided not only psychological comfort but a 'form' by which to place over, understand, and so control the world.
> (McKnight 2003: 54–5)

The partly dichotomous Ramist map, reproduced in Figure 5.1, shows not only the use of the term 'curriculum', but also a classification of curriculum subjects. As Peter Mack (1998, Vol. 8: 52–3) says, ' Ramus's method obliged him to avoid overlaps between subjects … He emphasised the need to select material, according to what we would now call disciplinary boundaries'.

The fact that puritans used Ramist logic not to promote free thought but to show the one true path that understanding must take (see Morgan 1986: 111) is a counterweight to an interpretation of puritan educational activity in the seventeenth century aligning it with cutting-edge educational reform in the sciences and in the humanities, associated with the ideas of Bacon (Parker 1914: ch. 1; Greaves 1969). If one concentrates, as Morgan does, on the *intentions* of puritan educationalists, these were far from embracing the new Enlightenment world that was beginning to emerge. They sought 'not man's intellectual dominion

TABVLA ARTIVM, QVAS IN
hoc Volumine coniunximus.

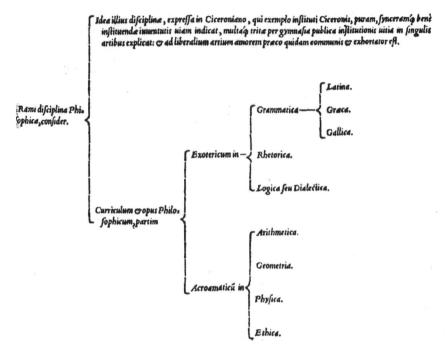

Figure 5.1 A Ramist curriculum map

Source: Hamilton (1990: 27).

in a rational universe, but rather a subordination of human reason to the demands of an enthusiastic faith' (Morgan 1986: 309). But *consequences* are a different story. As we have seen, Ramus's logic was anchored at its non-abstract end in experience of the world. This gave it a point of contact with the Baconians. As Morgan (ibid.: 111) writes,

> Ramus' insistence that logic should agree with nature may have meant that puritan educators conditioned an era of students to see 'truth' in an empirically approached natural world, even though the puritans themselves had no such intention of diverting scholarly attention, or of shifting the bedrock of 'reality', from the Word to the world.

All this provides background to the fact that by the late eighteenth century at least some of the Dissenting Academies were the site of advanced scientific teaching and crucibles of industrial progress.

Doubts about the role of the Dissenting Academies

Turning more globally from the seventeenth to the eighteenth century, we have seen reason to doubt the strong thesis that the modern curriculum was born in the Academies. Between 1750 and 1850 the Academies had little hand in the education of the laity, being predominantly, as Mercer tells us, theological colleges for the preparation of ministers; and other institutions from grammar schools to private academies were teaching a wide range of modern subjects.

But these two types of evidence are not conclusive. Mercer's thesis is only about what happened after 1750. He also states (2001: 35) that 'at the beginning of the eighteenth century at least half the Academies were open to students who intended following careers other than in the ministry'. There is a plausible reason, which he does not mention, why the proportion of Academies with lay students diminished after 1750 – from a half to about an eighth (ibid.: 35–6). From 1779 Dissenters were allowed by law to follow the teaching profession (although dissenting schools also existed outside the law before this time; Hans (1951: 58–62) describes several examples of these). Many dissenters moved from the Academies, as pupils and as tutors, into other institutions. I have given one example of this already in Chapter 3 – in the shape of Mill Hill School (see also Roach 1986: 176–7 for details of its 'full and varied curriculum for the time'); and I will come back to the topic more generally below. This line of thinking strengthens the case for the influence of the Academies on the modern curriculum, either directly, via their own teaching, or via their staff later teaching elsewhere.

There is more to be said, too, about Hans's thesis about the widespread presence of modern subjects in other eighteenth-century institutions. Although Hans (1951: 38–41) shows that these subjects were taught in two or three of the leading grammar schools, he does nothing to suggest that, by and large, grammar school education was not centred virtually exclusively on the classics. His evidence for modern subjects in private schools and academies is much more extensive, but he admits that 'very few of them published a detailed curriculum of studies' (ibid.: 63). Students were organised into groups according to their intended destinations (e.g. the universities, the navy, the army, business and law, some technical professions) and their curricula varied accordingly. But all students 'would study English, Arithmetic, Geography, Geometry, History; most of the pupils would take French and Drawing, and all would participate in Sports' (ibid.: p 64–5).

The curricular philosophy of these institutions was very different from that experienced by lay students in the Dissenting Academies. In most of the latter, lay students generally followed the first half of a four- or five-year divinity course (Mercer 2001: 38). In the post-1729 Northampton course outlined above logic, mathematics, natural philosophy and divinity were prominent in the first two years of a four-year course. At Warrington Academy in 1780 the first three years of a five-year course covered theology, ethics, logic, mathematics, theoretical and experimental natural philosophy, geography, history, commerce, theory of language, elocution and composition (ibid.: 39–40). In the Dissenting Academies, virtually the whole of the curriculum was common to all students in the first two or three years. It was planned – for the most part – as a unified whole: religious considerations were uppermost in framing it. It was meant to equip the believer, lay as well as clerical, with those forms of knowledge which would help him to understand the nature of God and of his world – to see both the big picture and also how the mass of details fitted into it. There is little evidence, according to Mercer (ibid.: 40), to support the belief that the leading dissenting businessmen and manufacturers who sent their sons to the Academies after 1750 were primarily guided by utilitarian motives.

In one important way, the English secondary school curriculum introduced in 1904 and reinforced in 1988 is closer to that of the dissenting than that of the private academy. It is a unity, not fragmented according to intended destinations. It is wholly common for all students, not common only in subjects seen as basic. Its elements are to be studied largely for non-instrumental reasons.

This is one reason why Hans's thesis does not undermine, as much as it perhaps appeared to, the claim that the Dissenting Academies had a major role in originating the modern subject-based curriculum. Another is this. In his conclusion, Hans (1951: 210) states that in the middle of the nineteenth century 'all the achievements and pioneering ideas of the eighteenth century were forgotten'. Why this should be so he saw as a 'problem worthy of deeper investigation'. His own provisional thought on this is that the industrial revolution in the latter part of the eighteenth century produced a gulf between employers and labourers which was reflected in diverging forms of education for each, the new industrial middle class blocking the way for newcomers from below (ibid.: 211). This eroded the eighteenth-century pattern, in which young people of lower social origin were more likely to enter the institutions Hans describes. Science, which had become prominent in eighteenth-century curricula, was henceforth demoted, as 'the social cleavage between employers of labour and employed labourers was reflected in the differentiation of social prestige, between the "classical" and "scientific" curriculum' (ibid.: 212).

Hans's thesis is that although the great variety of schools and institutions with which he deals successfully introduced new subjects and new methods and so 'started modern education in England' (ibid.: 209), the history of their influence is not continuous, there having been a major breach in this story caused by the industrial revolution. He does not say how the breach was healed. Neither is his claim that the 'scientific' curriculum became associated with employed labourers rather than employers plausible, science having been kept out of working-class curricula throughout the nineteenth century, as well as in the Morant reforms of 1904 which set a pattern which lasted well into the second half of the twentieth century.

The puritan curriculum in Scotland

The Dissenting Academies were not the only eighteenth-century institutions in which puritan origins foreshadowed a modern curriculum. Scottish schools and universities also played a significant part, not only in the Scottish, but also in the English story. Again, we are talking about upper secondary/higher education.

Presbyterian Scotland had its own educational system for its élite. As early as 1574–80, the Principal of Glasgow University, Andrew Melville, established a curriculum which became the basis of the university's work for two centuries. As Smith (1955: 68) notes, his system was similar to that in many of the Dissenting Academies:

Year 1: Humanities (Greek and Latin) and Ramus' dialectic
Year 2: Mathematics, Cosmography, Asronomy
Year 3: Moral and Political Science
Year 4: Natural Philosophy and History

By the beginning of the eighteenth century, despite variations, its four universities, all dating from the fifteenth and sixteenth centuries, tended towards a common pattern. This was to award MA degrees after a four-year course in theology, medicine or the arts. The latter was the staple curriculum; and its bent towards philosophy is again reminiscent of the Dissenting Academies, Greek tending to be taught in the first year; logic and metaphysics in the second; ethics and pneumatics ('covering such abstruse questions as the nature of angels, the human soul, and the one true God') in the third; and natural philosophy probably including some mathematics in the fourth (Knox 1953: 16–17).

A tilt was given to this curriculum in a more practical direction when, following the example of Perth in 1761, a number of Scottish towns set up academies offering a two-year higher secondary/university level course. In Perth's case:

The scheme of study included in the first year Natural Science, Mathematics, Navigation, Astronomy, and English; in the second, Natural Philosophy, Practical Geometry, Civil History, Logic and the Principles of Religion. All teaching and exercises were to be in English. In course of time, Fine Writing, Drawing, Painting, and Chemistry were included in the curriculum.

(Strong 1909: 161)

Later in the century a further attempt was made to bring more order into the 'chaotic medley' of Scottish schools, which were rapidly increasing. Confusingly, the new type of school – which covered a wider age-group than the academies, including the whole secondary age-group – was also called an 'academy'. One of the first, founded in 1793 for upper-class boys, was Inverness Academy. It taught 'English grammatically' in the first year; Latin and Greek in the second; writing, arithmetic, and bookkeeping in the third; mathematics, geography, navigation, drawing and fortification in the fourth; and civil and natural History, natural philosophy, chemistry and astronomy in the fifth (ibid.: 164–5). In the first half of the nineteenth century the curricula of these academies, which were erected all over the country, was copied by some of the grammar schools, although the classical tradition remained strong in others (ibid.: 168–9).

In the eighteenth century Scottish educational institutions had close links with the English dissenting communities. From the end of the seventeenth century, many dissenter students, who were barred from Oxford and Cambridge, went for their higher education to Glasgow and Edinburgh universities. Several of these became tutors in the Dissenting Academies, and occasionally some Scottish graduates, not trained in the Academies, also became tutors in them (McLachlan 1931: 29–30). The replacement of Latin by English as medium of instruction in the Academies probably owed something to Scottish influence (Smith 1955: 70).

University College London

University College London (UCL), which was founded in 1826, was patterned on Scottish university practice (Bellot 1929: 8). Prussian and American higher education – both also from the protestant thought-world – were further influences (ibid.: 8). UCL was originally conceived as a dissenting university, given the continuing exclusion (until the 1850s) of English dissenters from Oxford and Cambridge. Dissenting Academies, although considered, were by then unsuitable models (ibid.: 21). Many of UCL's teachers had dissenting connexions. As an example, the first professor of logic and the philosophy of the human mind (1830–1866) was the Rev. John Hoppus. He was an Independent minister, who had been educated at Rotherham Independent College and both Edinburgh and Glasgow Universities (ibid.: 109). The link between UCL and the dissenting world continued to some extent for much of the nineteenth century. As we have seen, Galton, Pearson, and McDougall were all connected with the college. So, indeed, was Burt in a later period.

UCL was divided into a medical and a general department, comprising arts, laws and science. At the beginning the general course was planned to cover four years (ibid.: 78–9):

> Years 1 and 2 Latin, Greek, Mathematics, with Natural Philosophy as alternative to Mathematics in Year 2
> Year 3 Logic and the Philosophy of the Human Mind, Chemistry and Natural Philosophy
> Year 4 Jurisprudence, Political Economy, Natural Philosophy, Moral and Political Philosophy
> French, German, English composition and history were among optional courses.

Not only was this course pattern very close to that of the Scottish universities – and therewith some of the Dissenting Academies, but the course itself was a general one, more specialised courses appearing only later in the century. In this respect, early UCL, like the Scottish universities and Dissenting Academies, was closer to the curriculum pattern found in the Scottish secondary schools described above. Both secondary and tertiary institutions provided a course of general education, based on separate subjects representing the main branches of human knowledge.

As a twentieth-century postscript to this section, I should mention A.D. Lindsay's work in helping to found Keele University (originally the University College of North Staffordshire) in 1949. This was a deliberate attempt to counter the specialisation of university courses which had begun in the later nineteenth century: like UCL's early general course, Keele's Foundation Year provided, and provides, a general course covering several disciplines across the arts and sciences. Born in Glasgow in 1879, and educated at Glasgow Academy, Glasgow University and Oxford, Lindsay himself was the son of the Principal of the United Free Church. Gallie (1960: 145–6) says of him 'In the language of his Calvinistic forebears, he had a sense – albeit in the least oppressive form – of being one of "the elect"'. Lindsay wrote about Keele in 1950: '… in some ways our experiment is inspired by memories of the old Glasgow MA as it still existed at the end of the last century' (Mountford 1972: 130). 'The "traditional" Scottish MA … covered seven subjects: humanity (Latin), Greek, mathematics, logic with metaphysics, moral philosophy, natural philosophy (physics) and English' (ibid.).

The story through to 1988

As we saw in Chapter 2, by the eighteenth century the dissenting communities in England had become a prominent part of the 'middling sort' of people, cut off as they were from the life and livelihoods of the Anglican establishment, and demarcated from the poor below. Their religiosity, as Tawney (1926) and others have taught us, brought them not only the conviction of salvation, but also worldly success. Hard work in dedication to a vocation chosen in line with God-given talents paid off in financial terms. The dissenters' success in commerce, banking and manufacture, spurred by a desire for social improvement as they interpreted this, played a major part in the industrialisation of the country in the late eighteenth century, some of them rising to great wealth. By the early nineteenth century, the dissenting middle classes, swelled now by many Methodists and evangelical Anglicans, were beginning to grow in political power and influence, and were merging, at their top end, with the old landed class of aristocrats and gentry.

In education, the same emphasis as we found at UCL on a common course based on a broad range of discrete disciplines is mirrored in the secondary education provided for dissenters' sons. Courses are understandably less abstract, excluding the logic and philosophy of mind that we find at UCL.

We saw above that after 1779 dissenters were legally allowed to become school teachers. Over the next sixty years middle-class nonconformists had their sons educated in new private and proprietary schools, as well as some reformed grammar schools. They pressed for the same kind of broad curriculum that had been found in the Academies, in opposition to the narrow classical education of the grammar schools. Brian Simon (1960: 102–25; see also Roach 1986: 237) gives a good account of these developments. He refers, for instance, to a report of 1834 about private schools in Manchester. Most had been established since 1820 and,

> a high proportion of teachers were dissenters. An analysis of the curricula showed that the average boys' school provided teaching in reading, writing, grammar, arithmetic, geography, history, mathematics and languages, up to the age of about fifteen. A few schools taught natural history and drawing and in some there was a little moral and religious teaching.
>
> (Simon 1960: 113)

The onward progress of the middle classes in wealth and political influence continued through the nineteenth century, fuelled now by the evangelical revival, and facilitated by the repeal of the laws excluding dissenters from public life. Soon after the middle of the century, official action was taken to tidy up the raggedness of what schools across the nation were offering, and to fit the content of the curriculum explicitly to a three-fold social class division. In the late 1850s and 1860s, while the Clarendon Commission pressed for the retention of the classical curriculum in the leading public schools, and the Newcastle Commission urged a three-'R's-based education for the masses, the Taunton Commission of 1864–8 recommended the general modern curriculum for second- and third-grade endowed and private schools, that is, largely for middle and lower ranks of the middle classes, among which dissenters were a prominent group. While 'second-grade' schools, for boys leaving at sixteen, were to have a curriculum based on Latin (but not Greek), English literature, political economy, mathematics and science, that of the 'third-grade' ones, stopping at about fourteen, 'should include the elements of Latin or a modern language, English, history, elementary mathematics, geography and science' (ibid.: 324).

The modern curriculum of the Prussian *Realschule* influenced the thinking of the commission, as did the curricular desires of different sections of the English middle classes. It is significant that Prussia was a protestant state (its Lutheran and Calvinist churches had been brought together in a unified Evangelical Church in 1817) and that its modern curriculum in the *Realschule* had been created in line with the wishes of the same commercial and industrial groups as were central to the English middle class – who had been pressing governments for many years but with little success to improve schooling for their children along modern lines.

Thus, while the Clarendon Commission of 1861–4 decided that the education of the upper classes (including now many of the upper middle classes) in the major public schools should continue to be devoted largely to classics, the plan for the bulk of the middle classes continued to be based on the traditional broad curriculum deriving originally from the dissenting tradition. Although the Taunton proposals were not put into effect, the pull of this curriculum was so great by the 1860s that it had begun to make inroads into the great public schools themselves (Roach 1986: 239). The Clarendon Report itself suggested that although classics (with history and divinity) was to have over 50 per cent of curricular time, there should also be room for mathematics, natural science, French or German, and music or drawing (ibid.: 240).

By the end of the nineteenth century the so-called 'traditional' (i.e. non-conformist) middle class had been joined by new middle-class members from Anglican or secular backgrounds, although the two groups often kept apart in fairly self-contained social networks and remained so in places until the 1950s (McKibbin 1998: 91). The twentieth century entrenched the middle classes – increasingly diverse, as we have seen, in their composition, and increasingly secular after mid-century – in the political influence which they had begun to attain by its early years. The 1906 election had returned 185 nonconformist MPs, nearly all sympathetic to the new Liberal government (Binfield 1977: 207); with the decline of the Liberal Party after World War I, the middle classes gravitated largely to the Conservatives. The old puritan notion of belonging to an elect destined for salvation had by then lost most of its force, but vestiges of it may have remained in the notion of an academic élite identified by mechanisms of selection.

In 1904 Morant created a gulf between the new local authority secondary schools and elementary schools. The secondary schools, as under the Taunton proposals, had to follow a broad subject-based curriculum, consisting in the 1904 case of:

> English language and literature, at least one language other than English, geography, history, mathematics, science, drawing, manual instruction (boys), domestic subjects (girls), physical exercise and organised games.

The reference here to girls' education deserves a comment. The 1904 scheme gives official blessing to the view that, at secondary level, girls should follow the same curriculum as boys, except in practical subjects. For most of the late nineteenth century, middle-class girls' education had been very different, orientated not towards scholarship but to their becoming 'decorative, modest and marriageable beings', and much of it taking place at home (Dyhouse 1981: 41–3). Even after 1904, in 1909, the regulations were changed so as to allow girls over fifteen to substitute domestic subjects for science and mathematics other than arithmetic (ibid.: 165).

Elementary schools, catering for some 75 per cent of children, were obliged to follow a less intellectual curriculum, which included no science beyond nature study, no foreign language, but much emphasis on (gender-differentiated) manual subjects (Board of Education 1929). For details of Morant's keenness that there should be more domestic science taught to girls in all schools, see Dyhouse (1981: 93–4, 98–9). The core of the middle class was thus able to differentiate itself more adequately from those below it, scholarships for the more able of the latter providing a frail ladder upwards.

A similar academic curriculum, based on a by now traditional list of curriculum subjects, lived on vigorously through the twentieth century, at first in the selective secondary sector and then in much of the secondary comprehensive system which largely replaced this from the 1960s. From mid-century onwards many egalitarian educational thinkers wanted the working classes to enjoy the same curricular advantages as those from the élite. In some cases – as in my own – this desire was intensified by personal experience of upward social mobility via the 'ladder' of scholarships into élite schooling. Comprehensive schools were also the home of innumerable attempts to move away from a totally subject-based curriculum towards new forms of curricular arrangement with more appeal and relevance to the mass of children.

In 1988 all innovation was blocked by the new National Curriculum, its ten compulsory subjects almost identical to Morant's in 1904, the only divergences being the inclusion of manual work/housewifery in 1904 and of technology and music in 1988 (Aldrich 1988: 22). The ground had been laid for this reversion by a steady campaign in favour of 'a traditional curriculum' begun by the *Black Papers* of the late 1960s and 1970s (with Cyril Burt and Hans Eysenck among the contributors) and continued in right-wing press articles and pamphlets in the 1980s.

Unlike in 1904, the broad compulsory curriculum was now for all children, not only a tiny élite. The subject-based curriculum was also extended from the secondary to primary schools. What began in the eighteenth century as a university/upper secondary level curriculum had percolated by 1988 into the infant school. ('Do not you delay, but be dropping in instruction as they are able, and as soon as they are able to understand any thing' (Morgan 1944: 53); see above p. 49.) In Chapter 6, I look again at the 1988 changes.

The twentieth century saw the triumph of what was once called the 'modern' curriculum, and now the 'traditional' curriculum, over its chief rival, the classics-based curriculum of the public schools. The division between the two had existed in the eighteenth century, as we have seen, but then schooling for dissenters had been more discrete from that of the landed establishment. The nineteenth century witnessed more overt conflict between the two curricular approaches. On the other hand, in the nineteenth century there was no question of rivalry between the modern curriculum and the basic curriculum provided for the masses. It was accepted on all sides within the competing élites – landed, financial and industrial – that the working classes had to have an education that would keep them in their station.

By the early twentieth century there had been a coming together of the older élites, as divisions of interest between the landed classes, the financial–commercial élite of London and the south-east, and northern industrialists became eroded (Rubinstein 1998). The political embodiment of this union was the Conservative Party, in power for some two-thirds of the century, and supported, as we have seen, by the bulk of the middle classes. In educational terms the merging of élites was reflected in the victory of the modern over the classical curriculum, even in the public schools – although classical traces remained, as in the minor public school I myself attended in mid-century, in the greater prestige of its 'classical' form over the 'science', and then 'modern', and then 'general' forms ranged below it.

The twentieth century was also marked by the threat to the new élite from the working classes and the Labour movement. This, too, had curricular consequences. The nineteenth-century policy of dividing curricula along class lines reached its apogee in the Morant reforms of 1904, and was still more or less in place by mid-century. After this time, there was growing pressure from the left for a common, non-class-divided, curriculum in the new comprehensive schools. Since the left's perception was that working-class children had been *excluded* from the science, languages and other elements of the traditional subject-based curriculum, the latter's sway was thus extended. The coming of the National Curriculum in 1988 sealed its victory. Right across the social spectrum, from housing estates to estates in the country, state schooling was now statutorily based on an identical range of subjects. If aspirations from below were to trouble the élite above, other ways would have to be found of containing them than by curricular division.

What had grown up in the eighteenth century as a curriculum suited to the religious beliefs of the minority community of Old Dissenters had become three centuries later, and through various transformations, the taken-for-granted curriculum of the whole nation. Throughout, it had maintained some kind of association with the middle classes, or the 'middling sort' as they were earlier known. Even from the end of the sixteenth century, puritans had been coming to see themselves as a distinctive social group with their own view of the world based around the notions of election, salvation, predestination, vocation and family life. This community began to contrast itself with the social groups on either side of it: the feudal nobility and the undisciplined rabble (George and George 1961: 170). The exclusion of Old Dissenters from English public life after the Act of Uniformity of 1662 potently helped to consolidate their apartness, their sense of belonging to a respectable, upright social world cut off from the Anglican establishment above and the mass of labourers, unemployed and criminals below. As many of them became richer through the industrialisation of the late eighteenth and early nineteenth centuries, class divisions between the 'middling sort', many of whom were Old Dissenters or Methodists or evangelical Anglicans, and the gentry above them were to some extent eroded. At the same time, throughout the nineteenth century the ranks of the middle classes were swollen by the growth of new professional groups – school teachers, engineers, surveyors and others. Although in the early twentieth century, divisions between nonconformist social networks and those of other middle-class groups were still present, as that century progressed the 'middle class' began to become the large, sprawling, often secular, unclearly-bounded group, stretching from the solidly affluent to the lower middle class of salaried or self-employed workers of all kinds, with which we associate the term today (Gunn and Bell 2002). The development of the modern/traditional curriculum mirrors, in its progress from excludedness to acceptance and finally to hegemony, the development of the middle classes.

The traditional academic curriculum today

Many of us tend to take today's traditional school curriculum for granted, as we do ideas about pedagogy, timetabling and assessment which have become associated with it over the last three centuries. It is a curriculum which makes a sharp distinction between mind and body, with physical education at its periphery. It is also centrally an *intellectual* curriculum, foregrounding subjects concerned with the pursuit of knowledge like mathematics, science, history and geography.

Artistic subjects – literature, the visual arts and music – are mainly nineteenth century additions to a narrowly intellectual core and still play second fiddle to the knowledge-seeking subjects. We may not see the imagination and the emotions as 'springs of false judgements' as the Old Dissenters did, but they are still given less priority than knowledge acquisition. Of the artistic subjects, English literature tends to be taken more seriously than the other two. This may be partly because it is more easily assimilable to a knowledge-seeking subject (see p. 112 for a historical source of this within the puritan tradition). In secondary schools, the intensity and delicacy of pupils' aesthetic response to drama, fiction and poetry are often rated less highly than their competence in evidence-based critical assessment.

Like the dissenters' curriculum of the eighteenth century, ours is dominated by non-instrumental goals. This is not to deny that science, for example, is often studied with extrinsic aims in view. An upper secondary student may have her mind on doing physics at university or on a job in pharmaceuticals. Something of the same outlook, *ceteris paribus*, must have been true of some lay students of Warrington Academy. But the *intended* goal of science teaching among the dissenters – intended, that is, by the establishment, not necessarily by each student – was to reveal the manifold glory of God's creation. In our own age, defenders of a traditional curriculum are often equally attached to non-utilitarian aims. They hold science, history and mathematics to be significant achievements of human culture in their own right. Schools should, as their primary purpose, inculcate a love of learning, rather than be vehicles of career advancement, citizenship, or self-exploration. (Sometimes, indeed, the term 'education' itself is defined in terms of intrinsic goods, with instrumental aims falling outside it, and belonging to 'training'.) Examples of this non-instrumental way of thinking are found in the works of educational philosophers like Richard Peters (1966), Paul Hirst (1965; Hirst and Peters 1970), and Michael Oakeshott (1971) as well as later writers like Anthony O'Hear (1991: 43–5), although the last two of these have been more traditionalist about the curriculum than Peters and Hirst, who saw themselves as basing a broad, disciplines-focused, curriculum on rational principles rather than a respect for what has been. I have explored elsewhere the indebtedness of 1960s philosophy of the curriculum to the dissenting tradition (White 2005).

In one way, this position is more purely non-instrumentally orientated than that of the dissenters. Behind the latter, after all, there was an extrinsic consideration of a sort, and one of great importance. Knowledge of God's world was linked in the dissenting mind with personal salvation, being believed to be a necessary condition of it. This did not necessarily make personal salvation an acknowledged *aim* of education; indeed, to have done so would have been arrogant towards God himself, since salvation was in his gift alone. The more recent position lacks this ambiguous relationship to purposes, or considerations, which lie beyond this. The learning is unalloyedly non-instrumental.

Yet this leaves the latter position worse off, in one respect, than the older one. It faces a difficulty over justification. *Why* should science or history be taught in a non-instrumental way? There is no obvious answer. While the dissenters could

– in some way, if not a crudely instrumental way – invoke salvation, contemporary defenders have no such recourse. Some make the value of academic learning-for-its-own-sake true by intuition (Downie *et al.* 1974: ch. 3), while others justify it in a Kantian way as presupposed to a rational life (Peters 1966: ch. 5). This may look promising, since it seems that human beings cannot, if they are rational, be endlessly pursuing means to ends without having some ends which they value, not as means to something yet beyond, but simply in themselves. But one problem facing any such argument is that good reasons have to be given for privileging academic goals of an intrinsic sort over other intrinsically valuable activities – from involvement in close personal relationships, to self-understanding, to a love of nature. There are many further twists in these justificatory claims and counter-claims; but I have perhaps done enough to show a main difficulty in the intrinsic position.

There are two more features which the modern subject-based curriculum shares with the dissenters'. First, the greater prestige given to more abstract subjects like mathematics and science. Logic was also prominent in the earlier curriculum, but its only counterpart today is in the 'thinking skills' which are now part of the official school curriculum. The second feature is the organisation of the curriculum around discrete subjects. There is no reason why it *has* to be arranged in this way, however inconceivable any departure from this may seem to some. The subject-basedness of the dissenting curriculum would seem to go back to the Ramist project of dividing and subdividing areas of knowledge in neat, visually presentable, ways. Attempts during the late twentieth century to play up interrelationships between areas of knowledge and play down discreteness made little headway, finally foundering in Britain when the rigidly subject-based National Curriculum was made mandatory in 1988. Five 'cross-curricular themes' which the government introduced at the same time quickly disappeared from the scene.

Timetabling

The formal curriculum is not the only feature of school life that has continuities with Old Dissent. I was struck, when reading McLachlan's (1931) book on the Dissenting Academies, by his diagram of the timetable for Warrington Academy around 1778 shown in Figure 5.2.

The similarity with a secondary school timetable today is remarkable. Time spent each day on studies may have been longer, but there is the same injection of knowledge in short bursts, with a shift to entirely different subject matter at the end of each period. (See also Comenius 1907, XXIX: 17.) The Old Dissenters had their own rationale for this. It was partly about the least wasteful use of time (on puritan time-valuation, see Thompson 1982); and partly reflected the Ramist tradition of classifying knowledge and packaging it into easily learnable chunks.

It was not his originality but his genius for layout and organisation that put Ramus on top of the textbook market, master of the most popular way of conveying complex information to beginners. His books on dialectic presented

Figure 5.2 Warrington Academy timetable

Hours.	Monday.	Tuesday.	Wednesday.	Thursday.	Friday.	Saturday.	Sunday.
7	Prayers	Prayers	Prayers	Prayers	Prayers	Prayers	Prayers
8	Arithmetic, Bookkeeping	Arithmetic, Bookkeeping	Arithmetic, Bookkeeping	Arithmetic, Bookkeeping	Arithmetic, Bookkeeping	Ancient Geography	—
	Breakfast	Breakfast	Breakfast	Breakfast	Breakfast	Breakfast	Breakfast
9	Algebra	Trigonometry	Algebra	Trigonometry	Algebra	Public Lecture	—
10	Greek Testament	Logic, Ethics, etc.	Theology	Logic, Ethics, etc.	Theology	Scheme Lecture	—
11	Geometry 1 2 3	English —	Geometry 1 2 3	Conic Secs.	Geometry 1 2 3	Geography Theological Society	Divine Service
12	Writing	Conic Secs. Drawing	Writing	English Drawing	Writing		—
1	Dinner	Dinner	Dinner	Dinner	Dinner	Dinner	Dinner
2	Classics	Classics	Classics	Classics	Classics	—	—
3	French	French	French	French	French	—	—
4	Do.	Do.	Do. —	Do.	Do.	—	—
5	Anatomy or Chemistry	—	—	Anatomy or Chemistry	Hebrew	—	—
6	—	—	—	—	—	—	—
7	Composition Society	Speaking Club	Book Club	Classical Club	Divinity Club	—	—
8	Supper	Supper	Supper	Supper	Supper	Supper	Supper
9	Prayers	Prayers	Prayers	Prayers	Prayers	Prayers	Prayers

N.B.—Evening Prayers are now at 7. Several Societies after Supper.
[1] Wilson's *Memorials*, II, p. 39, at New College, Hampstead.

Figure 5.2 Warrington Academy timetable

Source: McLachlan (1931: 227).

the method as applicable to all fields of learning, while other works extended his ideas to specific subjects, particularly mathematics, where the influence of his technique was strong. It was above all the dichotomous tables … that he made his hallmark and raised to new levels of popularity … Academic books, especially those meant for classroom use, routinely appeared as blocks of ordinary prose linked every few pages by a summary and a table, condensing the material into skeletal form, short and easy to remember. The point of this was to reduce the student's confusion and ease his labour.

(Copenhaver and Schmitt 1992: 238)

What rationale is there today for this kind of timetabling? It is another institution which we have come to take as read, but it sits ill with the greater attention we in contrast to dissenting teachers pay – in theory – to student motivation. Interest in a topic, once aroused, does not tend to come in forty-five minute episodes. Brave schools explore alternatives; but the norm is to cling to the older way.

Examinations

The Ramist approach to pedagogy also meant that curriculum material became examinable in a business-like way. From the start the notion of examination was a key concept in radical protestant thinking. In Chapter 3, we saw how Comenius (1907, XXIV: section 9, pp. 219–20) drew on Luther's belief that meditation, prayer and examination 'are essential to make a true Christian' in writing that:

> Examination is the continual testing of our progress in piety, and may come from ourselves or from others. Under this head come human, devilish, and divine temptations. For men should examine themselves to see if they are faithful, and do the will of God; and it is necessary that we should be tested by other men, by our friends, and by our enemies.

Given the weight that the puritan placed on knowledge as one condition of salvation, one would expect that the state of one's intellectual as well as moral progress would have been kept regularly under review in one's self-examination. Self-examination, as Comenius indicates, is not to be sharply divided off from examination by other people. The puritan was an individual, but not in an atomic sense: an individual was part of a community of like-minded individuals, who worked collectively to facilitate the salvation of each.

A fuller study than this present book would be needed to investigate the role that early puritan parents, ministers and schoolmasters played in the intellectual testing of young people. But if we look ahead from the sixteenth century to the end of the seventeenth, we see evidence from the history of the Dissenting Academies that, for older students at least, the notion of the scholastic examination in something like its modern sense was already in existence.

McLachlan (1931: 41) tells us that:

> In tests and examinations the academies maintained a standard far above that which obtained at the universities.

He goes on to provide textual evidence from the early eighteenth century of the amazingly easy questions which Cambridge undergraduates were expected – and failed – to answer for the BA degree:

> ... One of them was asked what was the English of Anno Domini, but the blockhead was unable to tell. Another was asked how long it was since our Savour's birth: he said, about a hundred years ...
>
> (ibid.)

Meanwhile, in the early Academies tutors frequently conducted tests and examinations; and in the later, 'the written work of the session was reviewed annually in public by persons appointed for the purpose' (ibid.: 42). As early as 1696 we find the United Brethren – Presbyterians and Independents – who funded scholars for the five-year course at Taunton Academy, insisting that their beneficiaries 'give satisfaction' of their 'skill in the Latin and Greek tongues' before being funded to read Logic and other subjects; and that

> those scholars in philosophy and divinity who have contributions from the Fund shall once a year pass under an examination before the Assembly, or such as they shall approve, as to their proficiency in learning.
>
> (ibid.: 71)

To judge by McLachlan's survey of all the Academies, it is in the Independent (Congregationalist) institutions that the practice of regular examinations is most widespread. There are references to this in his accounts of the Academies of Carmathen (ibid.: 56, 59), Kibworth (ibid.: 139), Northampton (ibid.: 148), Daventry (ibid.: 159), Rotherham (ibid.: 204–5), Hoxton (ibid.: 239–40), Blackburn (ibid.: 272–4). This no doubt stemmed from the fact that the – national – Congregational Fund arranged for the annual examination 'in humane learning and knowledge of divinity' of students whom they supported (ibid.: 3). Does this aspect of his Congregationalist background have any bearing on the attachment to examinations in Cyril Burt's family, not least in his own career (see p. 63 above)?

In the later Academies, annual examinations conducted by outside assessors often lasted two days and covered a number of fields. At Rotherham Academy in 1817, for instance, the examiners' report describes the testing of three classes in Hebrew and several in classics – including one class studying Cornelius Nepos, the Roman author whom Burt's father read to him in his cot (see p. 62 above). In addition,

Four students have entered on the study of the Syriac language, and several read French. Other subjects taken are Divinity, Logic, Ecclesiastical History, Biblical Criticism, and lectures on the sacred books, sermons and elocution – Mathematics in some degree, a little Chemistry, and branches of natural philosophy.

(ibid.: 205)

English (ibid.: 205), geography and history (each of ancient and modern Greece) (ibid.: 274) are other subjects examined in some Academies.

Again, in a larger study than this one, it would be interesting to chart how far, by the early nineteenth century, practices of formal scholastic examining had become detached from early protestant ideas about examination – not least self-examination – as a procedure of devotion. It would also be helpful to know how far Old Dissent's attachment to examinations was shared by other groups, bearing in mind among other things the blurring of distinctions, especially at the upper end of the social scale, between Dissent and Establishment.

Meanwhile, what seems uncontroversial is that the rise of the – often dissenting – middle classes during the nineteenth century was partly a function of the increasing use of examinations, both in directly vocational ways and also in general education.

Vocationally, upper-middle-class professions were the first affected. In the early nineteenth century churchmen and physicians were among the few university students who took a degree. The Law Society introduced examinations for solicitors in 1836 and the first examinations for the higher civil service and the Indian civil service date from the 1850s (Gunn and Bell 2002: 131). The new (post-1836) London University, itself largely an examining body, helped to spread the practice of getting degrees; by 1900 most Oxbridge students 'would have at least intended to take their degree' (ibid.).

Professionalisation based on examinations rather than apprenticeship also developed in the lesser bourgeoisie, in, for instance, accountancy, surveying and engineering.

As such elements began to perceive where their future lay they aspired to provide better education and professional training for their sons. To master their continuously elaborating professions, these men had to develop a steadiness and self-discipline that would carry them past severe academic and professional examinations; this they were prepared to do for there was no other way to advancement.

(Checkland 1964: 303)

Theoretical written examinations for accountancy were introduced in 1880 (Dore 1997: 18). The engineers became professionalised with the foundation of the Royal Institution of Civil Engineers in 1818, and although training continued to be by apprenticeship and self-study, after engineering became a proper university subject from the 1840s there was 'for members of the middle class, a short cut on the road to competence' (ibid.: 18–19).

Middle-class interest in examinations in the nineteenth century was vocationally motivated. As we have seen, these examinations included those for university degrees. As pressure to enter universities increased, schools became affected, too. Among the most popular examinations sat by university-bound school students in the later nineteenth and earlier twentieth century were those set by the Oxford Local Examinations Delegacy and the Cambridge Syndicate (Montgomery 1965: 56). In addition the London University Matriculation Examination was coming to be seen as a general school-leaving examination, even for those not aiming at London University (ibid.).

By the late 1860s, when Galton's work appeared and began to become influential, the role of examinations in the vocation–university–school network had more than begun to change the culture. Galton himself, as mentioned earlier in the book (pp. 57–8), was obsessed throughout his life by examinations, perhaps influenced by his failure to become a Wrangler in the Cambridge final honours examination (Fancher 1984). His interest in them comes out in his 1865 account of his Utopia:

> in which a system of competitive examination for girls, as well as for youths, had been so developed as to embrace every important quality of mind and body, and where a considerable sum was yearly allotted to the endowment of such marriages as promised to yield children who would grow into eminent servants of the State.
>
> (Galton 1865: 165–6)

It is also apparent in his remark, also discussed earlier in the book, that:

> I look upon social and professional life as a continuous examination. All are candidates for the good opinions of others, and for success in their several professions.
>
> (Galton 1978: 6)

For many middle-class men this was becoming increasingly true, with formal examinations playing a central role in the larger story. By the late 1860s England was rapidly turning into a more structured society, with more definite, less arbitrary tracks laid down for young people and their families to plan their careers and aim at vocational success. Cyril Burt's autobiographical account of his childhood in the 1890s shows this process at work very clearly. When he was ten he went to school in Warwick. In a passage already partly included in Chapter 3, he tells us that:

> As the examinations drew near, my mother regularly related how my father had once won so many prizes at St. Saviour's Grammar School that a cab was necessary to cart them home, and I felt I should be disgraced if I did not bring

back at least one prize. To make quite sure, I generally aimed at the Scripture prize, which nobody else seemed to covet.

(Burt 1952: 56)

At eleven Burt won a scholarship to Christ's Hospital, from which he won a scholarship to Jesus College, Oxford, having turned down a Grocers' Company exhibition to Cambridge. In another passage partially included in Chapter 3, he writes:

> My mother claimed that, from the age of nine, my education 'never cost my parents a penny'. Scholarships have thus played so indispensable a part in my life that, not unnaturally, one of my chief interests has been to widen, and if possible improve, the scholarship system and allied methods of examination and selection.

(ibid.: 57, fn 2)

Galton's vision, taken up by Burt and other eugenicists, of a society stratified according to intelligence level via intelligence tests and school and college examinations, appeared in the world, then, just at the time when the middle classes were becoming the dominant force in the country. The institution of the test or examination – historically *their* institution – was central to their victory. Galtonianism gave this institution a theoretical, political, indeed cosmic, rationale.

By the early decades of the twentieth century the more prosaic forms of the Galtonian revolution had become so embedded in the English state educational system as to be taken for granted. Burt's advocacy of streaming or 'treble-tracking' in elementary schools has already been described, as has the rationale that his theory of intelligence provided for the 11+ examination for secondary school selection after 1944 (see pp. 9–10). By this time, too – in 1904 – Morant had engineered his gulf between secondary and elementary education, for which Burt's theory furnished a theoretical justification. In 1907, a step on the way to the later 11+, 'free places' were introduced into secondary schools, allowing children to move to them from the elementary system by means of state scholarships. By 1950 the notions of selective schooling, intelligence testing, public examinations and a ladder of opportunity from one system to another had become accepted features of the English educational scene.

After the arrival of comprehensive secondary education after 1960, selection began to take place not *between* types of secondary school, except in those parts of England where the 11+ still existed, but *within* the comprehensive school itself, where one track led towards the GCE examination which opened the door to sixth-form and university study, and another towards the CSE exam which led nowhere at all, except for the ladder of equivalence between CSE grade 1 and a GCE pass. In 1988 the Thatcher regime introduced the National Curriculum and its assessment system. The latter has to be taken together with that other Thatcherite innovation – the publishing of league tables of school performance. Since these are based largely on results in National Curriculum assessment as well as in GCSE and A-level examinations, parents have been able to see at a glance which schools in their locality are performing 'better' than others, and try to choose accordingly. Although in 2006 all state schools follow a common statutory curriculum, the Thatcher changes, still largely in force, have meant that schools remain greatly divided – as they were in the days of overt selection – between those likely and those unlikely to lead to academic and professional advancement.

The link between the notions of examination and testing at work in Britain today and religious ideas of self-examination and mortal life as a testing ground for a life to come is no longer apparent to most of us. We live in a world which we see as modern and secular – as having rejected its religious antecedents. But our religious heritage still colours, however palely now, the way we think about and practise education. Not, of course, that it is anything like the sole influence. Like the traditional subject-based school curriculum and its timetabling, school tests and examinations have, among their roots, a root in the world of Old Dissent.

John Dewey and the traditional curriculum

In England, it was only in the twentieth century, and only gradually, that the traditional curriculum of discrete subjects achieved supremacy. So we are not likely to find critiques of this curriculum early in that century, taking it as read that this curriculum was already well-established. But in the USA things were different. John Dewey's essay My *Pedagogic Creed* of 1897 (Dewey 1972) provided the germ of his 1916 classic *Democracy and Education*. The earlier work states, among other things,

> I believe that the social life of the child is the basis of concentration, or correlation, in all his training or growth. The social life gives the unconscious unity and the background of all his efforts and of all his attainments.
>
> I believe that the subject-matter of the school curriculum should mark a gradual differentiation out of the primitive unconscious unity of social life.
>
> I believe that we violate the child's nature and render difficult the best ethical results, by introducing the child too abruptly to a number of special studies, of reading, writing, geography, etc., out of relation to this social life.
>
> I believe, therefore, that the true center of correlation on the school subjects is not science, nor literature, nor history, nor geography, but the child's own social activities.
>
> (Dewey 1972: 89)

Dewey lived in a country into which the puritan tradition had threaded deeper roots than it had in England. Many of his ideas about education can be read as a reaction, not necessarily always conscious, to that thought-world. As we saw in Chapter 3, he had been brought up in a New England Congregationalist family. Dewey later turned his back on religion, although not before he wrote at the end of his *Pedagogic Creed* in 1897: 'I believe that in this way the teacher always is the prophet of the true God and the usherer in of the true kingdom of God' (Dewey 1972: 95). *Democracy and Education*, by contrast, has a wholly secular feel to it. Yet even in the earlier work, as indicated, Dewey was laying the foundations of what came to be, in the latter, a full-blooded critique of traditional schooling – where 'traditional', in Dewey's world, was indissolubly connected with cultural attitudes towards learning derived from puritanism.

Key to Dewey's thinking in *Democracy and Education* is his rejection of the division made in traditional teaching between 'subject matter' and 'method'.

> The idea that the mind and the world of things and persons are two separate and independent realms – a theory which philosophically is known as dualism – carries with it the conclusion that method and subject matter of instruction are separate affairs. Subject matter then becomes a ready-made systematized classification of the facts and principles of the world of nature and of man. Method then has for its province a consideration of the ways in which this antecedent subject matter may be best presented to and impressed upon the mind …
>
> (Dewey 1916: 193)

He goes on to describe subject matter as 'information distributed into various branches of study, each study being subdivided into lessons presenting in serial cut-off portions of the total store' (ibid.: 220). In the seventeenth century it was still possible, since the store was still small, to have the ideal of a complete mastery of it; but although the store is now huge, 'the educational ideal has not been much affected' (ibid.).

The parallels with much older puritan ideas on the curriculum are striking. The Ramist legacy is echoed in the dichotomous thinking (Dewey's term is 'dualist') which divides world from mind, dealing first with subject matter in all its complexity and only then turning to how it is to be taught. We find the same preoccupation as in Ramus with classifying and subdividing branches and sub-branches of knowledge.

As in the Ramist scheme, 'method' mirrors the logical classification of subject-matter in its procession from abstract to concrete. In Ramist thinking, as explained in Chapter 4, this is because it is assumed that God has constructed the human mind so that it acquires more abstract knowledge before concrete. In *Democracy and Education* Dewey does not say much about why the abstract-to-concrete method of learning prevalent in his time was thought to make psychological sense. But his discussion of the method is interesting despite this. In describing contemporary science teaching, he writes:

> There is a strong temptation to assume that presenting subject matter in its perfected form provides a royal road to learning. What more natural than to suppose that the immature can be saved time and energy, and be protected from needless error by commencing where competent inquirers have left off? The outcome is written large in the history of education. Pupils begin their

study of science with texts in which the subject is organized into topics according to the order of the specialist. Technical concepts, with their definitions, are introduced at the outset. Laws are introduced at a very early stage, with at best a few indications of the way in which they were arrived at … The method of the advanced student dominates college teaching; the approach of the college is transferred into the high school, and so on down the line, with such omissions as may make the subject easier.

(ibid.: 257)

A few pages later he adds,

That science may be taught as a set of formal and technical exercises is only too true. This happens whenever information about the world is made an end in itself.

(ibid.: 267)

This last comment reveals Dewey's opposition to the idea that the rationale for teaching academic subjects is intrinsic. It links back to the discussion on pp. 125–7 above, with its suggestion that the modern defence of (something like) a traditional curriculum on intrinsic lines may well be a residue of a more ancient defence in the world of Old Dissent. This leads me to wonder how far Dewey, with his deep Congregationalist roots, was *aware* of this similarity – and indeed of other parallels mentioned in this section. Did he consciously connect his 'dualisms' with puritan 'dichotomies', his remarks on the separation between content and method with its likely historical antecedent in Ramist logic and pedagogy? How much did he know, in any case, of this history?

There are other passages in *Democracy and Education* which could well be taken as critical of puritan thinking:

- Where, for instance, Dewey talks of:

   … the feeling that knowledge is high and worthy in the degree in which it deals with ideal symbols instead of the concrete; the scorn of particulars except as they are deductively brought under a universal; the disregard for the body; the depreciation of arts and crafts as intellectual instrumentalities.

   (ibid.: 310)

- His attack on 'the persistent preference of the "intellectual" over the "practical"' (ibid.: 311).
- His statement about 'the antithesis supposed to exist between subject matter (the counterpart of the world) and method (the counterpart of mind)' (ibid.: 340).
- His comment that 'bare logic, however important in arranging and criticizing existing subject matter, cannot spin new subject matter out of itself' (ibid.: 349).

- His critical comments on the view that 'the intellect is a pure light; the emotions are a disturbing heat' (ibid.: 391).

A final passage is also interesting

> Under present conditions the scholastic method, for most persons, means a form of knowing which … includes making distinctions, definitions, divisions and classifications for the mere sake of making them – with no objective in experience … The doctrine of formal discipline in education is the natural counterpart of the scholastic method.
>
> (ibid.: 399)

Despite his references to the scholastic method, Dewey nowhere in his book makes any mention of that kind of scholasticism which entered the puritan bloodstream with the Ramist legacy. It may be, as hinted above, that he did not know of this provenance. This issue apart, Dewey's work remains a powerful critique of traditional subject-based schooling, unmatched as yet, for the reason given at the beginning of this section, by anything in Britain. It has not been appropriate in this context to examine the viability of Dewey's alternative vision of education, but echoes of his critique will be heard in the discussion of the 1988 National Curriculum in Chapter 6.

Conclusion

To summarise: the familiar school curriculum consisting of a range of discrete, largely academic, subjects – exemplified in the 1988 English National Curriculum – is rooted in puritan/dissenting ideas. There are difficulties in locating its origins in the Dissenting Academies, but the broader thesis that these origins lie in the puritan world has more to be said for it. Ramus's logic and its accompanying pedagogy helped to shape the curriculum for older students around discrete epistemological categories, with the more abstract in pride of place. Although by the eighteenth century one could find subject teaching in England in the private academies, only the Dissenting Academies and the schools and academies of Presbyterian Scotland appear to have provided a coherent, general, subject-based course. Its rationale was at root religious, given that salvation was thought to depend on a thorough knowledge of the varied features of God's creation, although the 'modern' curriculum, based on science, mathematics and other subjects, which thus took shape, was also increasingly valued for its utility. In the nineteenth century this curriculum became closely associated with the education of a (still largely dissenting) middle class, in opposition to the classics-based education of the Anglican establishment. This modern curriculum became standard in the twentieth century, at first for the new state secondary (grammar) schools created after 1904, and in 1988 for all state-school pupils. There are also echoes from the dissenting tradition in our contemporary practices in timetabling and examining. John Dewey's writings include an early critique of the traditional subject-based curriculum.

6 Contemporary perspectives

We are living at the beginning of the twenty-first century. How do things stand now? In Britain and in the USA traditional ideas about intelligence and about the curriculum are still with us, although increasingly under challenge. Are there still any links with the puritan/dissenting thought-world? In politics, psychology and education, has the growing secularism of the last century eroded all traces of this heritage?

Dissent in politics

In Britain, the nonconformist heirs of puritanism are no longer a major social force today – as they were a hundred years ago (see Chapter 5). Adherents are now fewer than they have ever been: nonconformist communities, like Anglican, unexpectedly increased in numbers towards the middle of the twentieth century but declined markedly between 1965 and 2000 (Brown 2001: 188).

Culturally, however, the traditional values of Victorian middle-class nonconformity seem to have been more tenacious, especially after 1980. Whether vociferous defence of these values has grown as the institutions and practices surrounding them – around organised religion, moral obligations (not least in sexual morality), personal responsibility, the traditional family, selective education, hard work, thrift, a conventional view of a 'successful' life with its categories of 'winners' and 'losers' – have become increasingly threatened is a speculation which could be taken further. Direct political influence seems also to have played a part. The result of the 2004 presidential election in the USA has underscored the electoral support which George Bush received from tradition-inclined protestant communities of the south and mid-west. A crucial contribution here, as in the 2000 election, seems to have come from the Scots-Irish, who number some 30 million people, and are descended from Ulster Presbyterians who emigrated *en masse* to the USA in the 1700s (Webb 2004).

Commentators on British politics have drawn attention to conservative nonconformist influence on the Thatcher regime from 1979 to 1990, emanating in policies favouring so-called traditional middle-class values. In the educational sphere these included support for selection and for the traditional subject-based curriculum.

That Margaret Thatcher was attached to the ideals of the Nonconformist Victorian middle classes is not surprising. Her father was a grocer in Grantham, Lincolnshire, a Methodist lay preacher who prided himself on 'hard work, high standards and integrity' (Campbell 2000: 15).

> He was not just a Methodist, but specifically a Wesleyan: an important distinction. In the middle of the nineteenth century Methodism had split. The Methodist Free Churches, which rejected authority and tended to be politically progressive, seceded from the main body. The Wesleyans, by contrast, adhered to what they held to be the tradition of John Wesley – who never wholly abandoned the Church of England – and became increasingly conservative, both theologically and socially. … Alfred Roberts' Methodism was a religion of personal salvation. His preaching, by all accounts, was fundamentalist, Bible-based, concerned with the individual's responsibility to God for his own behaviour. It was not a social gospel, but an uncompromisingly individualistic moral code which underpinned an individualistic approach to politics and commerce. A man's duty was to keep his own soul clean, mind his own business and care for his own family.
>
> (ibid.: 15–16)

Educationally, the most important innovation of the Thatcher era was the introduction of the National Curriculum in 1988. There is a curious story about how it came into existence, which touches on the puritan/dissenting tradition in its Scottish form. How strong a link should be claimed is another matter, and coincidence may play a greater part than cause. I will go into the details of this story below.

Whether there is any vestige of this tradition in the Labour administration which has been in power since 1997 is a further question. No doubt one should not make too much of the Scottish Presbyterian background of its former leader John Smith, or of the facts that the Chancellor, Gordon Brown's, father was a minister in the Presbyterian church in Scotland; that Tony Blair's mother, Hazel Corscadden, was from a protestant family in Donegal; and that David Blunkett, who was Secretary of State for Education before becoming Home Secretary, has in common with Thatcher a Methodist background, having trained and practised in his youth as a Methodist lay preacher. On the other hand, it has become clear over the last eight years that continuities with Thatcherite policies, not least in education, have been as remarkable as divergences from them. One example – of particular relevance to the theme of this book – is the Gifted and Talented initiative which Blunkett introduced in Labour's first term and which is still flourishing. I say more about this below.

Meanwhile I turn to recent developments in ideas about intelligence, especially as these affect the work of schools and teachers.

Intelligence and education

One might think that the Galtonian tradition of thinking about intelligence must have suffered a fatal setback in the mid-1970s with claims that Cyril Burt had fabricated evidence, favourable to the hereditarian case, about correlations between the IQs of identical twins reared apart (Kamin 1977; Hearnshaw 1979). But by the turn of the century the old association between intelligence and IQ was still influential in some quarters.

In 1994 Richard Herrnstein and Charles Murray published their *The Bell Curve* (Herrnstein and Murray 1994). This worked with the traditional, Galtonian notion of intelligence, achieving notoriety for its repetition of a claim first made by Arthur Jensen (1969) that the 15-point difference between the mean IQ scores of the white European population of the USA and those of the African-American population was largely due to innate factors.

More generally, the strides made in molecular genetics, partly via the US Human Genome Project (1990–2003), which sought to identify the roughly 20,000–25,000 genes in human DNA, have encouraged hopes of discovering the genetic basis of intelligence. Robert Plomin has been prominent in this research, having been credited in newspaper articles with the impending discovery of the first 'gene for IQ' (Richardson 1998: 174). As with the *Bell Curve* study, research in molecular genetics has taken IQ as a measure of intelligence, thus also committing itself to the traditional concept. As Richardson (1999: 77) writes, 'One reason for my misgivings ... is the idea of trying to identify genes for a character that no one can define'. He goes on to criticise the idea that 'genes (at least those related to evolved characters) can be identified as isolated, independent and additive charges ... the role of a gene in a complex character will vary with the genomic and environmental context' (ibid.).

Other recent research on intelligence has abandoned the traditional model in favour of a more catholic account. In the world of education the most influential of these alternatives has undoubtedly been Howard Gardner's 'multiple intelligences' (MI) theory (Gardner 1983). This identifies some eight or nine types of intelligence: not only the logico-mathematical and linguistic kinds said to be measured by IQ, but, also musical, spatial, bodily-kinaesthetic, intrapersonal, interpersonal, to which had been added by the turn of the century naturalist and possibly existential intelligences (Gardner 1999). Individuals have different strengths in these abilities, dependent partly on innate differences in the structure of their brains, and partly on their different developmental histories within the different intelligences.

This idea that children come hard-wired with a whole array of abilities in varying prominence has proven especially appealing to many teachers in schools. It has encouraged them to classify pupils according to their intellectual strengths and 'learning styles' and to vary their pedagogy and sometimes their curricular offerings accordingly.

I have fundamental misgivings about the truth of MI theory, which I have explored more fully elsewhere (White 1998, 2006). The basic one is that, surprisingly perhaps, Gardner has given no good reason in favour of picking out the 'intelligences' he does. What they have in common seems to have more to do with Gardner's way (and this is only one way out of many possible ways) of classifying important kinds of intellectual (including artistic) activity, than with close observation of individuals and their abilities. The roots of MI theory lie not in empirical psychology but in ethical judgements.

MI theory picks up on the important truth that intelligence is not especially to be connected with the kinds of logical, mathematical and linguistic ability picked out by the IQ, but has a far wider application in human life. The bare idea that intelligence can take many forms is both welcome and true. But it's hardly news. Many philosophers and psychologists have agreed with common sense that intelligence has a lot to do with being flexible in pursuit of one's goals. You want to buy a washing machine and check things out rather than rush into it. You vary your tactics against your opponent when you are playing tennis. Your child is being bullied at school and you work out what's best to do. There are innumerable forms in which intelligence can be displayed. We don't need a new theory to tell us this. Long ago the philosopher Gilbert Ryle (1949: 48) reminded us that 'the boxer, the surgeon, the poet and the salesman' engage in their own kinds of intelligent operation, applying 'their special criteria to the performance of their special tasks'. All this is now widely accepted.

This means that there are as many types of human intelligence as there are types of human goal. Gardner has corralled this huge variety into a small number of categories. In doing so, he has also weighted things towards intellectual and artistic pursuits at the expense of more practical ones. It is not surprising that his theory has been so warmly received in the world of education, since his categories of intelligence are close to the traditional categories of the subject-based school curriculum. At the same time, the enthusiasm with which many teachers embrace the idea that there are innate differences in the mix of intelligences with which their pupils are endowed leads them to classify pupils according to innate potential in a way which, although more pluralistic than the classifications of the Galtonian tradition, threatens to be almost as constricting.

Despite its self-proclaimed emancipation from this traditional view about the nature of intelligence, MI theory has central features in common with it. In its belief in the innate basis of the intelligences and in its intellectualistic orientation, it matches two features of Burt's definition of intelligence as 'innate, general, cognitive ability' (Burt 1955: 265), differing only in its rejection of general ability in favour of multiple abilities.

Contemporary intelligence research moves in other directions than the two just described – IQ based accounts, and MI theory. Robert Sternberg's work, for instance, gives practical intelligence the attention it deserves given its central importance in human life (see Sternberg 1996). In none of various kinds of recent research mentioned in this section have I come across any personal links with the puritan/dissenting world. This is not to say, as we have just seen, that ideas from the time of the pioneers which may be traceable to that religious tradition are not still at work in some contemporary writings.

The Gifted and Talented

Before leaving intelligence and passing to the school curriculum, I come back to the British government's Gifted and Talented (G and T) programme.

In 1999 David Blunkett as Secretary of State for Education inaugurated a National Strategy on Gifted and Talented Education. It was intended to improve the range and quality of gifted and talented education in England and has a number of strands, including special programmes for these pupils. A National Academy for Gifted and Talented Youth (NAGTY) has been set up for this at the University of Warwick for the most able 5 per cent of pupils in the country.

The government's Gifted and Talented initiative is in direct line of descent from Galton's study of eminent individuals in *Hereditary Genius*. Like Galton, Burt, Terman and others, the government is paying particular attention to people perceived as the most intellectually able. The motives are different: the cloudy desire to save the nation, or the human race, by improving its best stock has given way to something more hard-headed. In the DfES's own words, one of the aims is to 'help to attract parents back to inner city maintained secondary schools' (DfES 2002: 1). But the very fact that the government thinks that some middle-class parents can be wooed by a policy which assumes that they see their children as gifted and talented shows the persistence within the culture of a certain cast of mind – the belief that one's children are different from the ordinary run of children, that they have gifts which destine them for success, or would do so, provided those gifts were recognised and appropriately catered for. The old notions of belonging to an elect and of being rescued from a life of failure are not far in the background. The terms 'gifted' and 'talented' themselves have, as we saw in Chapter 2, religious connotations, belonging to an earlier thought-world in which personal salvation was partly a function of having discovered one's God-given vocation in line with one's God-given gifts. For most parents of G and T children today the religious associations have no doubt fallen away, but 'scientific' rationales have sometimes come to replace them, reliant, for instance, on the theory of 'multiple intelligences', already discussed. The latter lends itself particularly well to a belief in special talents in different areas. It is picked out by name in the DfES document, in its remark that the National Strategy 'is flexible enough to accommodate multi-dimensional models of ability, such as the 'multiple intelligences' approach' (DfES 2002: 2).

How, according to the British government, are 'gifted and talented' students identified? It states (ibid.) that the focus of its National Strategy for Gifted and Talented Education

> is explicitly on ability rather than attainment or achievement, so under-achieving pupils are a priority. Broadly speaking, 'gifted' pupils are defined as those with ability in one or more curriculum subjects, while 'talented' pupils are those with talents in sports or creative arts.

The strategy concentrates both on the 5–10 per cent in each school and the 5–10 per cent nationally who fall into these categories. The National Academy for Gifted and Talented Youth, as we have seen, caters for the latter group.

Why the distinction between 'gifted' and 'talented', as thus defined? And are the two categories seen as of equal status? To judge by the extensive use of the terms 'gifted children' and 'gifted education' the main emphasis appears to be on academic ability. This is what one would expect, given the greater cachet that is and has always been accorded to knowledge-based subjects (see Chapter 5, and also the discussion of the school curriculum in the next section. It is also interesting that the DfES definition, just quoted, uses the term 'curriculum subjects' in such a way as to exclude PE, music and art). In an article on 'Gifted Education: the English Model', the Director of the National Academy for Gifted and Talented Youth, Professor Deborah Eyre (Eyre 2004) states that 'today's gifted pupils are tomorrow's social, intellectual, economic and cultural leaders and their development cannot be left to chance'. She goes on: 'A major reason for a dedicated educational focus on gifted and talented pupils is their potential to play a leading role in their adult lives. If England is to be successful in a globalized world then it will need to produce leaders who can compete with the best'. This rationale for the programme reminds us again of the Galtonian project. It shares with it the belief that future leaders must be identified early and special provision made for them. In this it is also reminiscent of Morant's project.

By the end of 2004 the path to leadership was made easier for NAGTY members by requiring sixth-formers applying to university to confirm whether or not they belonged to the Academy. 'The Academy hopes that this will enable universities to better identify the most able pupils' (*TES*, 3 December 2004). It is not surprising in the light of such developments that 37,000 pupils were registered by this date with the Academy. Neither is it surprising that, as Eyre says (ibid.), NAGTY students

> see themselves as being educated in their 'home' school and also through NAGTY. 'My school friends and my NAGTY friends'. This second group comprises friends from all over England and from a variety of different backgrounds. For NAGTY students education is not only locally based it is regional, national and international and individuals become more mobile in pursuit of the specialist provision that will enable them to fulfil their potential.

How justified is what seems to be this deliberate fostering of an élite?

If there is some fair and reliable way of singling out the gifted and talented, such that it can be reasonably guaranteed that they will possess the qualities we are looking for, e.g. leadership qualities, and that other pupils are unlikely to attain these, the policy looks defensible. Is there such a way?

The government definition, quoted above, goes beyond actual achievement to include potential achievement. It describes this as 'ability'. This is because current policy makes the identification of underachieving able pupils a priority.

The 'actual achievement' criterion seems less problematic than the 'potential' one, but it still faces the difficulty that it is likely to favour children from more educated homes, including those whose parents take special steps to help them make the grade. It is the same problem as beset the 11+ exam.

This is why the notion of 'potential' achievement is important for a government, like the present Labour administration, eager to identify highly able, but underachieving, children from unprivileged backgrounds. But how do you identify what a child *might* achieve? What evidence do you go by?

Only two kinds of evidence are possible: behavioural and non-behavioural. The first is evidence of what the child is doing or has done. This is problematic, because we are back with actual achievements rather than potential ones. The force of this can be seen in a QCA checklist of characteristics of G and T pupils, whether achievers or underachievers (www.nc.uk.net/gt/general/01_characteristics.htm). The list, which it is recommended should be used with caution, is a long one. Its first four items, which are typical, are that gifted and talented children and young people are likely to:

- think quickly and accurately;
- work systematically;
- generate creative working solutions;
- work flexibly, processing unfamiliar information and applying knowledge, experience and insight to unfamiliar situations.

Teachers using characteristics like these, or teachers who use tests of cognitive ability, are still identifying G and T pupils by actual achievement, and so do not avoid the problem of privileging children from more educated homes. – Unless, that is, the extensive room for interpretation which categories like those from the QCA create allows subjective judgements on teachers' parts to creep in, allowing those impressed by the scheme's concern for the underprivileged to skew their identifications, perhaps unconsciously, in that direction.

The only other kind of evidence could be non-behavioural. Here one looks not at the outside of the child, as it were, to see what actions and activities he or she engages in; one focuses on internal features like characteristics of the brain, or – if the mind is different from the brain – of the mind. We have come across many examples of this approach in this book. It is the approach which Galton took, and which his followers – including his contemporary followers looking for the genetic basis of intelligence – have taken. It is an approach for which MI theory, with its suggestion of hard-wired intelligences, provides a new rationale.

The snag with this non-behavioural way of trying to identify highly able children is that the evidence required is as yet lacking. There is no reliable evidence of a genetic basis for differences in general intelligence or in any of the MI intelligences. This is why in practice teachers use the behavioural route, since evidence here *is* available (if not unproblematic, as we have seen).

As well as these problems in identifying G and T pupils, there are also issues about the wisdom of demarcating a certain group of children as special and having privileges others do not have. Is it supposed that they fall into a category with neat boundaries, such that all who fall within it are gifted and all who do not are not gifted? If so, further grounds have to be provided to show that this is how things are. If not, and giftedness is a matter of degree, why fix the percentage of the pupil population to whom the strategy is directed at 5–10 per cent in each school and 5–10 per cent nationally? Why exclude pupils who are nearly as 'gifted' between 10 and 20 per cent, or the somewhat less gifted between 20 and 30 per cent?

There may well be administrative and political reasons for drawing the boundaries where they are. This has certainly happened in the past: the figure of 5–10 per cent is somewhere between the percentage of children selected for Morant's secondary schools and those selected for grammar school education after 1944. Whatever the reasons, it is surprising that a Labour government has not considered the wider social effects of giving a small group of children a special label which carries with it all sorts of favourable associations as well as actual privileges. There must be many thousands of children who are not far from the 5–10 per cent boundary who now see themselves as 'not gifted'. How do they understand this? Do they think of themselves as unlucky in a competition in which in different circumstances they might have been among the winners? Or as lacking by nature some precious ingredient?

The Gifted and Talented initiative can be seen as the latest manifestation of Galton's project, taken up by Terman, Burt and many others, of identifying an intellectual élite and making special educational provision for them. If the hypothesis powering this book is correct, its deepest roots may go as far back as the thought-world of radical protestantism.

The school curriculum today

I turn now from intelligence and giftedness to recent developments in the English school curriculum. In 1988, the idea that school education should be an induction into a broad range of academic subjects finally prevailed. In the nineteenth century it was horns-locked with the view that the schooling of the élite should be based on classics. In the first half of the twentieth, following Morant's reforms in élite secondary education, it won out over its rival. In the second half, it permeated most of secondary education, élite or otherwise. Since 1988 it has become legally mandatory not only for all state secondary schools but also for all primary. Its triumph is complete.

Not that this was inevitable. Other, more defensible, ways of organising the curriculum could have succeeded instead. The 1988 curriculum was accompanied by a national assessment system, beginning in the primary school and culminating in public examinations at 16 and 18, which was itself tied in with national league tables, whereby schools could be compared with each other on their test and exam scores. This whole package of innovations, by design or by result, has favoured the middle classes. Their children are often better able than others to cope with the kind of academic curriculum historically familiar to parts of this group; and their parents are often better able to use league table evidence, combined with greater opportunities of persuasion, and even where necessary of moving house, to get their children into high-performing schools. Allocating children according to their intelligence to different types of school has thus been replaced by more complex but no less effective devices. Possibly connected with this, the gap between the proportions of middle-class and working-class children entering higher education almost doubled between 1994–5 and 2001–2 (Galindo-Rueda *et al.* 2004). And it is still the case that many young people, to whom academic schooling is an alien world, leave formal education as soon as they can. England is near the bottom of the list of twenty-nine developed states for young people continuing in education and training at age seventeen.

The 1988 curriculum arrived virtually aimless. Kenneth Baker laid it down that ten mainly traditional subjects were to constitute the National Curriculum from age five through to sixteen and that was that. No justifications were provided. In the Conservative circles in which mutterings, and more than mutterings, about reinstating traditional education had been heard for two decades, none were needed. The traditional curriculum was simply taken to be a good thing.

The 1988 Act did, it is true, lay down what the National Curriculum was for, so you might think that would give some rationale for why eleven years of compulsory maths and eleven years of geography and so on were thought so desirable. The aims were:

- [to] promote the spiritual, moral, cultural, mental and physical development of pupils at the school and of society;
- [and to] prepare such pupils for the opportunities, responsibilities and experiences of adult life.

(DES 1989: para. 16)

Churlish critics have objected that these were slightly on the thin side. Compelling children to spend years mastering all these academic subjects is not an ethically insignificant step and needs good arguments in favour. In effect, all we got were the ten so-called 'foundation' subjects. These were arranged in a hierarchy of importance. Three of them, English, mathematics and science, were 'core' subjects. In official documents the other seven were presented – and their successors still are – in a definite pecking order. Alphabetical order is never officially used. The full 1988 list went:

English, mathematics, science, technology, history, geography, (from age 11) a modern foreign language, art, music, physical education.

This order of presentation reveals the persistence of ancient ways of thinking. It shows the Old Dissenting tradition still extant.

The mind comes first, the body last. Why? Three hundred years ago, the question would not have been worth raising. The purpose of education was preparation for salvation – and salvation was of the soul, not of its animal appendage. These days, though, why relegate physical matters to the last spot? It is not as though we don't care that so many children are getting obese, take little exercise, eat the wrong sorts of food, as long as their minds are honed as carefully as possible. We do rightly care about the body – and given the basic importance of physical health in all our lives, there is as much reason to make physical education No. 1 as to make it No. 10.

On to the mind and the other nine subjects. At No. 9 comes music, and at No. 8 art. The aesthetic subjects are just above the body and below the transmission of knowledge. Why? Three hundred years ago, this would have made abundant sense – except that music and art would not have been on the map at all. Education was for salvation; and salvation depended on an understanding of God's world and putting that understanding to good use in furthering his purposes. Art was a distraction, a temptation toward sensuous delights which would take one away from life's true meaning. The positioning of music and art in our curriculum reflects in miniature the history of school education in the intervening centuries. Broadly, they acknowledge the change that the Romantic movement of the late eighteenth and early nineteenth centuries began to introduce into the culture (Taylor 1989: ch. 21, 23): the idea that the arts, together with the aesthetic appreciation of nature, help human beings in an age losing its faith to retain some hold on spiritual, or life-enhancing, values. Not that this became reflected in school art and music, if at all, until well into the twentieth century. Music secured a place in the elementary curriculum in the nineteenth partly because of the worries people in ecclesiastical circles had about the quality of choral singing in church (Plummeridge and Swanwick 2004: 128–9); and art as a subject in mass education had originally much more to do with training in hand–eye coordination to do with industrially applicable skills than with the appreciation of great masters (Steers 2004: 33).

English, at No. 1, is also partly an aesthetic subject, so the priority of knowledge over the arts in the hierarchy is not clear-cut. Even here, however, the practice of treating literature as yet another form of knowledge, which in Chapter 5 we saw occurring in some Dissenting Academies, has lodged deep in later ways of presenting English Literature, down to our times. Even today, enjoying fiction and poetry for its own sake often takes second place to being good at critical analysis.

The most favoured among the 1988 subjects are patently there to transmit knowledge, and for the most part propositional knowledge. Modern foreign languages and technology are the main exceptions here. These apart, we are left with mathematics, science, history and geography, the first two, at positions 2 and 3, being core subjects, and the latter two in respectable slots at 5 and 6. At the heart of the curriculum is what was at the heart of the dissenters' curriculum in England and Scotland in the eighteenth century: the acquisition of knowledge about the world. And – as in the dissenters' curriculum – the utility and applicability of the knowledge, although acknowledged, is not the first consideration. Everyone makes some use in later life of the basic arithmetic they learned, but few go on to use their geometry or their algebra unless they become some kind of specialist for whom mathematics is important. The same is true of school science. These subjects, like history and geography, are there primarily because they reveal the nature of the world – as in the eighteenth century. The old assumption that knowledge learned for this reason helps one's salvation-worthiness has long since fallen away (although it was still there in Fred Clarke's (1923: 2) remark that 'the ultimate reason for teaching Long Division to little Johnny is that he is an immortal soul').

The persistence of older patterns may not stop here. Why are mathematics and science at Nos 2 and 3 and history and geography at Nos 5 and 6? Why not the other way round? In the dissenters' thinking about the curriculum – going back to Ramism – abstract forms of knowledge had precedence over concrete.

I must stick to my promise of going further into the origins of the National Curriculum. According to one newspaper report of the time, the inspiration for this historic event came from Mrs Thatcher's hairdresser, worried about his daughter's poor progress at a South London primary school. This fired Mrs Thatcher, we are told, to put her money on something more basic than the ten-subject National Curriculum which actually materialised: a core of English, mathematics and science. The Secretary of State for Education at the time was Kenneth Baker. According to him, it was only his wife, a former secondary school teacher, who saved the nation from this meagreness. Writing of her in a later article in the *Daily Telegraph* (June 1 1996), he said: 'When I used to come back bloody and bowed from these meetings' – he was talking of his interactions with the prime minister – 'she would say, "No, you must stick out for a broad-based curriculum." I think this is the first time I've mentioned that. I should have acknowledged her role in this much more.'

What was her role? Why did she favour sticking out for a broad curriculum? Seeing from Kenneth Baker's autobiography (Baker 1993: 20) that his wife Mary is Scottish and 'has ensured that our children, who have all been educated at Scottish universities, are aware and proud of their ancestry', I wrote to him and told him about my historical thesis about the origins of the broad subject-based curriculum, including the role which the dissenting, including Scottish, tradition, via nineteenth century developments and the 1904 changes, had played in 1988. Did he think there was any link with his remarks about his wife?

He kindly wrote back at some length, confirming his disagreement with Margaret Thatcher and his determination to have a broad-based curriculum. He obtained it through the 'sheer exhaustion' of his cabinet colleagues, who, when they discussed the matter, 'reminisced from their own experience of school, which in many cases was not particularly relevant'. His own belief that children 'should be exposed to the widest range of cultural experiences as possible' was strongly reinforced by his wife 'who had been brought up in the Scottish tradition. She had attended school in England but nevertheless took Scottish Highers and went up to St Andrews. I received sterling reinforcement from her in the great Cabinet battles'.

The 1988 National Curriculum was built around its ten, largely traditional, subjects without any rationale for these in terms of wider aims. It looks as if it was simply assumed – as many people have assumed, including myself in the past – that something like the traditional pattern is best. How far do such unquestioning assumptions reflect deeper prejudgements within the culture, associated with the dissenting curricular tradition?

An important step in the history of the National Curriculum took place in 2000, with the publication in the new *Handbook for Teachers* (DfEE/QCA 1999) of an extensive set of 'values, aims and purposes' for the school curriculum (including religious education as well as the National Curriculum subjects). This followed the desire expressed by many teachers in the 1990s to have a clearer picture of what the National Curriculum was meant to be for. The new aims present a many-sided picture of the kinds of understanding and character traits which people will need in our society in order to lead a full and flourishing life as an individual, as a worker and as a citizen. Some 60 per cent of the items describe personal qualities, 30 per cent different kinds of knowledge, and 10 per cent skills. Although the aims are presented merely as a list – with a minimum of explanation, and although they would ideally need a full rationale as well as a thorough critical analysis, they are a good first shot at aims suitable for participants in a modern liberal democratic society.

The problem with the aims is that in their first four years they had no impact on the curriculum itself. If a government goes so far as to lay out its aims for schooling in an unprecedentedly extensive way, one would imagine it took them seriously. One would expect it to make sure that they were firmly incorporated into the curriculum. It now had the opportunity to monitor the curriculum subjects that already existed and see how far they were in sync with these overarching goals. One would expect it, too, to look more broadly at other ways of organising the curriculum in addition to subjects, if they are better able to meet the aims.

By the end of 2004 none of this had been done. An investigation, which I carried out in later association with a group of colleagues (White 2004), showed gross mismatches between the new overall aims on the one hand and the official internal aims and curricular specifics of most of the subjects. Only in the new subjects of PSHE (personal, social and health education) and citizenship and in the nearly new subjects of design and technology and ICT (information and communication technology) was there anything like a good match. Against this yardstick, most of the traditional subjects revealed themselves as locked into their own time-worn *modi operandi*, powered by internal aims that often failed to withstand critical scrutiny, and with much of their content apparently included because it always had been included. It was quite indefensible by the post-2000 criteria.

If the government takes its own aims for the school curriculum seriously, one would expect it to make them central to its curriculum planning. It is where the planning should start from. If it starts somewhere else – with subjects, say – the question always arises: what is this structure *for*? How does it relate to what schooling should be about? Better, then, to go straight for the aims – to get as clear as possible about these, and then – *only* then – think about what vehicles are best suited to realise them. There is no *a priori* reason to think that the traditional subjects – or any subjects at all – best fit this bill. The whole issue about vehicles needs to be thoroughly thrashed out. No doubt the traditional subjects will still get a piece of the action, and perhaps quite a large piece. It would be an odd education in which pupils learned nothing about the structure of the physical world or the history of their own society. But which parts of science, history and the other subjects would survive the winnowing; whether there are good grounds for continuing to teach them in their ancient confines rather than in collaborative units with other areas of knowledge; for how many years a separate subject would need to be taught on a compulsory basis to all pupils – to these questions there is no simple answer, certainly no answer that can be given before all options have been diligently explored.

Northern Ireland is so far the only part of the UK which has made a start on an aims-based curriculum. This, if implemented, will oblige each subject to work to internal aims in line with overall aims to do with personal development, education for employment, and education for citizenship. A more radical step would be not to assume a subject basis at all for a National Curriculum but work with whatever kind of vehicle best suits the aims.

Whether this will occur in England in, say, the first half of the twenty-first century is anyone's guess. Militating against it is the sheer institutional power of the traditional school subjects as a force against change. From the late nineteenth century, as the 'modern' curriculum became entrenched in the expanding world of middle-class secondary education, subject associations began to grow up in discipline after discipline. Not only did they bind together school teachers of these subjects: they also connected them within the same organisation with university teachers in the same field. Secondary schools became university recruiting grounds for bright students specialising at sixth-form level in geography and mathematics and other subjects. The twentieth century – the period of middle-class dominance in education as in other fields – saw the consolidation of subject-power as, in many quarters, a taken-for-granted part of the educational scene. The culmination came after 1988, when the ten foundation subjects were guaranteed a place – to which they had no legal right before – in the curriculum of all state schools. What was originally the dissenters' curriculum, which in the eighteenth century was at upper secondary/undergraduate level and intended for an excluded fraction of the population, and mainly for clerics within this group, has in the intervening centuries expanded downwards through the age group and outwards through the constantly enlarging middle classes, consolidating its institutional power throughout. In 1988 its sway was extended at a stroke – so that it expanded from secondary into primary education and now covered a whole nation.

Knowledge of the world is important. But as an educational goal it ought to take its place among other things which are also important. As adults, not all of us, by any means, are interested in exploring the infinitesimal calculus, or the evolution of life, or the history of the Renaissance. In fact, a scholarly turn of mind is not all that common – and there is no reason why it should be. Human life is so full of other worthwhile pursuits that it is not at all surprising that only a minority goes for the pursuit of knowledge in a serious way. Why, then, should schools tilt things so much in favour of this particular life-ideal? It is hard to justify the bias, but easier to explain it. I hope the argument of this book has helped to do this.

Although I have chided the Labour administration for not acting on its own overall aims between 2000 and 2004, there are signs in early 2005, the time in which I am now writing, that things may change. The QCA has now launched its *Futures* programme, inviting widespread discussion on the future of the school curriculum. It focuses among other things on such questions as: 'How effectively do subjects contribute to the wider aims, purposes and values of education?' 'How might we organise the national entitlement to deliver the curriculum's aims, purposes and values of the curriculum?' 'How can we adequately define future learner needs across subject boundaries?' It has also organised a series of seminars largely for subject specialists, a main remit being how the various subjects contribute to the aims, values and purposes of the curriculum.

We must wait and see whether the QCA initiative has repercussions in future government policy. Meanwhile the present government announced in February 2005 that it rejected the central recommendation of the Tomlinson Enquiry on education and training 14–19 (DfES 2004) that separate academic and vocational routes through the qualifications system should be brought together under an overarching diploma. The decision to maintain a dual system preserves the integrity of the academic subject-based curriculum and its traditional reputation for superiority over alternatives. It may be interpreted as the final chapter so far in the story of that curriculum from its puritan beginnings.

Success in life

The school curriculum is not a thing in itself. It is a vehicle to realise larger aims. When we ask what those aims should be – what schools are for – we quickly reach rock-bottom questions about what kind of society we want and what kind of life is best for the individual. The school curriculum is – or should be – a vehicle to enable young people not only to lead a fulfilled personal life, but also to help other people, as friends, parents, workers and as citizens, to lead as fulfilled a life as their own.

I imagine few would object to this. The difficulty is, we don't all see eye to eye on *what it is* to lead a fulfilled life. Here, too, remnants of the puritan/dissenting thought-world are still buried in our own.

Take the notion of success. As we saw in Chapter 2, New England parents in the seventeenth century wanted their children, as they put it, 'to do well'; and we have the same ambition for our own. Doing well in the earlier period was a religious concept. It meant living a godly life. It meant following one's vocation, doing what God has called one to do to one's best ability. We, too, make a tie between doing well in life and vocational success, although the religious connotations have largely gone. Like the puritans, too, we also make a connexion between both of these things and education at school and university. In our case, it helps us to 'get on' via the examination system, to hold down a 'good job'. In the puritan tradition, education – at home, in the academy and via apprenticeship – passed on the knowledge of God's world required for election, including the knowledge necessary for one's vocation as minister, farmer or apothecary.

'She has never stopped working 19 hours a day,' says her friend Lord Archer. 'She has nothing else in life. She can't stop and she doesn't know how to. She starts at 6 a.m. and they have to drag her to bed at night' (Paul Vallely in *The Independent* 27 May 1995). As with Margaret Thatcher, hard, unremitting work was central to the puritan life. It still is for many of us. We take it as natural that, once our education is over, we will – if we can find it – be going into paid work which will fill much of our life until retirement. From this point of view, the success of women's liberation over the last half century has made no difference. Until then, the hard, unremitting work that women did was almost wholly in the home – just as it had been when puritan culture began to form our modern conception of the affection-based family. Since then, women tend to work just as hard, but now outside the home as well as within it.

How far should we welcome or reject these relics of older attitudes towards work? Has the protestant work ethic had its day? My young friend Chris, who is an astonishingly good surfer and can negotiate the big waves of Mundakka and Hawaii with fearlessness and grace, would no doubt say it had. But is he right?

The salvationist reason for endless hard work is now behind us. Has anything taken its place? Whenever I meet an old retired colleague he tells me that he is still writing as much as ever: 'yesterday was a good day: I managed 3,500 words' – and so on. He is a driven man, a workaholic. I am sure he does not have his Judgement Day in mind. He just enjoys the relentlessness. It is how he wants to live, his preference.

Hard work can be personally valuable if autonomously chosen. The justification leads us back to the ways different individuals have of finding personal fulfilment. Not all of us are workaholically inclined and there is no reason why we should be. Accomplishing something with one's life – a constant stream of publications as with my colleague, making a garden, teaching people – is an ingredient of a fulfilled life, but not the only one. So – among other things – is enjoying being with one's friends, using one's senses in aesthetic or other pursuits, physical exercise. Most of us are drawn to all these things to some extent, making our own resolutions about the importance we attach to each. Some of us are more monomaniac, weighting getting things done above all else. My colleague is one of those. But there is no legitimate ethical pressure on the rest of us to be like this.

The life of ceaseless industry *can* have a justification, but it is a very different one from the puritan's. It comes from a different ethical perspective. It starts from what is personally fulfilling for the individual, not from moral duty. But personal fulfilment also lies, you may reply, at the root of the puritan perspective. Why do one's moral duty and work hard unless for salvation and beatitude in the next life? The difference from the contemporary justification is that the latter assumes this is the only life we have. As autonomous persons, within this confined time-frame some of us find our highest fulfilment in industriousness.

Another way the two justifications differ is that the contemporary – or liberal – one does not insist that *everyone*, or virtually everyone, spend their life in hard labour. For the puritan, this was a religious duty incumbent on all. As such, a distinction which is of the first importance to us today is not made, or at best is blurred. This is the distinction between work that is autonomously chosen and work that is not. The liberal justification only applies to autonomous work. The life of ceaseless industry is a good one only for those who choose it: no reason has been given for imposing it on those who do not. A faith that saw this-worldly ethics in terms of moral obligation rather than personal flourishing was different. Given, too, its belief in God-given stations in life, it made no difference whether one's labouring took place in, say, living out one's passion for the improvement of education or in dragging coal along a mine shaft.

For many of us it makes all the difference. Work you ideally don't want to do – non-autonomous work – is a brake on the good life, a barrier to it that can be overcome only by some desideratum like money. I feel we need to be clearer about this – at least in Britain, and probably America, too. The culture is still dominated by work, most of it non-autonomous. We still think of it, here and there, as 'good for the soul', however boring or unpleasant it may be. While France has introduced a thirty-five hour week, British working hours are still among the longest in Europe. We need to de-fetishise non-autonomous work, to reduce it to what is necessary, collectively and individually, for a flourishing life (White 1997).

Autonomous work aside, people work not only for money, but also for status. This happens everywhere; but in Britain part of the story goes back to the experience of puritan/dissenting communities, whose religiously inspired diligence in work led to increased affluence, which, reinforcing their sense of being a people apart, deepened the gulf between them and the poor below them. Hard work – *their* kind of work, that is, not the drudgery of the poor – became associated with superior social status. It earned them badges of rank: comfortable houses, carriages, better education for their children.

The snobbery, the class-consciousness that foreigners have associated with the English has some of its roots in this story. As the nonconformist middle classes – of higher status like the Galtons, lower like the Burts – were reintegrated into national life in the nineteenth century, the need to preserve these marks of difference became more urgent. (Galton's own obsession with 'reputation', discussed in Chapter 2, may be an example of this.) Hence by the early twentieth century the receptiveness of the now more disparate middle classes to ways of marking differences between individuals and between social groups, including intelligence tests and the distinction between élite and mass curricula.

A successful, fulfilled life is, in the eyes of some of us today, one in which, among other things, you enjoy benefits you know other people can't afford and partly *because* you know they can't afford them – a second home between the Pyrenees and the Mediterranean, dining out at £60 a head, private education, a centre dress circle seat at the Royal Opera House. It is this notion of success which admen exploit when they associate their products with exclusiveness. Is this conception of a successful life valid? Are these so-called 'positional goods' *genuinely* fulfilment goods?

Personal fulfilment

This takes us into central issues about the nature of human well-being. A fulfilled life has two sorts of requirement. The first is infrastructural. Certain needs have to be met – for adequate food, clean air, health, income, security and so on. The other has to do with the goals one pursues given these needs are satisfied. The goals are the tricky part. One might be inclined to say that a life is more fulfilled the more one succeeds in achieving one's goals. But suppose one of the things you want to engage in is binge-drinking; and suppose you hate yourself for this: you know it's stupid, you want to kill the habit, but you keep finding yourself getting tempted. What this shows is that we can have wants at different levels: there are wants that – at a higher level – we don't want to have.

Is fulfilment, then, a function of satisfying one's desires – not just any old desires, but those with which one can identify, those which are really important to one in one's life? This is where positional goods come in. For some of us, possessing or enjoying things which set us apart from other people, things we know they can't have, is a really important preoccupation. We cannot always satisfy such ambitions. But when we do, does this count towards a fulfilled life? If satisfying one's most important desires is a mark of fulfilment, it must do so.

This may be an unwelcome thought. Can *any* life be a flourishing one, merely given that the person who lives it is able to attain his or her keenest aspirations? What if he wants, all things considered, to spend as much time as he can playing slot machines or gambling in the casino? What if he gets his highest kicks from knowing that others are suffering?

Examples like this challenge the claim that personal fulfilment is satisfying one's preferred desires. What else, though, could it be? An alternative view makes it an objective affair, not wholly dependent on subjective factors like individual preferences. According to this account, certain goods – and only these – are ingredients of personal fulfilment. Individuals' preferences come in at the point where these goods can be weighted differently by different people; but they do not come in *at the start*, that is when the broad contours of fulfilment are being mapped out.

What are these goods? Philosophers who go for the objective account usually include things like (the list varies): close personal relationships, understanding oneself and the world in which one lives, the enjoyment of beauty, accomplishing something with one's life, acting autonomously, working for other people's benefit, physical exercise, the bodily pleasures of food, drink and sex.

This is not the place to go much more deeply into the philosophy of fulfilment. I have explored the topic elsewhere (White 2002b). All I would add is that the objective theory has problems of its own, notably the task of justifying the items in its list. Intuitively they seem acceptable enough. But why these? Are they deducible from our common human nature? Do we know that all human societies have prized intimate personal relationships or leading an autonomous life of one's own? Are some at least of the items – these last two, perhaps – culture-sensitive in some way? If so, is the notion of personal fulfilment at least partly culturally relative? Or can this conclusion be avoided (Raz 1986: ch. 12; 2003: 15–36)?

The philosophy of personal fulfilment, or personal well-being, is much in its infancy. It may seem strange, but it has been only in the last two decades that Anglo-Saxon philosophers have begun assiduously to engage in it. Partly this reflects the domination of ethical philosophy by *moral* issues for most of the past four centuries – a fact in part connected with the continued influence of Christianity over that period and relative lack of interest in personal flourishing in this world as distinct from the next.

Over the next decades we may hope that the controversies now wracking the academy about whether fulfilment is subjective or objective, culturally relative or a constant for our species, will be at least partially resolved. At least we know now that personal fulfilment must be a central topic for politics in general and for educational policy in particular. We want to create a society in which people will be better able to live flourishingly. And – as we saw when discussing the justification of the school curriculum – defensible aims of education have a lot to do with enabling the pupil to lead a life of well-being and helping others to do so too.

Three more points before we leave these more philosophical realms. First, living a personally flourishing life does not imply that one has this as one's *aim*. Flourishing depends on success – in intimate personal relationships, in worthwhile and absorbing activities, in family life, in self-understanding, aesthetic enjoyments and in other things – but being successful can, and as often as not does, occur *as a result of* wholeheartedly engaging in these things, regardless of whether or not one has had one's sights on success from the start. This has enormous implications for how we conceive of educating young people. What is important is not that they have life-targets in mind from an early age and strive to reach them; but that somehow they get involved, caught up, in valuable activities such as those mentioned.

The second point is also educationally significant. If you argue for personal fulfilment as an educational aim, you may be accused of wanting young people to become selfish or self-centred, to live for Number One. But this does not follow. As we have just seen, arguing for personal fulfilment as a systemic aim of schooling does not imply arguing that young people *themselves aim* at their own fulfilment. It points towards getting them absorbed in worthwhile activities and relationships. Being absorbed in this way benefits themselves, certainly, but not typically *only* themselves. Engaging in teaching, farming, parenting, making furniture, friendship is taking part in cooperative activities which serve the well-being of a number of people. In the religious traditions which still inform a more secular age, the demands of morality are sharply segregated from appeals to self-interest, in the shape of earthly happiness or pleasure. Education has been traditionally orientated to the former, moral, aims, the acquisition of knowledge being itself, in protestant circles, a major moral obligation for the Christian child. But there is no good reason for this segregation. Personal fulfilment is no rival to concern for others. If we conceive it aright, they are inseparable.

The third point is that a fulfilled life need be nothing high-flown. There are degrees of fulfilment. One person may lead not quite so flourishing a life as another but still be flourishing. There may some temptation to think that 'real' fulfilment must be of an optimal sort, but there is no reason for going along with this. Educators, for instance, sometimes say that the aim of schooling is 'the fullest development of the individual's potentialities'. Leaving aside possible implicit assumptions here about innate abilities and about their biological unfolding, why 'fullest'? Why, more generally, should the ideal be a life in which one's experience of worthwhile activities and relationships is as rich, as perfect as possible? Why this, rather than experience which is very good even though it could be better? Why aim, like utilitarians, at the greatest happiness of the greatest number (for a recent account, see Layard 2005: ch. 8), when most of us would willingly settle for happiness which is merely great? One strand in this perfectionism goes back to salvationist thinking. Being *nearly* saved can never be good enough: success and failure are absolute categories. In our post-salvationist world, where for most of us this life is the one life we think we have, perfectionism is a hindrance.

Conclusion

Given the comments in the last paragraph, a fulfilled human life is within the reach of nearly all of us. Ill-luck can sometimes prevent it. Ill-luck can never be wholly eliminated, although much can be done to reduce it. If we wished, we could create a society in which virtually everyone is able to lead a reasonably flourishing life. This egalitarian perspective does not necessarily go so far as flat equality of wealth or income, although great discrepancies in these militate against this goal. The perspective is at odds with attempts described in this book to divide people from an early age into [a] those bound for a successful life as conceived by the religious or social conventions of the time – and [b] the negligible remainder, 'democracy's ballast'.

Countries like Britain or the United States are wealthy enough to make personal fulfilment for all – or virtually all – a practical political goal. Basic needs – for food, housing, adequate income etc. – can be satisfied. The burdens of unwanted work can be minimised, partly by changing attitudes towards non-essential consumption, partly by compensating for drudgery by more income or more free time, partly by spreading what burden still remains more evenly across the whole population. Time can be freed up for people to engage in worthwhile activities and relationships of their own choice. Schools can be given the purpose of equipping young people for such a life.

Economically all this is within our grasp. But we remain under the spell of past thinking. This calls instead for division and for classification. Taking it as read that the good life is not for everyone, it demands resources and energy be put into providing its conditions for only some. In so doing, it is likely to misconstrue the nature of human well-being and associate it with greater wealth, comfort, power and recognition than a flourishing life requires. It devises ideological structures, partly to do with the innateness of intelligence and a sacrosanct traditional curriculum, to reinforce the power of the more privileged. Behind this thinking, historically speaking, is discernible the thought-world of salvation. We need to become aware of these roots of our conventional perspectives so that we can, where appropriate, make ourselves free of them.

Conclusion

This book has suggested that roots of both the psychology of intelligence and the subject-based school curriculum are located in the same place – the world of puritanism and its descendants. 'Roots', not '*the* roots'. Historical phenomena have complex antecedents, and this book is not a comprehensive account of all causal factors: it makes a more limited claim. The evidence supporting it is laid out above for others to challenge or confirm.

The early part of the book is about the nature of intelligence. Philosophical doubts about the adequacy of the Galton–Burt notion of it as innate, general intellectual ability prompts the question how such a very odd conception can have originated in the first place. Eugenics is plainly part of the story, but a part which takes us back no further than a magazine article by Galton of 1865. Clues as to what may have been earlier influences come from parallels between this approach to intelligence and ideas, associated with the puritan lineage, about predestination, salvation and damnation, gifts, work and vocation, the family, and education.

That these parallels are almost certainly more than coincidences is suggested by an examination of the family background of early psychologists of intelligence in the Galtonian tradition. Whether one looks at the United States or at Britain, the answer is the same: virtually all of the leading figures in this paradigm had a puritan pedigree. I give full details in Chapter 3. Here I also examine counter-examples, including those in the Galtonian tradition like Charles Spearman who are not known to have radical protestant backgrounds, as well as scholars like Watson and Dewey who came from such backgrounds but *rejected* this approach to mental ability. The fact that nearly all the pioneers are united by a similar religious background has not, as far as I know, been picked up before. This may be partly because most of these men, anxious to put the new discipline of psychology on an objective footing, constantly reiterated the scientific nature of their work. Psychological textbooks have followed them in this, presenting them as among the early creators of a new branch of human science which they helped to split off from philosophy by putting psychology on an empirical rather than an *a priori* basis. Recent work in the history of psychology (e.g. by Fancher (2001) and Richards (2002)) takes the pioneers less at their self-evaluation and puts more weight on continuities between their work and the religious worlds which most of them – but not Goddard, who remained a committed Quaker – ignored or thought they were leaving behind them. I build on this in Chapter 3 to show the underlying religiosity of the eugenics project, following Galton's repeated presentation of this as a new religion; the latent theological basis of Burt's view of the mind; as well as traits of character manifest in the achievements of these early pioneers which seem best explained by reference to their specific religious heritage. I am aware that there is much more digging to be done in mining this seam.

A psychology of intelligence need not centre on abstract thinking. The fact that the Galtonian approach did so becomes more intelligible once one appreciates the role of logic in puritan thought. This goes back as far as the beginnings of puritanism in the sixteenth century. The French logician Ramus, little known outside specialist circles, was hugely influential in the world of ascetic protestantism for his easily assimilable method of organising and passing on knowledge of God's world. This began with the most abstract and general categories and moved thence in a series of dichotomies towards the concrete and particular. Ramist logic was taken up by protestant educators, including Comenius on the continent and puritan teachers in old and New England. It helped to form the peculiar character of puritan and post-puritan education – its interest in subdividing knowledge into manageable chunks for learning, in classification, in time- and money-saving efficiency, in testing what has been learned. It was both a window on to God's created world in general and also a guide to the nature of human thinking, which was held to be pre-programmed along Ramist lines. In the latter respect logic was closely allied with pneumatology, the subject on the puritan/dissenting curriculum which dealt with the nature of both the human and of the divine mind. Both subjects, logic and pneumatology, remained part of this curriculum into the nineteenth century, both in Britain and especially in the United States. There is clear evidence from the latter country that early academic psychology grew out of this older, religious tradition. In Britain, there is also some reason for believing that Galton's early views about individual differences in ability may have been indebted to the phrenologist George Combe, who was of Scottish Presbyterian stock. The interest that grew up in both countries in classifying types of human intellectual ability seems to have been a specification of the more general puritan/dissenting penchant for classifying the phenomena of creation.

Later chapters of the book have more to say about the puritan origins of a school curriculum based on a broad range of discrete subjects. The Ramist legacy included dividing and subdividing realms of knowledge so as to leave no grey areas: each item to be taught and learnt was allocated unambiguously to its own superordinate category. Abstract subjects had pride of place. These included logic, mathematics and, increasingly, natural philosophy or science. Learning was conducted as efficiently as possible, with doses of knowledge administered via tight timetables thanks to which no moment was wasted. All this had a clear religious rationale, in that a comprehensive understanding of God's created world was adjudged a necessary condition of personal salvation. By the eighteenth century, religious colleges in America, Dissenting Academies in England and institutions also called academies in Presbyterian Scotland played their part in this project of personal liberation. In England we can trace a line from here, through middle-class education in the nineteenth century, to the subject-based curriculum typical of secondary schools, and later all state schools, in the twentieth.

In the twentieth century, too, the curriculum story and the intelligence story intermeshed. Although they never worked together, two men sharing a Congregationalist upbringing, Robert Morant and Cyril Burt, helped to bring this about in England. On what were originally eugenic grounds, IQ tests classified children into different intellectual strata and allocated their schooling accordingly. The prize for the most capable was the intellectually demanding subject-based schooling described above. As confidence in the IQ waned, the later part of the twentieth century saw this traditional curriculum extended to more and more children, and finally, in 1988, to all.

This brings the narrative up to our own time. Curriculum and intelligence are today still intertwined in England as elsewhere. This is partly owing to the phenomenal popularity of multiple intelligence theory among teachers and policy-makers. With evidence on every hand of problems in motivating the not-particularly-academically-inclined pupil to take pleasure in the more abstract core subjects of the traditional curriculum, MI theory's assurance that being smart at mathematics is on all fours with being smart at sport, drama, playing guitar and craft activities has been a pedagogical lifeline. MI is also a useful selective tool for those who run the government's Gifted and Talented strategy in English schools. This is in direct line of descent from eugenic attempts from the 1860s to the 1930s to identify and provide for the most intellectually endowed, although for understandable reasons an explicit eugenic rationale is absent. To what extent recent British politics has been directly, if vestigially, influenced by the puritan legacy is unclear – although a far more than residual influence seems evident in Republican circles in George W. Bush's USA.

Across the countries of the United Kingdom there are now, in 2006, signs that the ice-floes of the traditional curriculum are beginning to break up. The curriculum authorities of first Northern Ireland, then Scotland, and now England have been drawn to the idea of an aims-based curriculum. This starts not with the givens of academic subjects but with the goods of a fulfilling life, personally and as worker and citizen. If these projects succeed, traditional subjects will lose the meal ticket granted to them in the twentieth century: in the twenty-first they will have to earn their keep. They will have to show that they, or relevant parts of them, can compete with other forms of curriculum organisation as ways of realising the overall aims.

All this means hard philosophical and practical thinking about the components of a flourishing personal and civic life. Being a success in life rather than a failure is a central value here. It was a central value in the puritan tradition in Britain and America, at first with a predominantly salvationist connotation, and gradually, as religion became increasingly entwined with industrial and commercial developments, in the more worldly sense in which we use the term today. Now there are reasons for moving beyond this money/status/celebrity-focussed life-ideal to a more modest and therefore more universally achievable vision of a successful life, founded on wholehearted and satisfying engagement in self-chosen activities and relationships.

Bibliography

Aldrich, R. (1988) 'The national curriculum: an historical perspective', in D. Lawton and C. Chitty (eds) *The National Curriculum*, London: Institute of Education University of London.

Allen, B.M. (1934) *Sir Robert Morant*, London: Macmillan.

Anderson, R.D. (1983) *Education and Opportunity in Victorian Scotland*, Oxford: Clarendon Press.

Arnold, M. (1869) *Culture and Anarchy*, London: Smith, Elder and Co.

Baker, K. (1993) *The Turbulent Years: My Life in Politics*, London: Faber and Faber.

Barrelet, J.-M. and Perret-Clermont, A.-N. (1996) *Jean Piaget et Neuchâtel*, Lausanne: Payot.

Bebbington, D.W. (1989) *Evangelicalism in Modern Britain: A History from the 1730s to the 1980s*, London: Unwin Hyman.

Bellot, H.H. (1929) *University College, London 1826–1926*, London: University of London Press.

Bevington (n.d.) http: //www.rootsweb.com/~cotswold/MONTACUTE51.htm.

Binfield, C. (1977) *So Down to Prayers: Studies in English Nonconformity 1780–1920*, London: J.M. Dent.

Blum, J.M. (1978) *Pseudoscience and Mental Ability: The Origins and Fallacies of the IQ Controversy*, New York: Monthly Review Press.

Board of Education (1929) *Handbook of Suggestions for the Consideration of Teachers and Others Concerned in the Work of Public Elementary Schools* (6th impression), London: HMSO.

Brett-James, N. (n.d.) *The History of Mill Hill School 1807–1923*, Reigate: Surrey Fine Art Press.

Briggs, J.H.Y. (1994) *The English Baptists of the Nineteenth Century*, Didcot: Baptist Historical Society.

Brookes, M. (2004) *Extreme Measures: The Dark Visions and Bright Ideas of Francis Galton*, New York: Bloomsbury.

Brown, C.G. (2001) *The Death of Christian Britain*, London: Routledge.

Burt, C.L. (1937) *The Backward Child*, New York: Appleton.

—— (1947) *Mental and Scholastic Tests* (second edition; first published 1921), London: Staples Press.

—— (1952) 'Cyril Burt', in E.G. Boring, H.S. Langfeld, H. Werner and R.M. Yerkes (eds) *History of Psychology in Autobiography*, Vol. IV, Worcester, MA: Clark University.

—— (1955) 'The evidence for the concept of intelligence', *British Journal of Educational Psychology*, 25: part 3; reprinted in S. Wiseman (ed.) (1973) *Intelligence and Ability*, Harmondsworth: Penguin.

—— (1959) 'The examination at eleven plus', *British Journal of Educational Studies*, 7(2): 99–117.

—— (1969) 'The mental differences between children', in C.B. Cox and A.E. Dyson (eds) *Black Paper Two*, London: Critical Quarterly Society.

Campbell, J. (2000) *Margaret Thatcher, Vol. One: The Grocer's Daughter*, London: Jonathan Cape.

Cattell, R.B. (1933) *Psychology and Social Progress: Mankind and Destiny from the Standpoint of a Scientist*, London: C.W. Daniel.

—— (1974) 'Raymond B. Cattell', in G. Lindzey (ed.) *History of Psychology in Autobiography*, Vol. VI, Englewood Cliffs, NJ: Prentice Hall.

Checkland, S.G. (1964) *The Rise of Industrial Society in England, 1815– 1885*, London: Longman.

Clarke, F. (1923) *Essays in the Politics of Education*, Oxford: Oxford University Press.

—— (1940) *Education and Social Change: an English Interpretation*, London: Sheldon Press.

Combe, G. (1828) *The Constitution of Man Considered in Relation to External Objects* Edinburgh: Maclachlan and Steward.

Comenius, J.A. (1907) *The Great Didactic*, trans. M.W. Keatinge, London: Adam and Charles Black.

Cooter, R. (1984) *The Cultural Meaning of Popular Science: Phrenology and the Organization of Consent in Nineteenth-century Britain*, Cambridge: Cambridge University Press.

Copenhaver, B.P. and Schmitt, C.B. (1992) *Renaissance Philosophy*, Oxford: Oxford University Press.

Cowan, R.S. (1977) 'Nature and Nurture: the interplay of biology and politics in the work of Francis Galton', in W. Coleman and C. Limoges (eds) *Studies in History of Biology 1*, Baltimore, MD: Johns Hopkins University Press.

Cox, C.B. and Dyson, A.E. (eds) (1969) *Black Paper Two: The Crisis in Education*, London: Critical Quarterly Society.

Creelan, P.G. (1974) 'Watsonian behaviorism and the Calvinist conscience', *Journal of the History of the Behavioral Sciences*, X: 95–118.

Davidoff, L. and Hall, C. (1987) *Family Fortunes: Men and Women of the English Middle Class 1780–1850*, London: Hutchinson.

Department for Education and Employment/Qualifications and Curriculum Authority (DfEE/QCA) (1999) *The National Curriculum Handbook for Teachers in England* (two versions: primary and secondary), London: DfEE and QCA.

Department for Education and Skills (DfES) (2002) *Overview of the National Strategy for Gifted and Talented Education* (presented to its National Conference on Gifted and Talented Education 12–13 November 2002), London: DfES.

Department for Education and Skills (DfES) (2004) *Final Report of the Working Group on 14–19 Reform*, London: DfES.

Department of Education and Science (DES) (1989) *The Education Reform Act 1988; The School Curriculum and Assessment*, London: DES.

Dewey, J. (1916) *Democracy and Education*, New York: Macmillan.

—— (1972) 'My pedagogic creed', in J. Dewey (ed.) *The Early Years of John Dewey 1882– 1898, Vol. 5*, Carbondale, IL: Southern Illinois University Press, pp. 84–95. First published 1897.

—— (1990) 'Mediocrity and individuality', in *The Middle Works of John Dewey 1899– 1924, Vol. 13*, Carbondale, IL: Southern Illinois University Press.

Doddridge, P. (1763) *Lectures on Pneumatology, Ethics and Theology*, included in P. Doddridge (1803) *Works*, Vol. IV, published in Leeds.

Dore, R. (1997) *The Diploma Disease: Education, Qualification and Development*, London: Institute of Education University of London. First published 1976.

Downie, R.S., Loudfoot, E.M. and Telfer, E. (1974) *Education and Personal Relationships*, London: Methuen.

Dyhouse, C. (1981) *Girls Growing up in late Victorian and Edwardian England*, London: Routledge and Kegan Paul.

Eaglesham, E.J.R. (1967) *The Foundations of 20th Century Education in England*, London: Routledge and Kegan Paul.

Ellis, N.C. (2001) 'Alfred North Whitehead 1861–1947', in J. Palmer (ed.) *Fifty Major Thinkers on Education: From Confucius to Dewey*, London: Routledge.

Eyre, D. (2004) *Gifted Education: The English Model*, Warwick: National Academy for Gifted and Talented Youth.

Eysenck, H.J. (1975) 'Educational consequences of human inequality', in C.B. Cox and R. Boyson (eds) *Black Paper 1975*, London: J.M. Dent.

—— (1990) *Rebel with a Cause*, London: W. H. Allen.

Fancher, R.E. (1984) 'The examined life: competitive examinations in the thought of Francis Galton', *History of Psychology Bulletin*, 16: 13–20. Also at http://htpprints. yorku.ca/archive/00000130/.

—— (2001) 'Eugenics and other Victorian "Secular Religions"', in C.D. Green, M. Shore and T. Theo (eds) *The Transformation of Psychology*, Washington, DC: American Psychological Association.

Galindo-Rueda, F., Marcenaro-Gutierrez, O. and Vignoles, A. (2004) *The Widening Socio-economic Gap in UK Higher Education*, London: National Institute Economic Review.

Gallie, W.B. (1960) *A New University: A.D. Lindsay and the Keele Experiment*, London: Chatto and Windus.

Galton, F. (1865) 'Hereditary talent and character', *Macmillan's Magazine*, 12: 157–66; 318–27.

—— (1907) *Inquiries into Human Faculty and its Development*, London: J.M. Dent. First published 1883.

—— (1978) *Hereditary Genius*, reprint of 1892 edition, first published 1869, London: Friedmann.

Gardner, H. (1983) *Frames of Mind: The Theory of Multiple Intelligences*, London: Heinemann.

—— (1999) *Intelligence Reframed: Multiple Intelligences for the 21st Century*, New York: Basic Books.

George, G.H. and George, K. (1961) *The Protestant Mind of the English Reformation*, Princeton, NJ: Princeton University Press.

Gibbon, C. (1878) *The Life of George Combe*, London: Macmillan.

Gibson, H.B. (1981) *Hans Eysenck*, London: Peter Owen.

Gillham, N.W. (2001) *A Life of Sir Francis Galton*, Oxford: Oxford University Press.

Goddard, H.H. (1912) *The Kallikak Family: A Study in the Heredity of Feeble-mindedness*, New York: Macmillan.

—— (1920) *Human Efficiency and Levels of Intelligence*, Princeton, NJ: Princeton University Press.

Gould, S.J. (1981) *The Mismeasure of Man*, New York: Norton.

Grafton, A. and Jardine, L. (1986) *From Humanism to the Humanities: Education and the Liberal Arts in Fifteenth- and Sixteenth-century Europe*, London: Duckworth.

Greaves, R.L. (1969) *The Puritan Revolution and Educational Thought: Background for Reform*, New Brunswick, NJ: Rutgers University Press.

Gunn, S. and Bell, R. (2002) *Middle Classes: Their Rise and Sprawl*, London: Cassell.

Hamilton, D. (1990) *Curriculum History*, Geelong: Deakin University.

Hans, N. (1951) *New Trends in Education in the Eighteenth Century*, London: Routledge and Kegan Paul.

Hearnshaw, L.S. (1979) *Cyril Burt: Psychologist*, London: Hodder and Stoughton.

—— (1987) 'Burt, Sir Cyril Lodowic', in R.L. Gregory (ed.) *The Oxford Companion to the Mind*, Oxford: Oxford University Press.

Henking, S.E. (1992) 'Protestant religious experience and the rise of American sociology: evidence from the Bernard papers', *Journal of the History of the Behavioral Sciences*, 28: 325–39.

Herrnstein, R.J. (1971) *IQ in the Meritocracy*, Boston, MA: Atlantic Monthly Press.

Herrnstein, R.J. and Murray, C. (1994) *The Bell Curve*, New York: Free Press.

Hirst, P.H. (1965) 'Liberal education and the nature of knowledge', included in P.H. Hirst (1974) *Knowledge and the Curriculum*, London: Routledge and Kegan Paul.

Hirst, P.H. (1974) *Knowledge and the Curriculum*, London: Routledge and Kegan Paul.

Hirst, P.H. and Peters R.S (1970) *The Logic of Education*, London: Routledge and Kegan Paul.

Hofstadter, R. and Smith, W. (1961) *American Higher Education: A Documentary History* Vol. I, Chicago, IL: University of Chicago Press.

Hufton, O. (1995) *The Prospect Before Her: A History of Women in Western Europe, Vol.1: 1500–1800*, London: HarperCollins.

Jackson, William Fritz (1893) *James Jackson et ses Fils: notice sur leur vie. et sur les établissements qu'ils ont fondés ou dirigés en France*, Paris: Chamerot et Renouard.

Jensen, A.R. (1969) 'How much can we boost IQ and scholastic achievement?', *Harvard Educational Review*, 39(1): 1–123.

Jonçich, G.M., (1968) *The Sane Positivist: A Biography of Edward L. Thorndike*, Middletown, OH: Wesleyan University Press.

Jones, R.T. (1962) *Congregationalism in England 1662–1962*, London: Independent Press.

Kamin, L.J. (1977) *The Science and Politics of IQ*, Harmondsworth: Penguin.

Kleinig, J. (1982) *Philosophical Issues in Education*, London: Croom Helm.

Knox, H.M. (1953) *Two Hundred and Fifty Years of Scottish Education 1696–1946*, Edinburgh: Oliver and Boyd.

Layard, R. (2005) *Happiness: Lessons from a New Science*, London: Penguin.

Lippman, W. (1922) 'The abuse of the tests', *The New Republic*, 15 November: 297–8.

Mack, P. (1998) 'Ramus, Petrus 1515–1572', in E. Craig (ed.) *Routledge Encyclopaedia of Philosophy*, Vol. 8, London: Routledge.

Maclure, J.S. (ed.) (1965) *Educational Documents: England and Wales 1816–1967*, London: Chapman and Hall.

McDougall, W. (1930) 'William McDougall', in C. Murchison (ed.) *History of Psychology in Autobiography*, Vol. I, Worcester, MA: Clark University.

McKibbin, R. (1998) *Classes and Cultures in England 1918–1951*, Oxford: Oxford University Press.

McKnight, D. (2003) *Schooling, the Puritan Imperative and the Molding of an American National Identity*, Mahwah, NJ: Lawrence Erlbaum.

McLachlan, H. (1931) *English Education under the Test Acts: Being the History of Nonconformist Academies 1660–1820*, Manchester: Manchester University Press.

Martin, J. (2002) *The Education of John Dewey*, New York: Columbia University Press.

Mensh, E. and Mensh, H. (1991) *The IQ Mythology*, Carbondale, IL: Southern Illinois University Press.

Mercer, M. (2001) 'Dissenting academies and the education of the laity, 1750–1850', *History of Education*, 30(1): 35–58.

Miele, F. (2002) *Intelligence, Race and Genetics*, Boulder, CO: Westview Press.

Miller, P. (1939) *The New England Mind: The Seventeenth Century*, New York: Macmillan.

—— (1953) *The New England Mind: From Colony to Province*, Cambridge, MA: Harvard University Press.

Minton, H.L.(1988) *Lewis M. Terman*, New York: New York University Press.

Montgomery, R.J. (1965) *Examinations*, London: Longmans.

Morgan, E.S. (1944) *The Puritan Family*, Boston, MA: Trustees of the Public Library.

Morgan, J. (1986) *Godly Learning: Puritan Attitudes Towards Reason, Learning and Education, 1560–1640*, Cambridge: Cambridge University Press.

Mountford, Sir J. (1972) *Keele: An Historical Critique* London: Routledge and Kegan Paul.

Mulder, E. and Heyting, F. (1998) 'The Dutch curve: the introduction and reception of intelligence testing in the Netherlands, 1908–1940', *Journal of the History of the Behavioral Sciences*, 34(4): 349–66.

Norton, B. (1980) 'The meaning of intelligence', in J.V. Smit and D. Hamilton (eds) *The Meritocratic Intellect*, Aberdeen: Aberdeen University Press.

Oakeshott, M. (1971) 'Education, the engagement and the frustration', *Proceedings of the Philosophy of Education Society of Great Britain*, 5(1): 43–76.

O'Hear, A. (1991) *Father of Child-centredness: John Dewey and the Ideology of Modern Education*, London: Centre for Policy Studies.

Palmer, J. (ed.) (2001) *Fifty Major Thinkers on Education: From Confucius to Dewey*, London: Routledge.

Parker, I. (1914) *Dissenting Academies in England. Their Rise and Progress and their Place Among the Educational Systems of this Country*, Cambridge: Cambridge University Press.

Passmore, J. (1957) *A Hundred Years of Philosophy*, London: Duckworth.

Pastore, N. (1949) *The Nature-Nurture Controversy*, New York: King's Crown Press.

Pearson, E.S. (1938) *Karl Pearson: An Appreciation of Some Aspects of his Life and Work*, Cambridge: Cambridge University Press.

Pearson, K. (1914–30) *Life, Letters and Labours of Francis Galton*, 3 Vols, Cambridge: Cambridge University Press.

Peters, R.S. (1966) *Ethics and Education*, London: Allen and Unwin.

Piaget, J. (1952) 'Jean Piaget', in E.G. Boring, H.S. Langfeld, H. Werner and R.M. Yerkes (eds) *History of Psychology in Autobiography*, Vol. IV, Worcester, MA: Clark University.

Plato *Republic*, many editions.

Plummeridge, C. and Swanwick, K. (2004) 'Music', in J. White (ed.) *Rethinking the School Curriculum: Values, Aims and Purposes*, London: RoutledgeFalmer.

Popper, K.R. (1963) *Conjectures and Refutations*, London: Routledge and Kegan Paul.

Ramus, P. (1969) *The Logike of the Moste Excellent Philosopher P. Ramus, Martyr*, trans. R. MacIlmaine (1574), ed. C.M. Dunn, Northridge, CA: San Fernando Valley State College.

Raz, J. (1986) *The Morality of Freedom*, Oxford: Clarendon Press.

—— (2003) *The Practice of Value*, Oxford: Clarendon Press.

Reid, T. (1785) *Essays on the Intellectual Powers of Man*, 1969 edition, Cambridge, MA: MIT Press.

Richards, G. (2002) *Putting Psychology in its Place*, New York: Routledge.

Richardson, K. (1998) *The Origins of Human Potential*, London: Routledge.

—— (1999) *The Making of Intelligence*, London: Weidenfeld and Nicolson.

Roach, J. (1986) *A History of Secondary Education, 1800–1870*, London: Longman.

Rose, S., Kamin, L. and Lewontin, R.C. (1984) *Not in Our Genes: Biology, Ideology and Human Nature*, Harmondsworth: Penguin.

Ross, D. (1972) *G. Stanley Hall: The Psychologist as Prophet*, Chicago, IL: University of Chicago Press.

Routley, E.R. (1961) *The Story of Congregationalism*, London: Independent Press.

Rubinstein, W.D. (1998) 'Britain's élites in the interwar period, 1918–1939', in A. Kidd and D. Nicholls (eds) *The Making of the British Middle Class?*, Stroud: Sutton.

Rudolph, F. (1962) *The American College and University: A History*, 1990 edition, Athens, GA: University of Georgia Press.

Ryan, A. (1995) *John Dewey and the High Tide of American Liberalism*, New York: Norton.

Ryle, G. (1949) *The Concept of Mind*, London: Huchinson.

Schultz, D.P. and Schultz, S.E. (2000) *A History of Modern Psychology* (7th edition), Fort Worth, TX: Harcourt College Publishers.

Seacoe, M. (1975) *Terman and the Gifted*, Los Altos, CA: William Kaufman.

Simon, B. (1960) *Studies in the History of Education, 1780–1870*, London: Lawrence and Wishart.

—— (1974) *The Politics of Educational Reform 1920–1940*, London: Lawrence and Wishart.

Smith, J.W.A. (1955) *The Birth of Modern Education: The Contribution of the Dissenting Academies 1660–1800*, London: Independent Press.

Steers, J. (2004) 'Art and Design', in J. White (ed.) *Rethinking the School Curriculum: Values, Aims and Purposes*, London: RoutledgeFalmer.

Sternberg, R.J. (1996) *Successful Intelligence*, New York: Simon and Schuster.

Stowe, H. B. (1869 [1987]) *Oldtown Folks*, New Brunswick, NJ: Rutgers University Press.

Strong, J. (1909) *A History of Secondary Education in Scotland*, Oxford: Clarendon Press.

Tawney, R.H. (1926) *Religion and the Rise of Capitalism*, West Drayton: Penguin.

Taylor, C. (1989) *Sources of the Self: the Making of the Modern Identity*, Cambridge: Cambridge University Press.

Terman, L.M. (1916) *The Measurement of Intelligence*, Boston, MA: Houghton Mifflin.

—— (1919) *The Measurement of Intelligence* (English edition of Terman 1916), London: Harrap.

—— (1922) 'Were we born that way?', *World's Work*, 44.

—— (1923) 'Editor's Introduction', in V.E. Dickson, *Mental Tests and the Classroom Teacher* Yonkers, NY: World Book Company.

—— (1932) 'Autobiography', in C. Murchison (ed.) *History of Psychology in Autobiography*, Vol. II, Worcester, MA: Clark University.

Thompson, E.P. (1982) 'Time, work-discipline and industrial capitalism', in A. Giddens and D. Held (eds) *Classes Power and Conflict*, London: Macmillan.

Thomson, G.H. (1947) *The Trend of National Intelligence*, London: The Eugenics Society.

—— (1969) *The Education of an Englishman*, Edinburgh: Moray House.

Thurstone, L.L. (1952) 'L.L.Thurstone', in E.G. Boring, H.S. Langfeld, H. Werner and R.M. Yerkes (eds) *History of Psychology in Autobiography*, Vol. IV, Worcester, MA: Clark University.

Triche, S. and McKnight, D. (2004) 'The quest for method: the legacy of Peter Ramus', *History of Education*, 33(1): 39–54.

Vann, R.T. and Eversley, D. (1992) *Friends in Life and Death: the British and Irish Quakers in the Demographic Transition, 1650–1900*, Cambridge: Cambridge University Press.

Vernon, P.E., (1978) 'The Making of an Applied Psychologist', in T.S. Krawiec (ed.) *The Psychologists*, Vol. 3, Brandon, VT: Clinical Psychology Publishing.

Walvin, J. (1997) *The Quakers*, London: John Murray.

Walzer, M. (1966) *The Revolution of the Saints*, London: Weidenfeld and Nicolson.

Watts, I. (1996) *Logic: or the Right Use of Reason in the Inquiry after Truth*, Morgan, PA: Soli Deo Gloria (first published 1724).

Watts, M.R. (1978) *The Dissenters: Vol I: From the Reformation to the French Revolution*, Oxford: Clarendon Press.

Webb, J. (2004) 'Secret GOP weapon: the Scots-Irish vote', *Wall Street Journal*, October 19, available at www.opinionjournal.com/extra/?id=110005798.

Weber, M. (1930) *The Protestant Ethic and the Spirit of Capitalism*, London: Allen and Unwin.

White, J. (1969) 'Intelligence – the new Puritanism', *Times Educational Supplement*, 24 October: 4.

—— (1970) Correspondence with Cyril Burt 1969–70 (unpublished).

—— (1974) 'Intelligence and the logic of the nature–nurture issue', *Proceedings of the Philosophy of Education Society of Great Britain*, 8(1): 30–51.

—— (1975) 'The end of the compulsory curriculum: a historical investigation', in *The Curriculum: The Doris Lee Lectures*, London: Institute of Education, University of London.

—— (1997) *Education and the End of Work: A New Philosophy of Work and Learning*, London: Cassell.

—— (1998) *Do Howard Gardner's Multiple Intelligences Add Up?*, London: Institute of Education, University of London.

—— (2002a) *The Child's Mind*, London: RoutledgeFalmer.

—— (2002b) 'Education, the market and the nature of personal well-being', *British Journal of Educational Studies*, 50(4): 442–56.

—— (ed.) (2004) *Rethinking the School Curriculum: Values, Aims and Purposes*, London: RoutledgeFalmer.

—— (2005) 'Reassessing 1960s philosophy of the curriculum', *London Review of Education*, 3(2) 131–44.

—— (2006) 'Multiple invalidities?', in J.A. Schaler (ed.) *Gardner Under Fire: A Rebel Psychologist Faces His Critics*, Chicago, IL: Open Court Publishing Company.

Williams, R. (1961) *The Long Revolution*, London: Chatto and Windus.

Woodworth, R.S. (1932) 'R.S.Woodworth', in C. Murchison (ed.) *History of Psychology in Autobiography*, Vol. II, Worcester, MA: Clark University.

Yerkes, R.M, (1932) 'R.M. Yerkes', in C. Murchison (ed.) *History of Psychology in Autobiography*, Vol. II, Worcester, MA: Clark University.

Young, M. (1958) *The Rise of the Meritocracy 1870–2033*, London: Thames and Hudson.

Zenderland, L. (1998) *Measuring Minds: Henry Herbert Goddard and the Origins of American Intelligence Testing*, Cambridge: Cambridge University Press.

Index